IMAGES
of America

BURR RIDGE

On the Cover: From left to right, A. Hockemeyer, Howard Hoyt, and George Gear prepare the wagon for a visit to local schools in 1915. (Courtesy of Flagg Creek Heritage Society.)

IMAGES
of America

BURR RIDGE

Sharon L. Comstock, PhD

ARCADIA
PUBLISHING

ISBN 978-1-4671-1339-7

Published by Arcadia Publishing
Charleston, South Carolina

Printed in the United States of America

Library of Congress Control Number: 2014946510

For all general information, please contact Arcadia Publishing:
Telephone 843-853-2070
Fax 843-853-0044
E-mail sales@arcadiapublishing.com
For customer service and orders:
Toll-Free 1-888-313-2665

Visit us on the Internet at www.arcadiapublishing.com

This book is dedicated to the story-keepers of each generation and Judge David Hall (1952–2014), who generously shared and modeled his committed passion for genealogy, local history, and family.

Contents

Acknowledgments		6
Introduction		7
1.	Early Years	9
2.	Working the Land	19
3.	Turn-of-the-Century Life	27
4.	Industrious Families	39
5.	Church Life	47
6.	Plainview and Pleasantdale Schools	61
7.	Gower and Anne M. Jeans Schools	69
8.	High School Spirit	81
9.	Farms to Farmalls	93
10.	Harvester and Burr Ridge	111

ACKNOWLEDGMENTS

They say that history is written by the conquerors. I suggest it is written by those who have the privilege of access to living memories of place, faces, names, and narrative. Without having been granted the opportunity to meet and sit down with so many who have been and continue to be a part of the Burr Ridge story, the images—and the stories they tell—would have remained in the quiet place of silent memory.

I would like to thank Hazel (Martin) Sharp, whose lifelong dedication to local history mirrors that of her mother, Ruth (Vial) Martin, who was a leading advocate for the Flagg Creek Heritage Society and Museum. I thank Flagg Creek Heritage Society leaders Alice Latham, Sandi Bulthuis, Linda Petrasek, and Betty Tompkin. I thank the village of Burr Ridge, village administrator Steven Stricker, and, especially, village clerk Karen J. Thomas for her many late hours and rigorous curiosity. I thank Jim Martin, whose collection of memorabilia from growing up on the International Harvester research farm are treasures. He and his wife, Loretta (Lorry), were gracious hosts as we learned about life with his father, Kile Martin, who worked the IH farm. I thank family archivist Sandra (Comstock) Browning and her husband, Richard, whose photos rival any historical society's. I thank our oldest area religious institutions: Lyonsville Congregational United Church of Christ and Trinity Lutheran Church. I thank Gower School District 62, Anne M. Jeans School Community Consolidated School District 180 (AMJSCCS), Pleasantdale School District 107, Lyons Township High School District 204, and Hinsdale South High School District 86. I thank Dr. George P. Godfrey, Citizen Potawatomi, for his insight into his own genealogical line of Shabbona. I thank Indian Prairie Public Library librarian Mary Krelkelburg, whose experience was encouraging. I thank Bonnie Kohout and Julie Ryan of King-Bruwaert House. I thank family members David P. and Pat J. Comstock, Nina (Bonham) Schmidt, Lorrie (McHugh) Soltwisch and her daughter Jenny (Soltwisch) Vazquez, John McHugh, and Adam Orozco-Comstock, all of whom helped to locate and scan images.

Finally, I ask in advance for your forgiveness for those aspects not represented in these pages. May you feel inspired to view this title as a beginning, not an end, to the Burr Ridge narrative.

INTRODUCTION

Burr Ridge. The name evokes images of oak trees and rolling hills, certainly the very ones we see today and that will—we can safely say—remain. The narrative of the place, however, is much deeper and complex than even the roots of the prairie plants and hard woods that once covered these lands.

The story of Burr Ridge doesn't begin on October 20, 1956, when 76 votes were cast for (and 67 against) incorporation as the village of Harvester, inspired by the International Harvester research and engineering farm at the corner of Plainfield and County Line Roads. Nor did it start when the Village of Harvester changed its name to Burr Ridge in 1962, when it annexed an area known as Burr Ridge Estates, a 1950s development of five-acre tracts once owned by the Busby family, who—so it is said—named it for a grove of burr oaks on what they called a ridge on their land on County Line Road near Plainfield across from International Harvester.

The story of Burr Ridge isn't about annexations. Burr Ridge's history is a story of place, family, and community. It is one of hard work and families seeking and consciously building home—not "a" home, but that sense of knowing you've arrived somewhere special, that you don't have to search any longer. What defines home is permanence and relationship, both the physical and emotional comfort of rootedness.

The continuity of the generations may not be visible, but in fact, the descendants of many of the earliest families are still here to a greater or lesser extent. Names like Bachman, Behm, Bielby, Boness, Buege, Bulthuis, Carrington, Craigmile, Durland, Gauger, Godar, Harder, Honeck, Hoyt, Jeans, Keller, Marwitz, McClintock, McNaughton, Rediehs, Rodgers, Ruthe, Sass, Tietd, Vial, Wachter, and so many others formed the character of what eventually became Burr Ridge today.

These early families settled the land to build better lives on the edge of a prairie as farmers, entrepreneurs, and educators. They came from Scotland, England, Holland, and Germany, among other European countries, to build the earliest institutions, from churches to post offices and schools to now-disappeared towns. They practiced their faiths and formed churches. Lyonsville Congregational (1843) and Trinity Lutheran (1865) are the two earliest founded by first families. They built the earliest schools, such as Plainview (now District 106) in 1843; Flagg Creek School, which became Pleasantdale (or "Pleasant Dale," as it was known then), in 1861; Byrneville (now Anne M. Jeans) in 1910; and Gower Schools (Gower was its own town, with its first teacher noted in 1891). Then, of course, there were Lyons Township High School (1888) and Hinsdale High School (1879). These families farmed, educated, governed, built, married, and grew. And the area grew right along with them.

What drew these families to this place? Why here? Let's take a step back for a moment and look down at the land beneath our feet by way of some explanation. When the last glacial retreats occurred around 25,000 to 14,000 years ago in West Cook and DuPage Counties, a series of moraines to the south and west were formed. As the temperatures warmed and the glacier that became known as the Lake Michigan Lobe retreated, areas between the moraines became natural paths of fast-running meltwater, Salt Creek becoming one of these. (Flagg Creek, which borders Burr Ridge and was deepened in the 1950s, is a part of the Salt Creek Watershed.) The glacial clay and dolomite limestone formed firm ground for wetlands to develop. Those wetlands eventually became complex prairie and woodland ecosystems. Hardwood trees, such as maple, hickory, and oak, of the eastern forests met the western prairie grasses. When early settlers arrived, they burned off these grasses, often to flush game and clear land for farming; improved travel; and used the forest hardwood for lumber. These processes revealed the rich soil that the farming families later found so bountiful. Despite the clearing, the enduring burr oak survived, and groves remained, usually on upland areas and along river edges. Keep in mind, however, that some naturalists' estimates are that only 15 percent of this area was hardwood; the rest was prairie. Common wildlife included bears, cougars, and other game animals.

What Europeans found were not "discoveries," however. We are only four generations away (if we are fortunate) from living memory of the Potawatomi who lived among the earliest settlers in the 1830s to 1850s. In their oral histories, our oldest residents today still remember digging up arrowheads along Flagg Creek as children or that fathers, uncles, and brothers discovered them churned up from farming plows. Maps of the time show Potawatomi on the Plainfield Road Trail. Robert Vial—son of Joseph Vial, one of the first settlers of the area—recounts in his own writing of Potawatomi chief and friend Shabbona stopping to see his father at their Plainfield Road home. One written source from the turn of the 20th century cites "old-timers" recalling Potawatomi camps even along what became County Line Road. After the Chicago Treaty of 1833, however, the last in a series of treaties, the Potawatomi agreed to be relocated west of the Mississippi. Chicago was only a village of 350. With the Potawatomi, the Ojibwe and Ottawa also moved west.

The area we call Burr Ridge, then spanning the Lyons and Downers Grove Townships and the Cook and DuPage County line, became open for the earliest of settlers to purchase land. Plat by plat, families, such as those of David Craigmile and Nancy Harrison, purchased acreages by the hundreds, farmed, raised families, and eventually sold to others over time—in Craigmile's case, to International Harvester (IH) in 1917. The iconic Farmall tractor was perfected on the IH research facility and working farm on that acreage on Plainfield between County Line and Madison Roads. It inspired a whole new generation of innovators and settlers, fueling a post–World War II growth spurt that mirrored the nation's, and a village, Harvester (later renamed Burr Ridge), to incorporate on an October day in 1956. Names like Whittaker, Molnar, Tennyson, and Hall, as well as others who we will learn more about in the unfolding pages of this book, entered as leaders.

So, Burr Ridge isn't about annexation, no. It's about the growth of a place we can proudly claim as "home."

This book can in no way tell every story Burr Ridge holds, but it may inspire all of us to learn, listen, and tell our stories for the next generations of "Burr Ridgers" to come.

One

Early Years

The Plainfield Road. The Joliet. The Indian Trail. The German Church. The "crick." The old Vial Place. All of these are early family vernacular for what we term Burr Ridge today. Creating markers from the vast land gave meaning to the early landscape and allowed newer settlers and entrepreneurs to find their way into or through the area.

The area in the early 1800s was spacious yet well traveled. Plainfield and Joliet Roads are our earliest local trails. Potawatomi—a largely peaceful Algonquian-speaking nation—were the most numerous in and around what would become Chicago. Fort Dearborn, which the US Army built in 1803, served as a commercial hub for traders, soldiers, and families of all nationalities: French, English, Sac, Ojibwa, Potawatomi, Fox, American, and others.

The Black Hawk War (1832) was a defining moment in the area's history. Because of increasing violence as the US government sought more land, Fort Dearborn was ordered to evacuate. Although Potawatomi chief Shabbona warned settlers of an impending assault by Sac chief Black Hawk and aided the Army against the Sac, many of Fort Dearborn's troops and civilians were killed during their retreat. The government permanently moved the Potawatomi and other nations west of the Mississippi River in response. The Potawatomi were incredulous: "Their Great Father in Washington must have seen a bad bird which had told him a lie, for that far from wishing to sell their land, they wished to keep it." Shabbona, however, remained friends with local families, primarily the Vials. Young Samuel Vial described many visits during which Shabbona would enjoy stories and meals and would sleep in a blanket near the Vials' fireplace at their rough-hewn home on Plainfield Road near Flagg Creek.

By 1840, the mix of Indian and Euro American traders had lost their primary place in the economy, and land speculation boomed. Sedentary farming and livestock drove growth throughout the mid- to late 1800s. Settlement grew in earnest, and the rest, as they say, is (local) history.

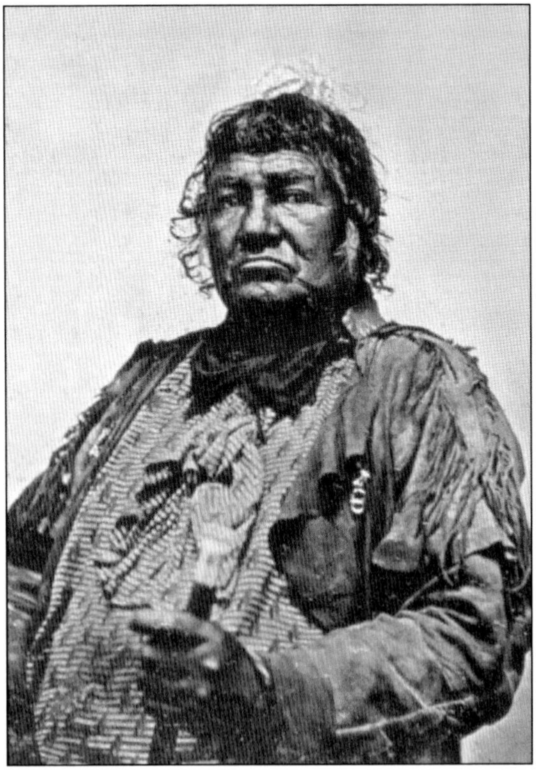

Chief Shabbona is illustrated here around 1850. Joseph Vial's eldest son, Samuel, is quoted on July 21, 1889, in the Chicago newspaper the *Inter Ocean* as saying that Shabbona "was in the great battle where old Tecumseh was killed, and I never can forget how vividly he portrayed what happened in that famous fight to a crowd of settlers at my father's house one bright moonlight [sic] night." (Courtesy of George Godfrey and Flagg Creek Heritage Society.)

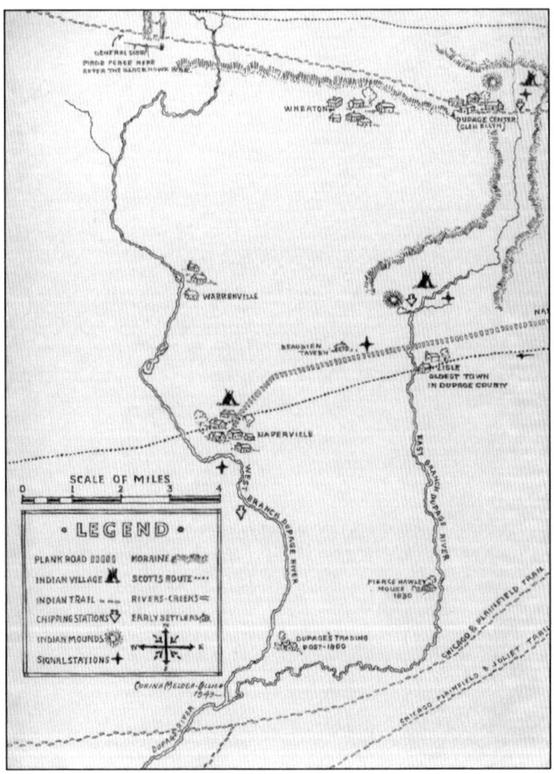

A majority of what became Burr Ridge was bounded in the 1800s by the Chicago and Plainfield Trails to the north, bisected by the Joliet Trail (Historic Route 66), and bounded by the Illinois and Michigan Canal (1848) to the south. Travel was long and difficult. Trips to Chicago were often necessary for business. Joseph Vial wrote, for the week of Sunday, May 31, 1835, "Returned [to] house. Clear good weather. Carney came here told me he had no pre-emptions and wanted I should give up the papers [for land sale]." For the week of June 7, 1835, he wrote: "Ploughed and planted potatoes. Saml. [Samuel] started with load for peck. Went to Chicago with team. Returned same day. Very wet. Land sale commenced. Finished planting." (Courtesy of Indian Prairie Public Library.)

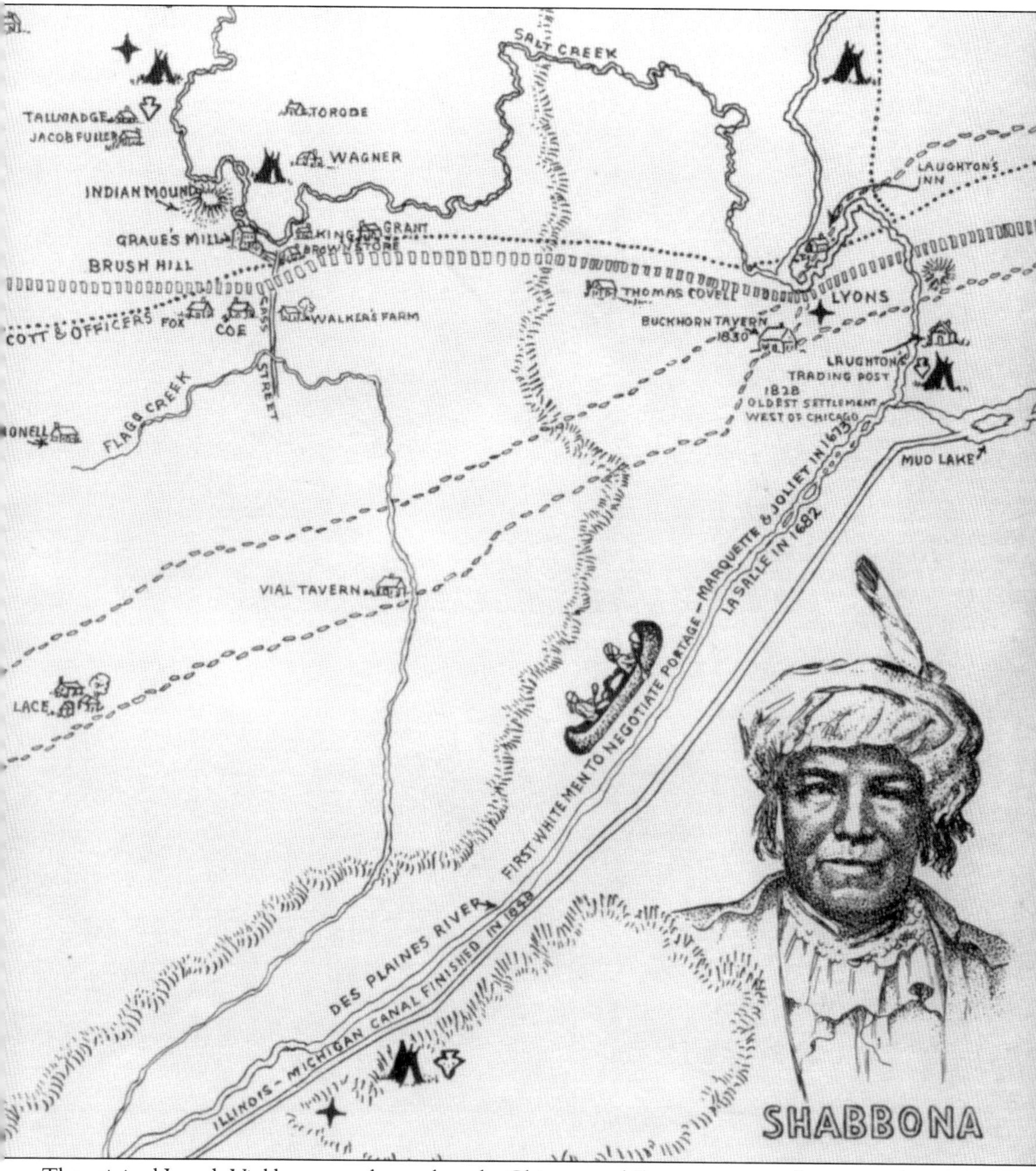

The original Joseph Vial home was located on the Chicago and Ottawa stagecoach route, making it the "Vial Tavern" noted on this map. In an *Inter Ocean* article from July 21, 1889, titled "Before Chicago Was," Samuel Vial is described as "one of the few remaining pioneers who came to Cook County in the early days when Fort Dearborn was more widely known than Chicago" who "little dreamed . . . that the vast . . . vicinity of the old fort would ever be the site of the largest city on the western hemisphere. It was a dreary place when he came. 'A few scattered log-houses, a general merchandise store, and the fort comprised the town,' [Vial said]." (Courtesy of Indian Prairie Public Library.)

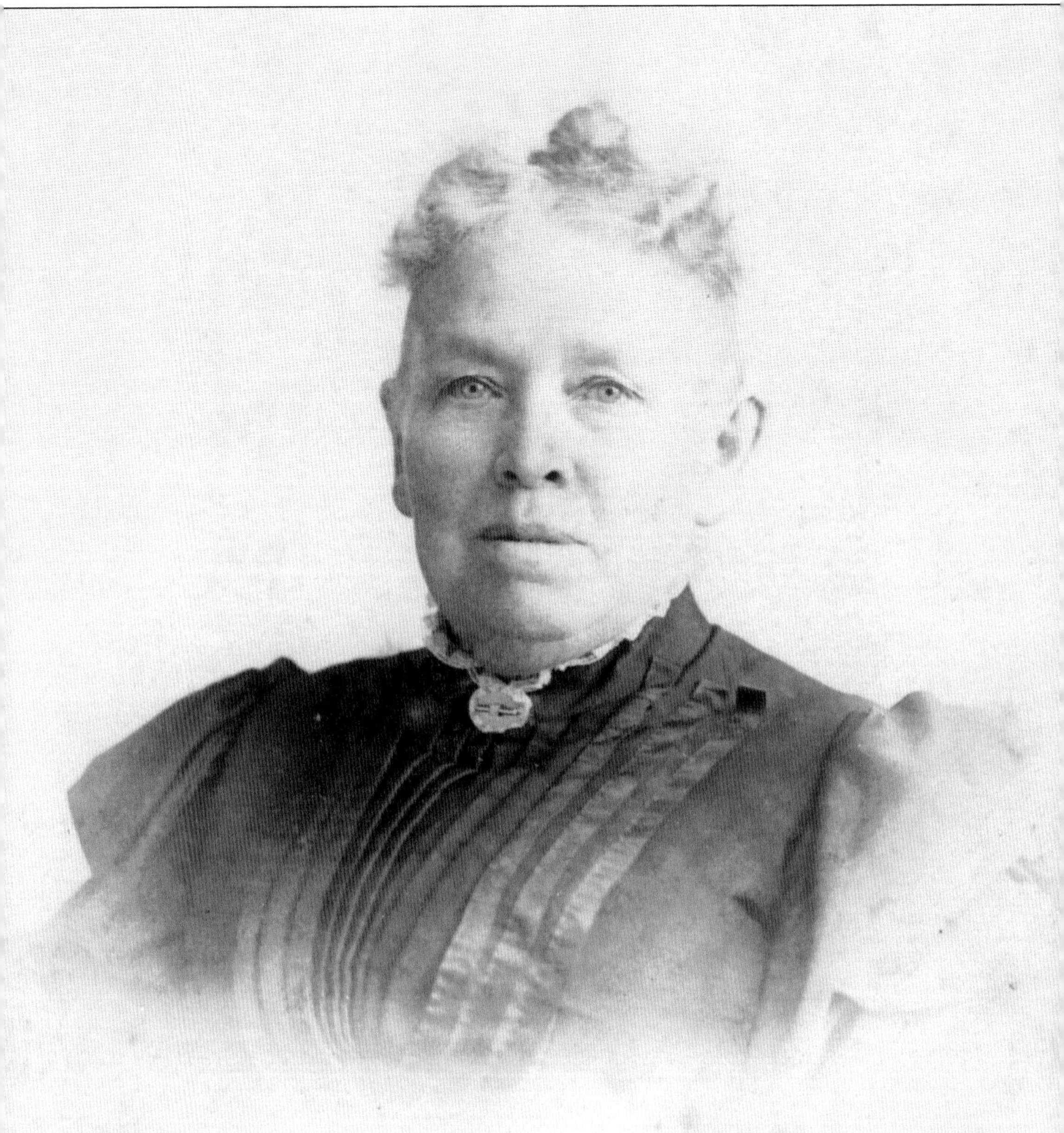

Mary Roe Ketchum married Robert, the second son of the Joseph and Louisa Vial family. Their 1856 home originally stood near the corner of Plainfield and Wolf Roads and was relocated in 1989 to the Pleasantdale Park District and Flagg Creek Heritage Society, at 7425 Wolf Road in Burr Ridge. After extensive renovation, Mary and Robert's home was made a National Historic Landmark in 2007. (Courtesy of Flagg Creek Heritage Society.)

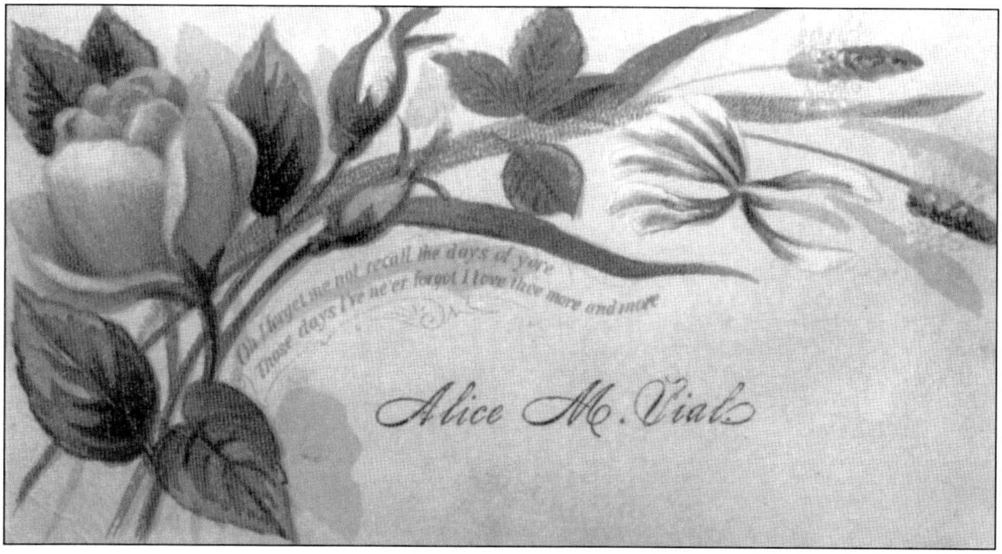

The Robert and Mary Vial family assumed leadership roles within the community. Robert Vial became postmaster in 1853, inheriting the role from his father Joseph. He was appointed Lyons Township supervisor, treasurer of Lyons Township High School, and deacon in what became Lyonsville Congregational Church. Mary served to support these roles at church and home, visiting the sick and tending women in childbirth. Robert had come a long way from his childhood in some ways. One Vial oral history says that he was called "papoose" by the Potawatomi who traded with his father, Joseph. He thoroughly disliked the term because he was 10 at the time "and not a baby." Six of Robert Vial's children grew to adulthood in the area: Mary L., Edmund, Eugene, Fredrick, Robert C., and Alice. They represented a class of institution-building families. As such, etiquette conventions were followed. This is hinted at by these visiting (or calling) cards for Alice and "Robbie." Alice would be among the first to graduate from Lyons Township High School and become a schoolteacher (Both, courtesy of Flagg Creek Heritage Society.)

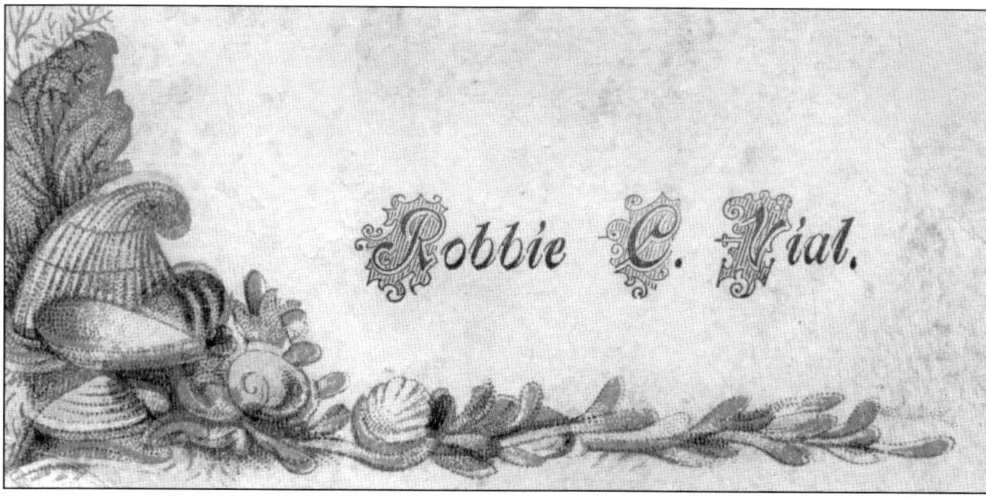

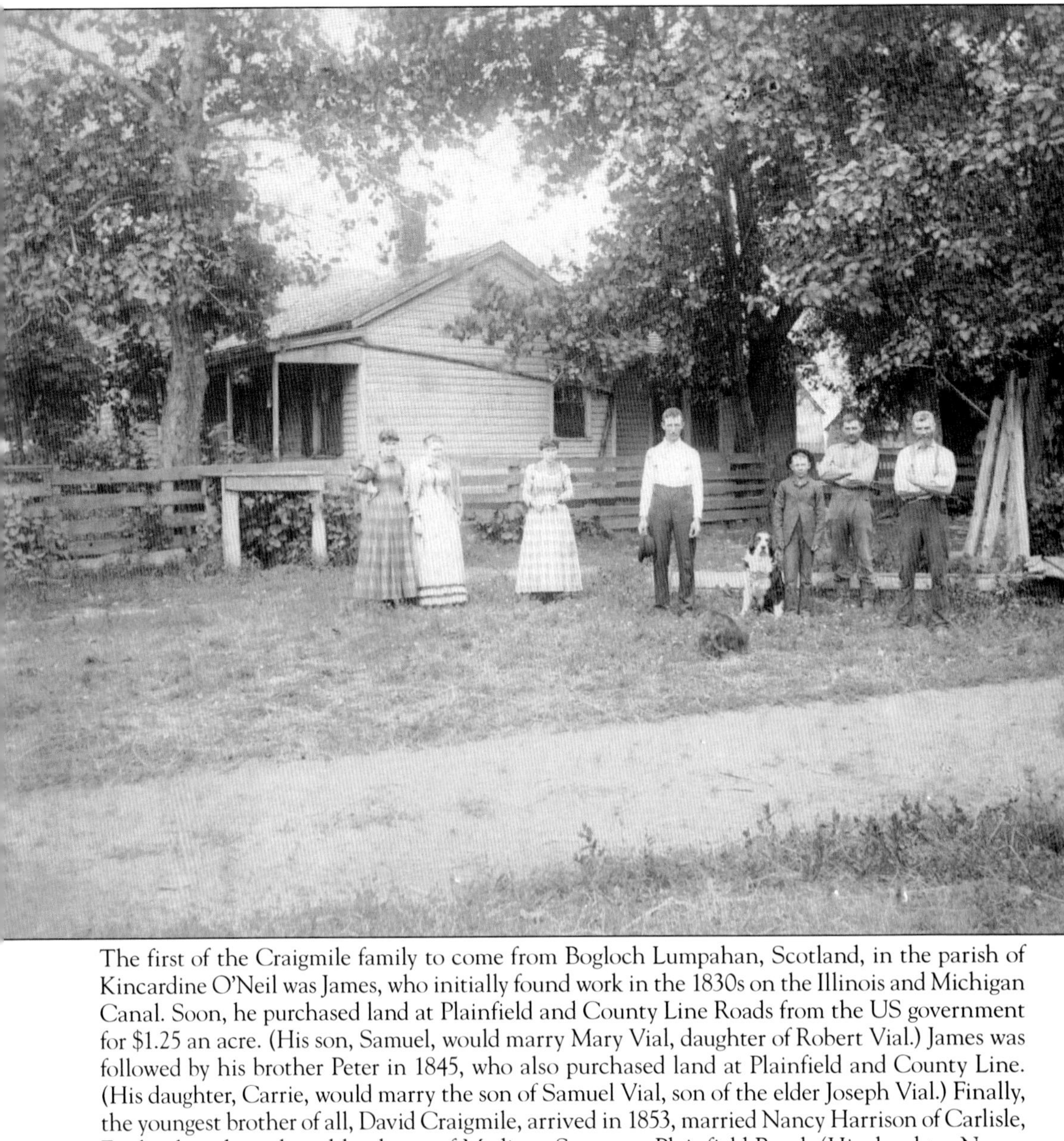

The first of the Craigmile family to come from Bogloch Lumpahan, Scotland, in the parish of Kincardine O'Neil was James, who initially found work in the 1830s on the Illinois and Michigan Canal. Soon, he purchased land at Plainfield and County Line Roads from the US government for $1.25 an acre. (His son, Samuel, would marry Mary Vial, daughter of Robert Vial.) James was followed by his brother Peter in 1845, who also purchased land at Plainfield and County Line. (His daughter, Carrie, would marry the son of Samuel Vial, son of the elder Joseph Vial.) Finally, the youngest brother of all, David Craigmile, arrived in 1853, married Nancy Harrison of Carlisle, England, and purchased land east of Madison Street on Plainfield Road. (His daughter Nancy would marry Eugene Vial.) In total, the Craigmile brothers had 450 acres. These later became the largest part of the International Harvester farm in 1917. This photograph was taken at "the homestead" on the east side of Plainfield Road and Madison Street. Pictured around 1890 are, from left to right, daughters Ruth, Sarah, and Esther; sons Francis and Ira; a Craigmile brother; and David. (Daughter Nancy is not pictured.) (Courtesy of Sandra Browning.)

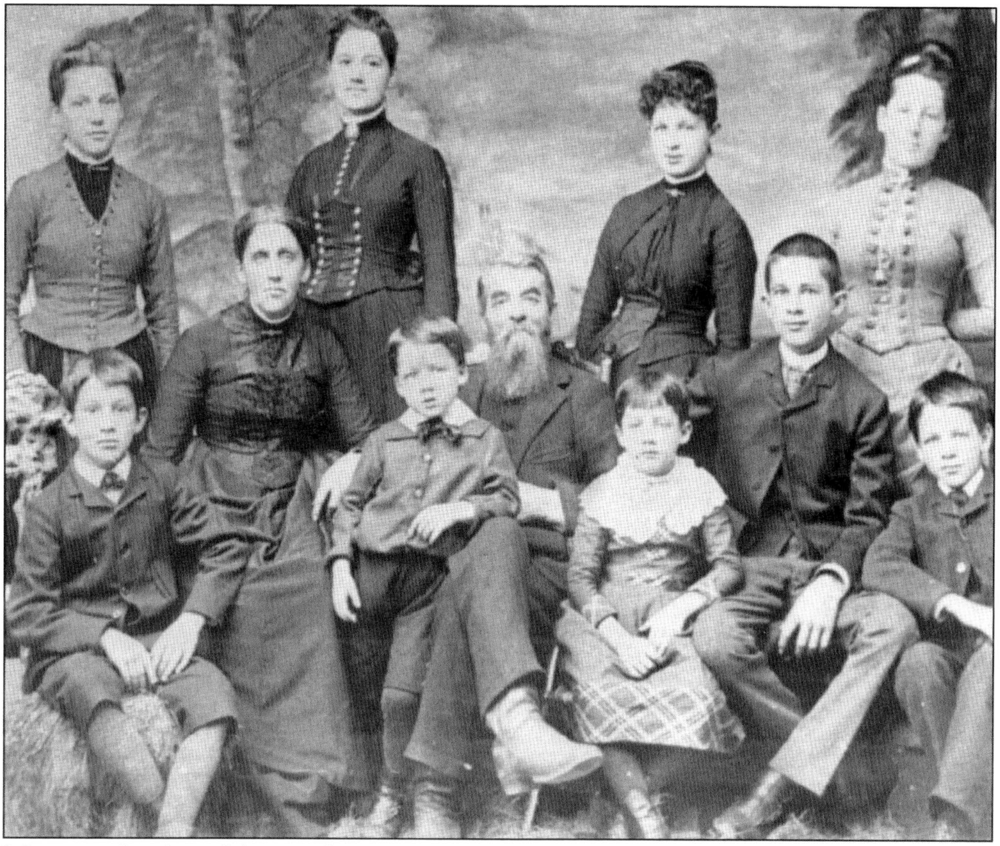

Like many families of the era, the Hoyt-Durland family was a large one. The Durland family arrived from New York in the 1860s, and their youngest son married Louisa Vial, who became one of the earlier Pleasantdale schoolteachers. The Hoyt family was already established by the 1850s; this 1870s photograph of the Hoyt clan includes, from left to right, (first row) Howard, mother Sybil (Durland), George, Alfred, unidentified sister, Walter, and Jonathan; (second row) Emma Nathe, Alta, and Jessie. (Courtesy of Sandra Browning.)

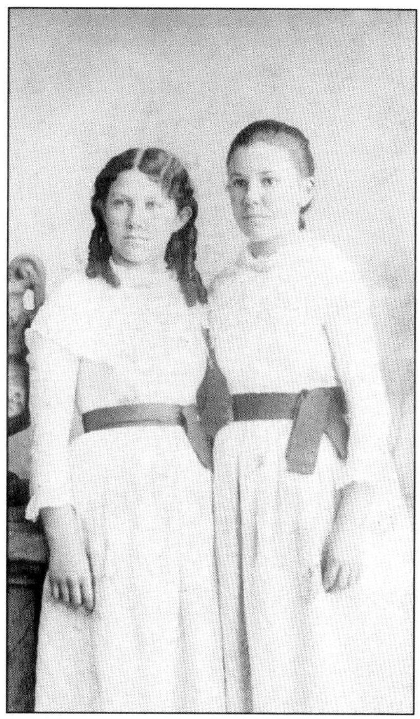

David Craigmile lost his wife, Nancy (Harrison), when their children were young and never remarried. The eldest daughter, Sarah, was said to have cared for the younger sisters with tenderness. Two of those sisters, Esther (left) and Ruth, are seen in this 1888 family photograph. David was known to be a religious man who, his daughter Esther recounts in her diary, read the Bible aloud nightly with a strong Scottish cadence. After selling his acreage to International Harvester in 1917, the girls' father would move to 26 South Grant Street, Hinsdale, and tend his "in-town" orchard until his death in 1919. (Courtesy of Sandra Browning.)

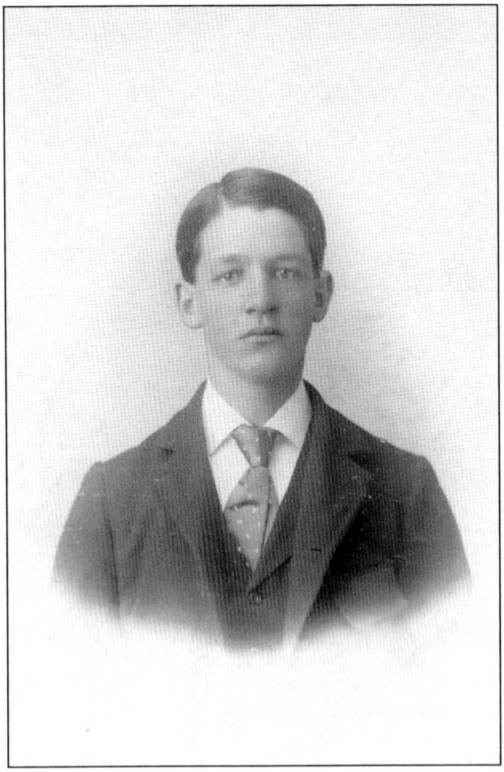

Howard Hoyt, seen here in the 1880s, was one of eight children. He remained in the area and attended Lyonsville Congregational Church, where he would meet his future wife, (Margaret) Ruth Craigmile. (Courtesy of Sandra Browning.)

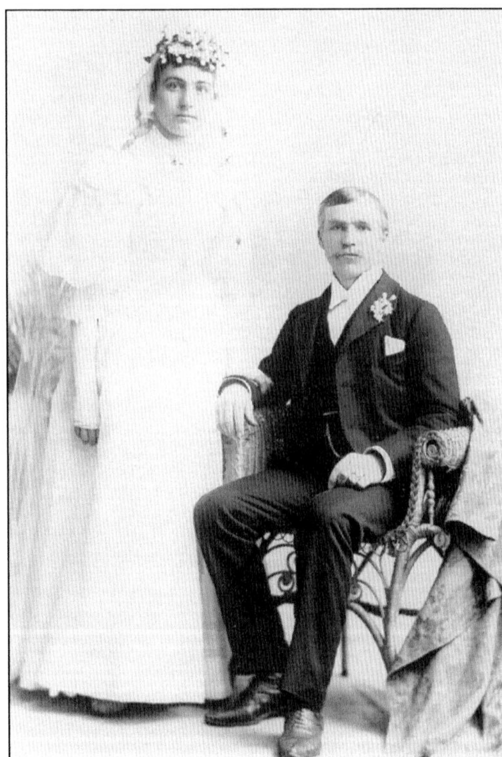

Founding farming families from Germany anchored the southern edges of what became Burr Ridge as early as 1839. From these early settlers, Trinity Evangelical Lutheran Church grew into being and was officially built in 1865. What became the "German Church Road" was a corridor of the early German community, around which the Buege, Knapp, Marwitz, Pantke, Rediehs, Sass, and Tiedt familes, among others, settled and grew. Members of the community—such as Emma Buege and August Boness, shown here celebrating their wedding day in 1896—valued church and family life. (Courtesy of Flagg Creek Heritage Society.)

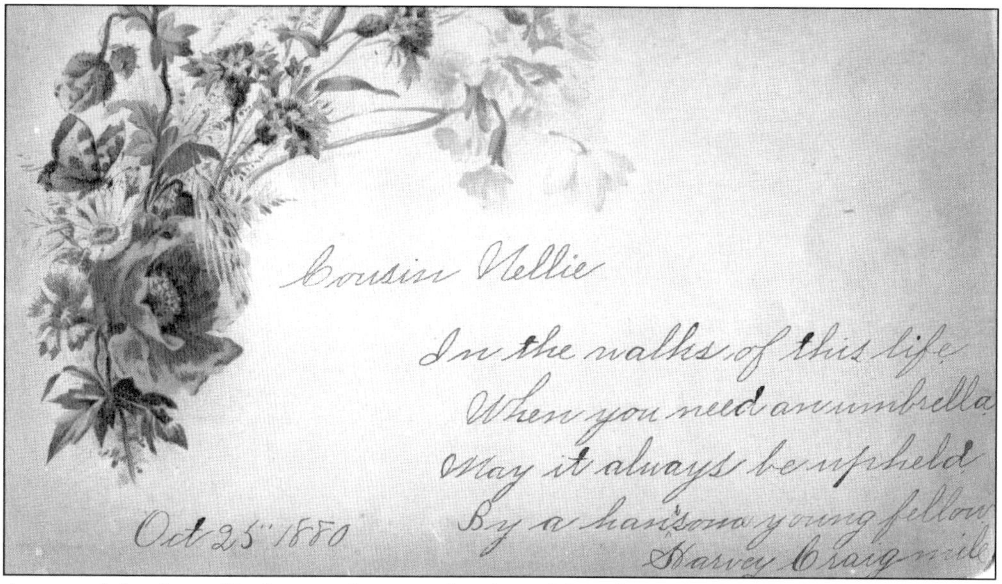

Autograph books and little notes between family and friends were common in an age that relied on the written word. Nellie Craigmile received one such playful poem from her cousin Harvey Craigmile. (Courtesy of Flagg Creek Heritage Society.)

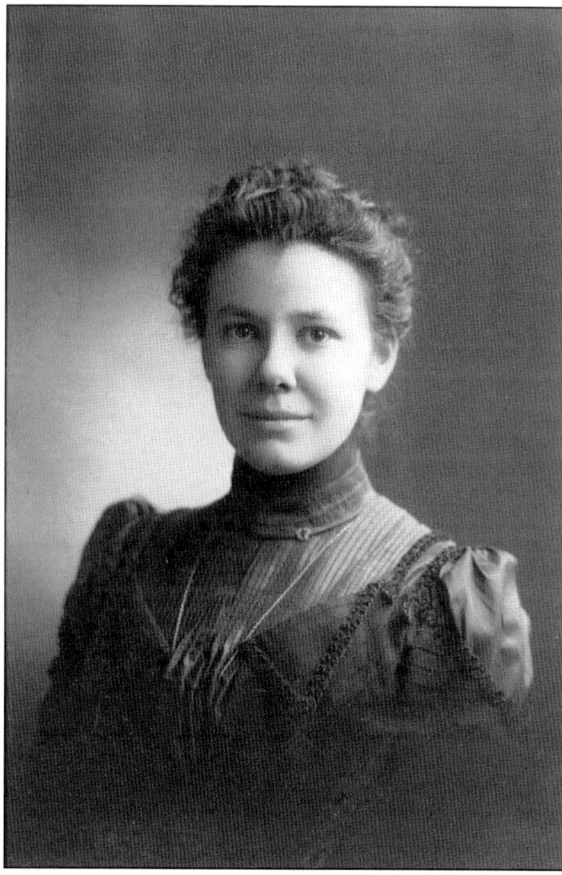

Ruth Craigmile, pictured here around 1890, married Howard Hoyt, making a home and raising children as Howard worked the land with his team and tended his own dairy cows on, at first, Craigmile land and then at County Line and Plainfield Roads. The Carrington family land was nearby along County Line, and the family owned several head of Swiss cattle. (Courtesy of Sandra Browning.)

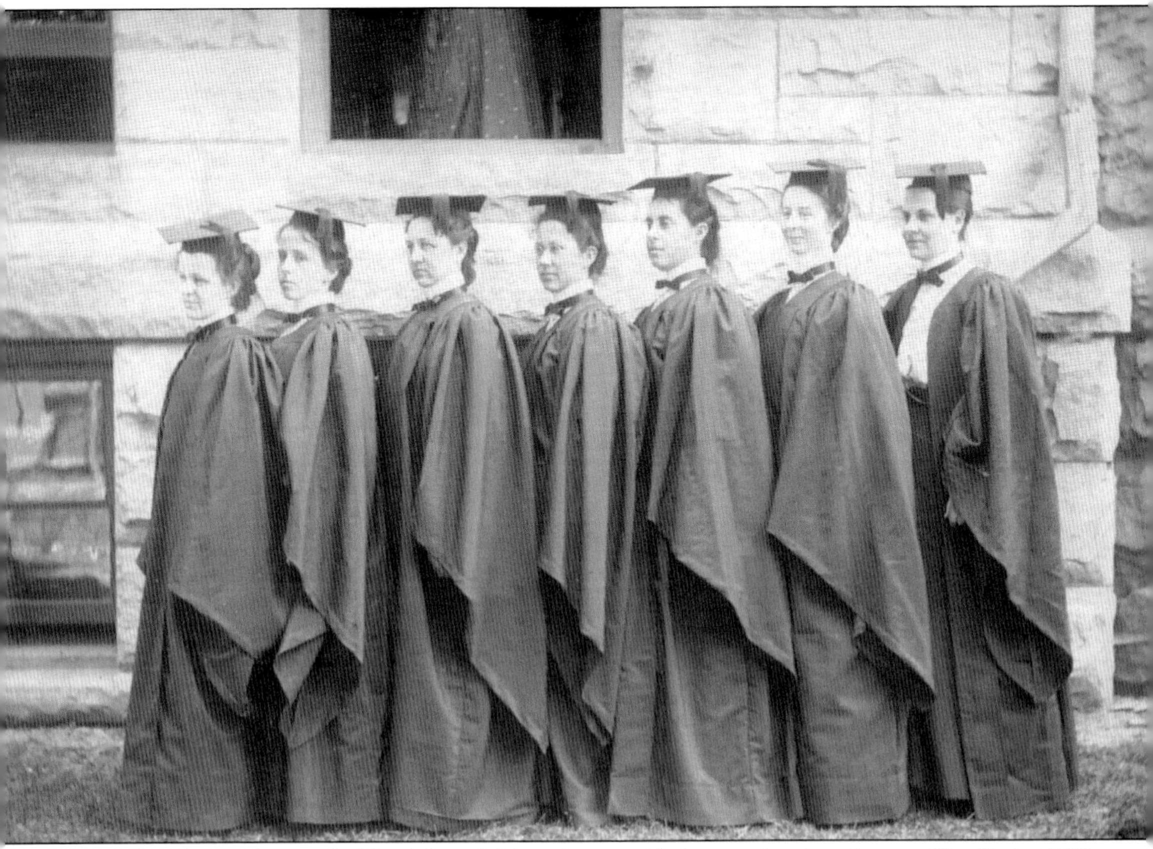

Esther Anne Craigmile (third from left) is shown with her graduating class at Oberlin in 1899. Esther was the only daughter of David not to marry, choosing instead an education career. She studied for one year at the University of Illinois–Urbana-Champaign but transferred to Oberlin College in Ohio to study ornithology. (Courtesy of Sandra Browning.)

Two

WORKING THE LAND

The turn of the 20th century saw a shift toward a growing agrarian economy that drew more and more people. By the first decade of the 1900s, Chicago had grown from a muddy fort to a city and had burned nearly to the ground (in 1871), only to be raised again more burly than ever on the backs of industry and immigrants. Railroads bustled grains, coal, limestone, and kerosene across the Midwest. Towns emerged along these routes, and businesses boomed to entertain and offer respite to an emerging working middle class. And here? Towns with names like Tiedtville, Byrnesville, and Gower appeared (and disappeared). Hinsdale and La Grange were the places folks meant when they said they were going "into town." One-room schools grew to bursting, filled with the children of these industrious farming families. Families were necessarily entrepreneurial in spirit: if you raised it, you sold it (presumably excluding the children).

Innovation and industrial production were the new drivers. The McCormick Harvester Machine Company, Deering Harvester Company, and Plano Manufacturing merged in 1902, forming International Harvester (IH) with its hub in Chicago and the surrounding farm land. By 1910, it had an estimated 17,000 employees in the area and grossed a reported $100 million in sales. In 1917, IH purchased the farmlands along Plainfield Road at County Line Road to Madison Road. There the company developed dairy and harvesting machinery inventions. Life in the immediate area became "modern"—plumbing and electricity, while luxuries for some, were becoming more expected. Horse-and-buggy travel was still the norm, of course, but Model Ts and even the occasional touring models were seen (often stuck in the unpaved roads, however, according to oral histories). A new generation was coming of age, still working the land—and often still with horsepower—but modernity had come with increasing income, stability, and growth.

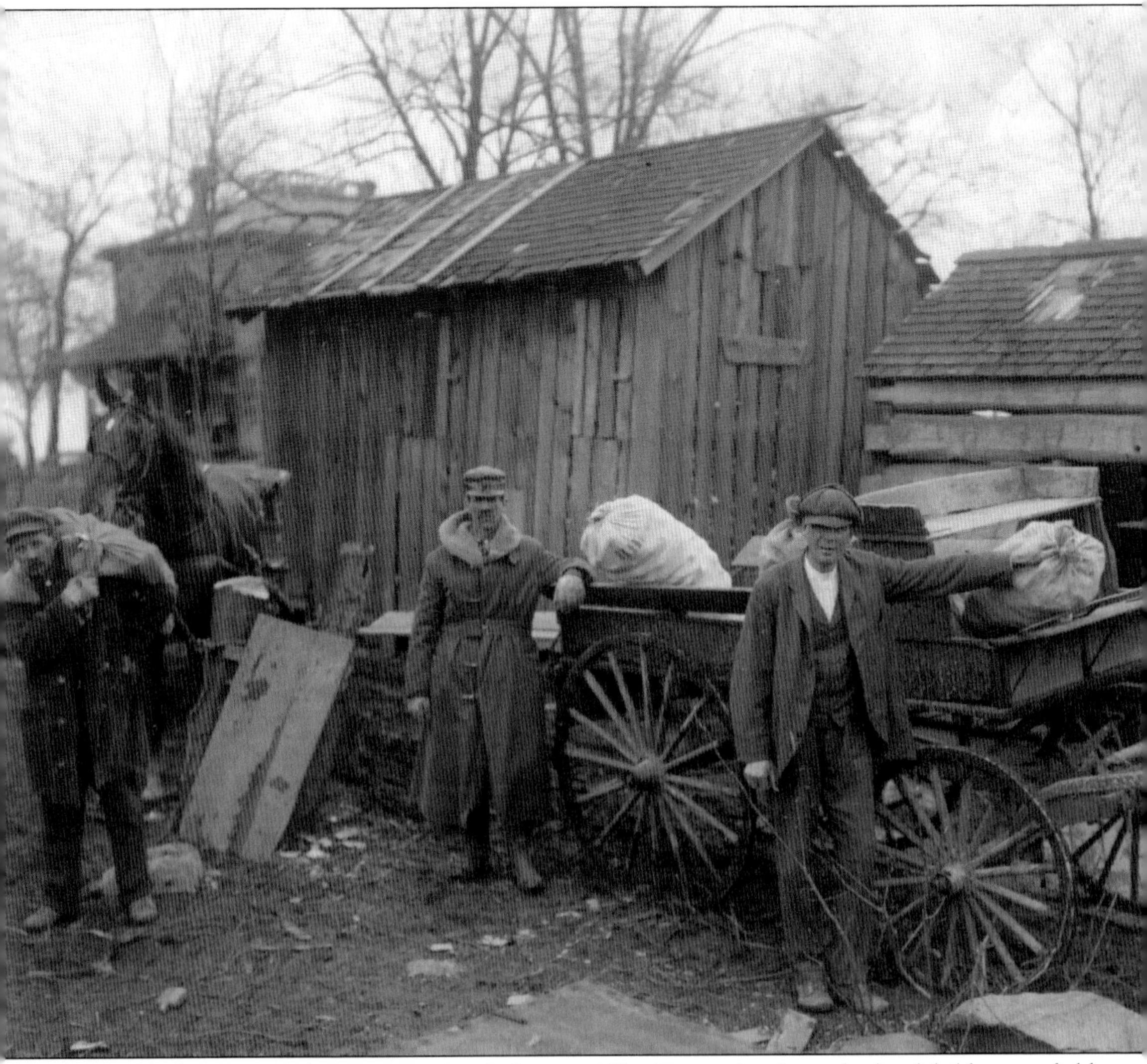

Both the Hoyts and Gears were family farmers. The Gears often hosted schoolchildren on field trips to learn more about the trade. This 1915 photograph, in which A. Hockemeyer, Howard Hoyt, and George Gear are loading a wagon in preparation for a visit to the school, shows a typical scene. Hoyt's daughter, Harriet, in an interview by a Pleasantdale School student, recounted that as a girl she "always took care of the cows" and "went to church in a buggy pulled by a horse and never went to a restaurant or a show." Another oral history described "the Plainfield Road" as often muddy and uncrossable without getting stuck at Flagg Creek (where I-294 is now). (Courtesy of Flagg Creek Heritage Society.)

The area was known in print more commonly as the land "south of Hinsdale" after 1900. This 1903 advertisement highlights the pastoral wealth of the Sedgeley Farm estate. Note the Swiss cow Thilda and the interior picture promoting the modern dairy barn to the left. Featured prominently in the center are proprietor E.M. Barton; his superintendent, W.E. James; and, almost as prominently, French Coach stallion Indre. (Courtesy of the Village of Burr Ridge.)

Sedgeley Farm employed many local families who had knowledge of modern practices. The Hoyts, the Comstocks, and others would work one farm and—literally—cross the street to the next. Such is the case with Sedgeley and Four Pines Farms. Maynard Comstock recalled, "In 1916 I took over the management of the Four Pines Farm on South County Line Road south of Hinsdale for the late Fred Babson. Across the road was one of the Sedgeley Farms operated by the late Howard Hoyt. It happened I had Mr. Babson's Italian Lancia out at the farm at the time, and took the boys [working the two farms] into Chicago for a site seeing trip. The car caused quite a stir and the boys felt pretty important." (Courtesy of the Village of Burr Ridge.)

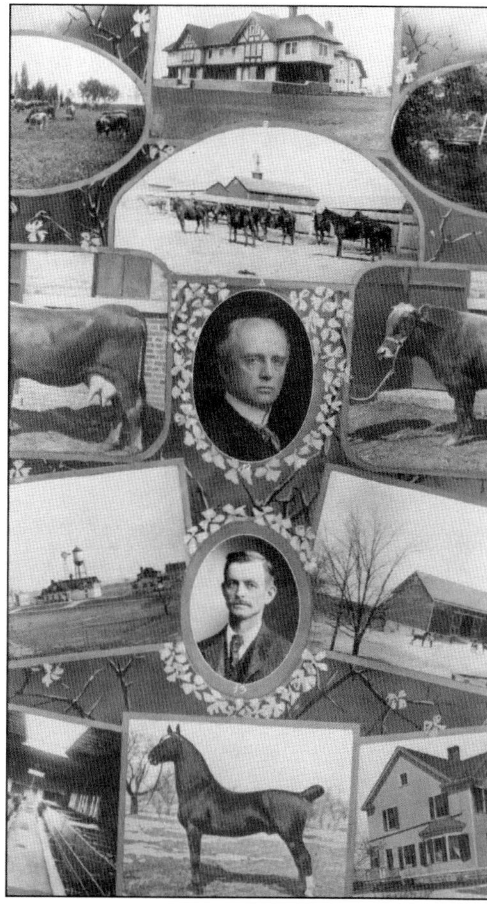

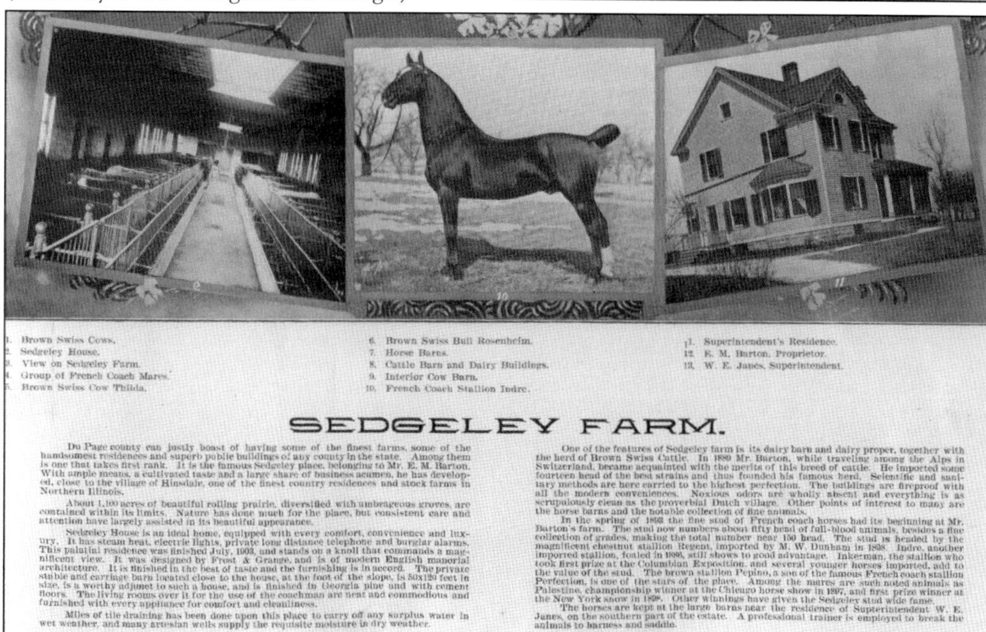

1. Brown Swiss Cows.
2. Sedgeley House.
3. View on Sedgeley Farm.
4. Group of French Coach Mares.
5. Brown Swiss Cow Thilda.
6. Brown Swiss Bull Rosenheim.
7. Horse Barns.
8. Cattle Barn and Dairy Buildings.
9. Interior Cow Barn.
10. French Coach Stallion Indre.
11. Superintendent's Residence.
12. E. M. Barton, Proprietor.
13. W. E. Janes, Superintendent.

SEDGELEY FARM.

Du Page county can justly boast of having some of the finest farms, some of the handsomest residences and superb public buildings of any county in the state. Among them is one that takes first rank. It is the famous Sedgeley place, belonging to Mr. E. M. Barton. With ample means, a cultivated taste and a large share of business acumen, he has developed, close to the village of Hinsdale, one of the finest country residences and stock farms in Northern Illinois.

About 1,100 acres of beautiful rolling prairie, diversified with umbrageous groves, are contained within its limits. Nature has done much for the place, but consistent care and attention have largely assisted in its beautiful appearance.

Sedgeley House is an ideal home, equipped with every comfort, convenience and luxury. It has steam heat, electric lights, private long distance telephone and burglar alarms. This palatial residence was finished July, 1903, and stands on a knoll that commands a magnificent view. It was designed by Frost & Grange, and is of modern English manorial architecture. It is finished in the best of taste and the furnishing is in accord. The private stable and carriage barn located close to the house, at the foot of the slope, is 50x120 feet in size, is a worthy adjunct to such a house, and is finished in Georgia pine and with cement floors. The living rooms over it for the use of the coachman are neat and commodious and furnished with every appliance for comfort and cleanliness.

Miles of tile draining has been done upon this place to carry off any surplus water in wet weather, and many artesian wells supply the requisite moisture in dry weather.

One of the features of Sedgeley farm is its dairy barn and dairy proper, together with the herd of Brown Swiss Cattle. In 1889 Mr. Barton, while traveling among the Alps in Switzerland, became acquainted with the merits of this breed of cattle. He imported some fourteen head of the best strains and thus founded his famous herd. Scientific and sanitary methods are here carried to the highest perfection. The buildings are fireproof with all the modern conveniences. Noxious odors are wholly absent and everything is as scrupulously clean as the proverbial Dutch village. Other points of interest to many are the horse barns and the notable collection of fine animals.

In the spring of 1893 the fine stud of French coach horses had its beginning at Mr. Barton's farm. The stud now numbers about fifty head of full-blood animals, besides a fine collection of grades, making the total number near 150 head. The stud is headed by the magnificent chestnut stallion Regent, imported by M. W. Dunham in 1898. Indre, another imported stallion, foaled in 1886, still shows to good advantage. Inkerman, the stallion who took first prize at the Columbian Exposition, and several younger horses imported, add to the value of the stud. The brown stallion Pepino, a son of the famous French coach stallion Perfection, is one of the stars of the place. Among the mares are such noted animals as Palestine, championship winner at the Chicago horse show in 1897, and first prize winner at the New York show in 1898. Other winnings have given the Sedgeley stud wide fame.

The horses are kept at the large barns near the residence of Superintendent W. E. Janes, on the southern part of the estate. A professional trainer is employed to break the animals to harness and saddle.

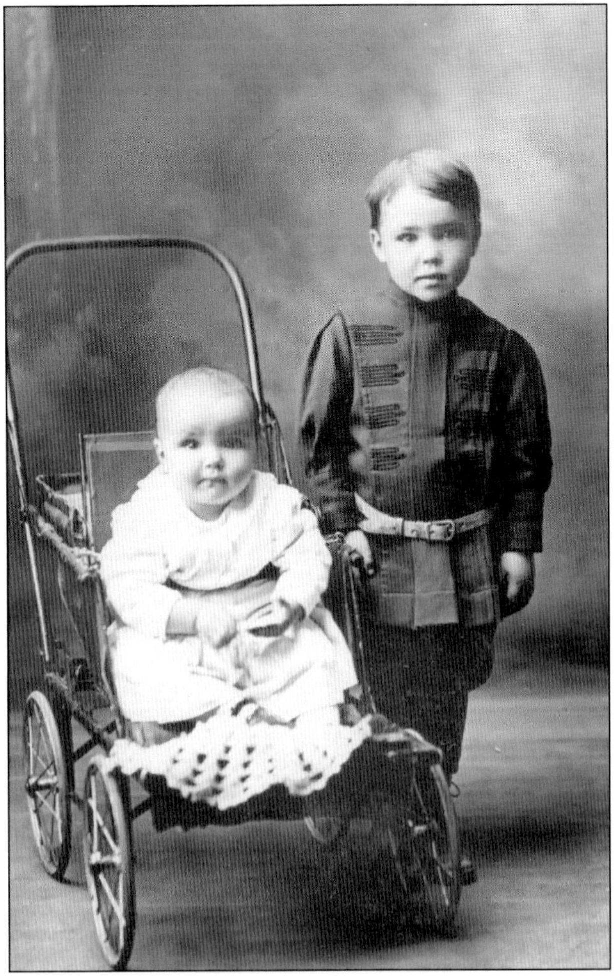

New families were coming into the area, attracted by land and employment. A rising middle class, while expecting children to work and contribute to the farm, were also focusing on raising educated children. Professional portraits of families—and especially children—were intended to signal a certain class or status, even if it was only aspirational. Martha and Leonard Comstock patiently posed for one such portrait in 1909. (Courtesy of Sandra Browning.)

For the Boness family, success seemingly had come, revealed here in a casual and joyous romp in a touring car during a 1912 picnic on their family land on 91st Street. The Boness family were active in the busy Trinity Lutheran Church community. Their descendants remain in the area. (Courtesy of Flagg Creek Heritage Society.)

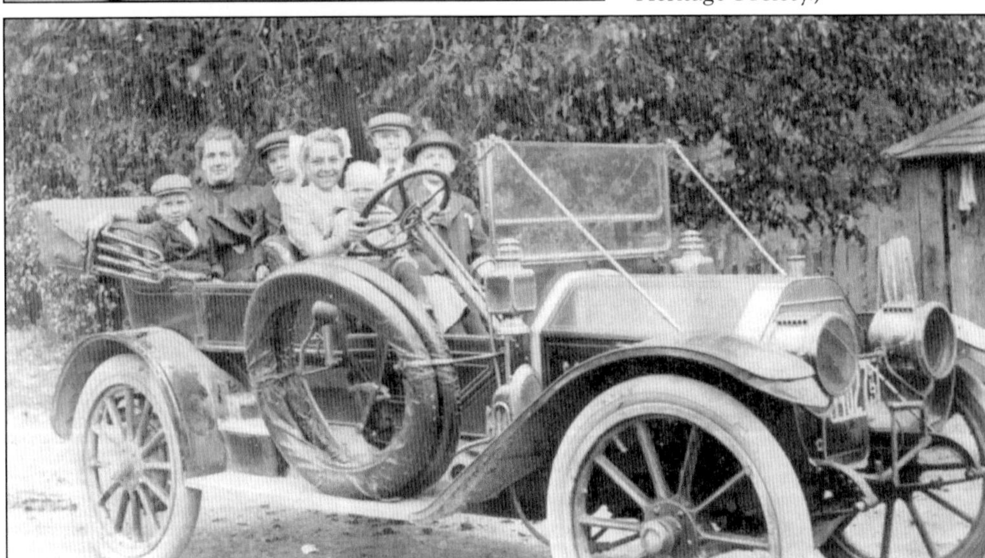

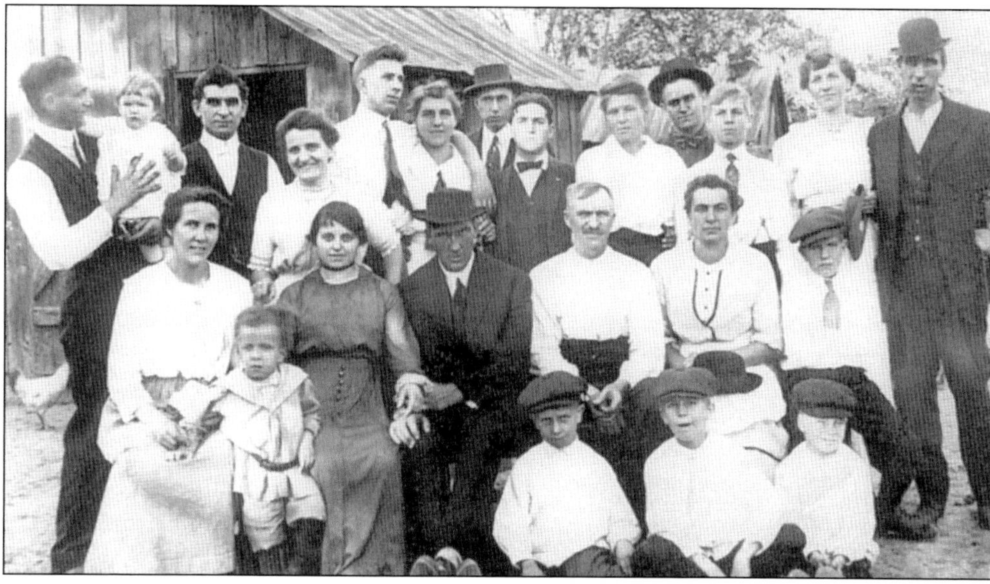

Even as the Boness family expanded, hard work remained a priority. The Bonesses are shown on their 91st Street land around 1915. (Both, courtesy of Flagg Creek Heritage Society.)

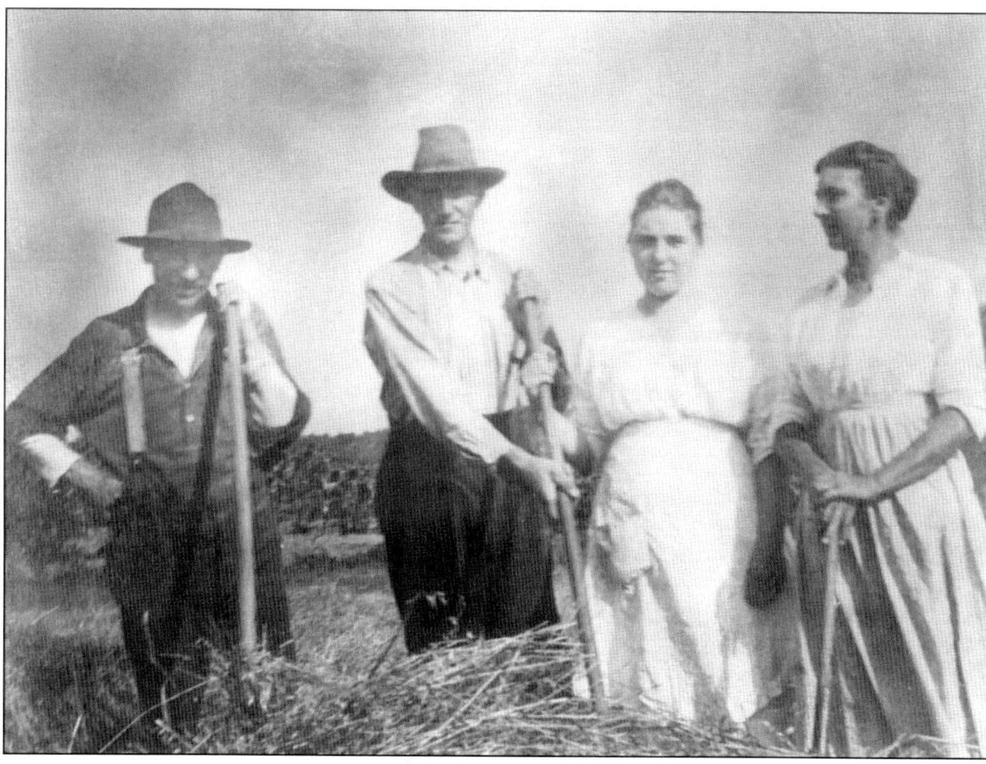

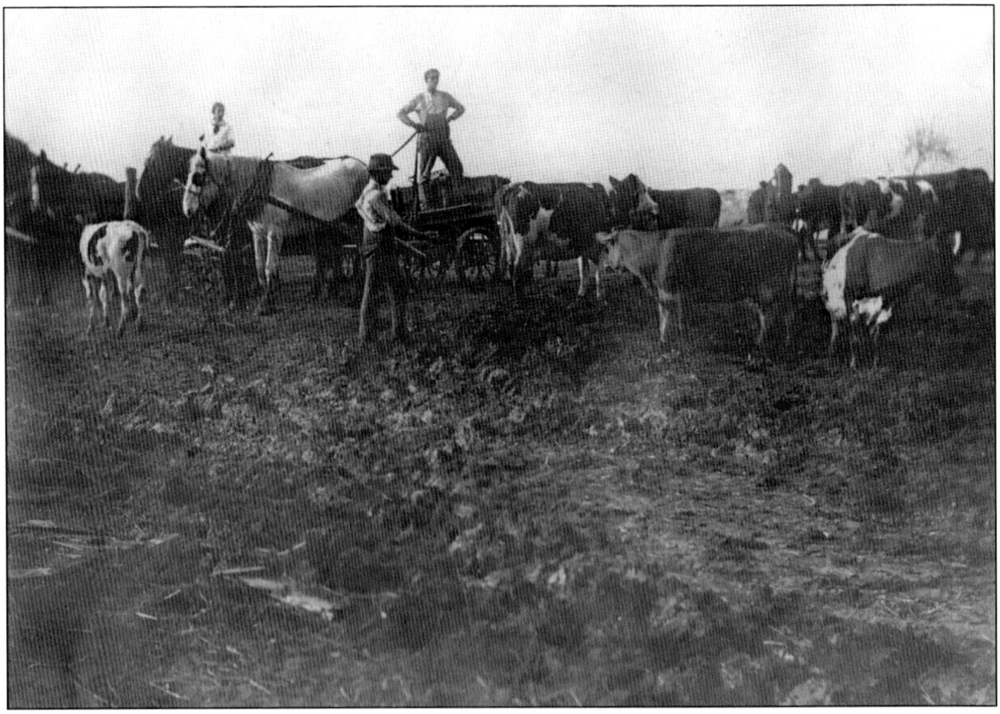

Dairy farming was an established industry and included Kraml Dairy (which had business in Chicago but also had herds here) and what would become Four Pines Farm on County Line Road. International Harvester, too, had dairy herds and tested new types of milking equipment. For most "dairymen," it was hands-on work. Note the teenager at left as she tends the herd in this 1914 photograph. (Courtesy of Flagg Creek Heritage Society.)

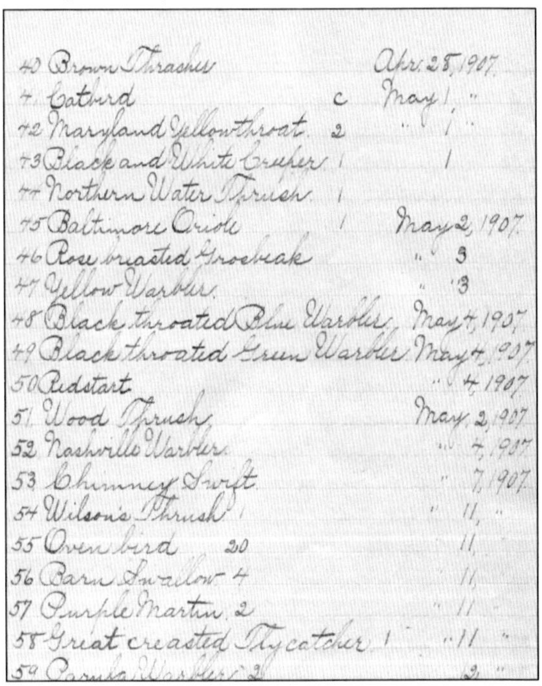
40 Brown Thrasher Apr. 25, 1907
41 Catbird c May 1 "
42 Maryland Yellowthroat 2 " 1 "
43 Black and White Creeper 1 1
44 Northern Water Thrush 1
45 Baltimore Oriole 1 May 2, 1907
46 Rose breasted Grosbeak " 3
47 Yellow Warbler " 3
48 Black throated Blue Warbler May 4, 1907
49 Black throated Green Warbler May 4, 1907
50 Redstart " 4, 1907
51 Wood Thrush May 2, 1907
52 Nashville Warbler " 4, 1907
53 Chimney Swift " 7, 1907
54 Wilson's Thrush 1 " 11 "
55 Oven bird 20 11
56 Barn Swallow 4 11
57 Purple Martin 2 " 11
58 Great creasted Flycatcher 1 " 11 "
59 Parula Warbler 2 2 "

The wooded ridges, wetlands to the south, Flagg Creek and DesPlaines River plain, and open grasslands were all inviting habitat for birds. Esther Craigmile studied ornithology at Oberlin and later became a published scholar and director of the Illinois Audubon Society. An avid birder, she kept bird counts throughout her life. These notes from 1907 reveal the area's avian diversity. (Courtesy of Sandra Browning.)

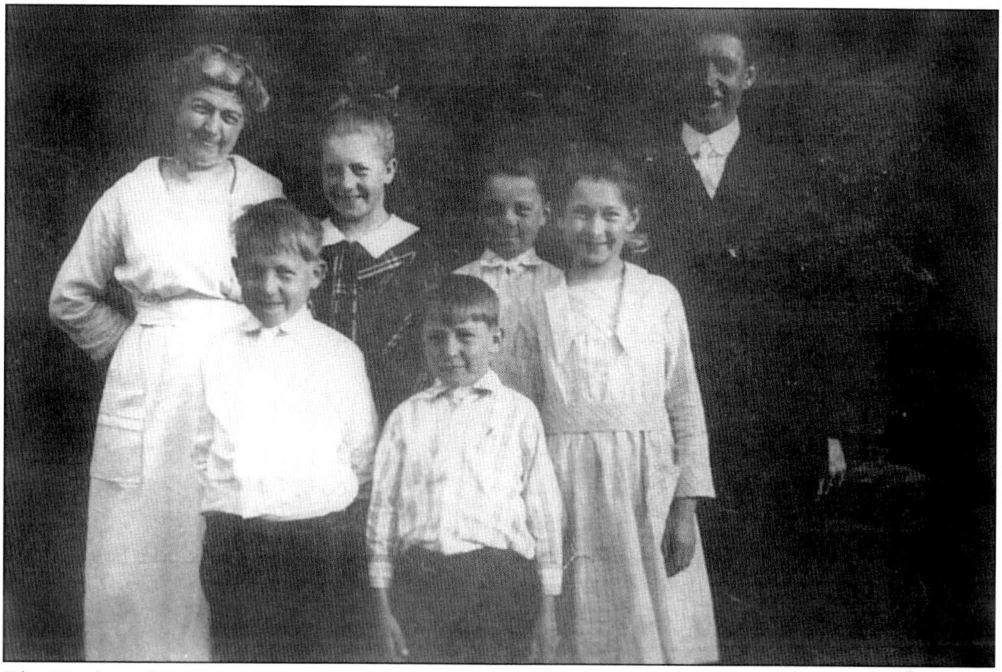

The Tiedt and Sass families were well-known, active early families both within and outside the Trinity Lutheran Church community. Fred Tiedt—born in 1868 at Wolf Road and 91st Street—by the late 1800s, was a saloonkeeper, storekeeper, and local businessman. His services were so popular that the area became known as "Tiedtville." He even persuaded the Santa Fe Railroad to make weekend stops to bring weary, Chicago-worn workers and families to his acreage, which he had converted to a picnic and recreation area. By the turn of the 20th century, he had added horse and bicycle races. The Tiedt family was also known for hosting the beloved Farmer's Harvest Day Picnic, at which farmers could celebrate and share their bounty. Louise Tiedt Sass, Edward Sass, and their family, seen here around 1900, were part of Tiedtville's next generation. (Courtesy of Flagg Creek Heritage Society.)

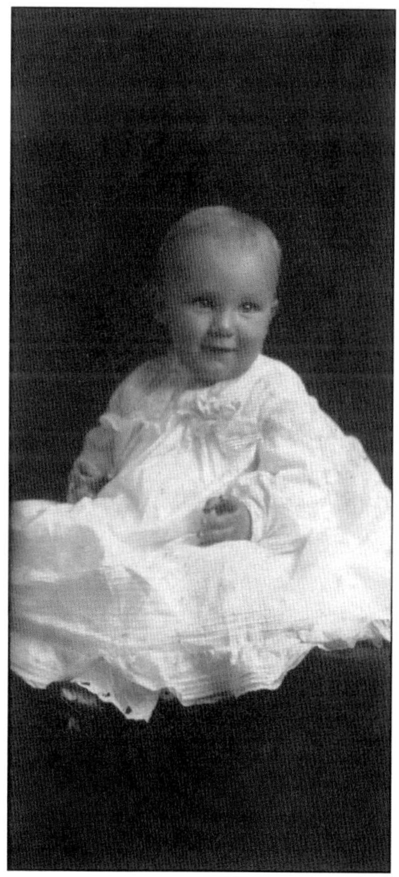

Howard and Ruth Hoyt's family was growing, like most farm families. Raymond Hoyt is shown here around 1903. (Courtesy of Flagg Creek Heritage Society.)

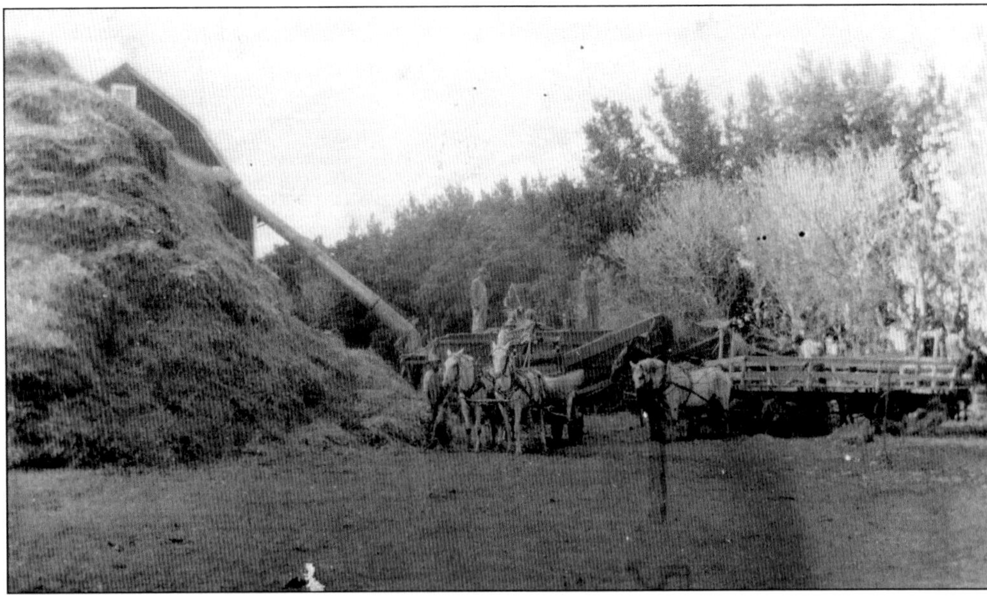

Threshing had not yet been mechanized for most, but it couldn't come soon enough. As seen in these photographs, taken around 1900, men worked late days to bring in the harvest (hay and otherwise). (Both, courtesy of Flagg Creek Heritage Society.)

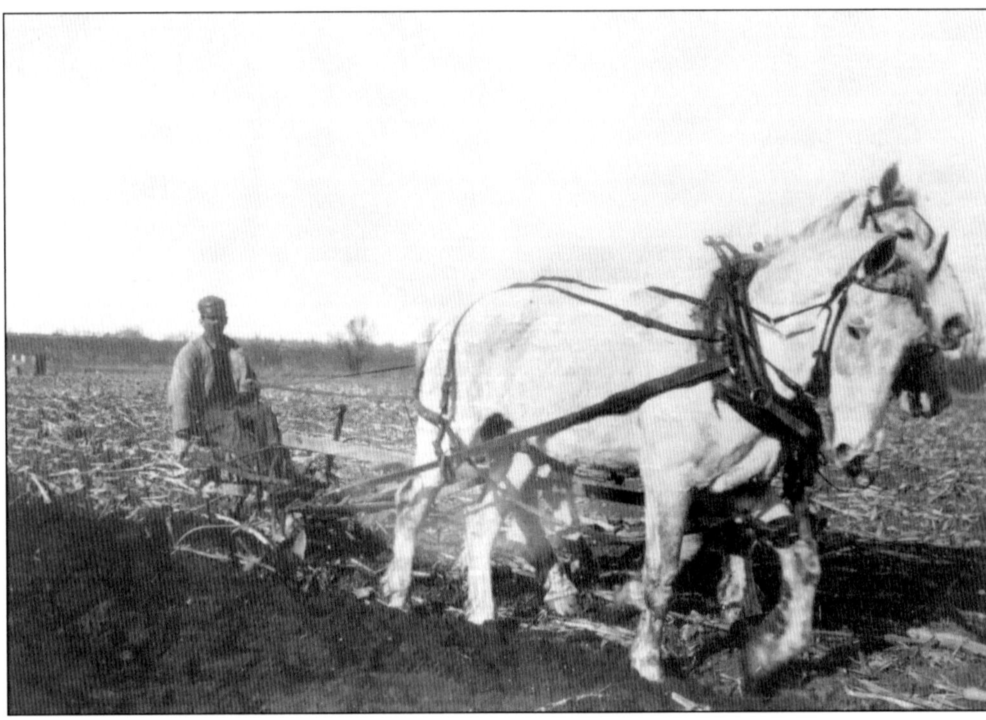

Three

Turn-of-the-Century Life

While there was rollicking Tiedtville, there was also another area that had grown into being: Byrneville. Far more sleepy, it was located in what is now the Palisades area of Burr Ridge at the southern end of Madison Street and was not much more than a train stop and a one-room schoolhouse. The train stop was particularly useful to local dairy farmers, who were able to transport their milk. And the school? It was founded by residents William C. Jeans, John Doolin of Lemont, F.C. Tiedt, and William Wachter to solve the problem of their children walking three miles to Cass School each day. The Byrneville School was completed in 1910, and its first teacher was the locally noted Anne M. Jeans. She remained its only teacher until 1947. The Jeans family lived near Madison and 91st Streets and had extended family farther south in "the Palisades." Anne, family, and friends took the following photographs at the turn of the 20th century, revealing a rare glimpse into the everyday life of not only a respected teacher but also a young woman at home with family and friends. These images are all from the personal scrapbook of Anne, which remains in the care of the school that bears her name: Anne M. Jeans School Community Consolidated School District.

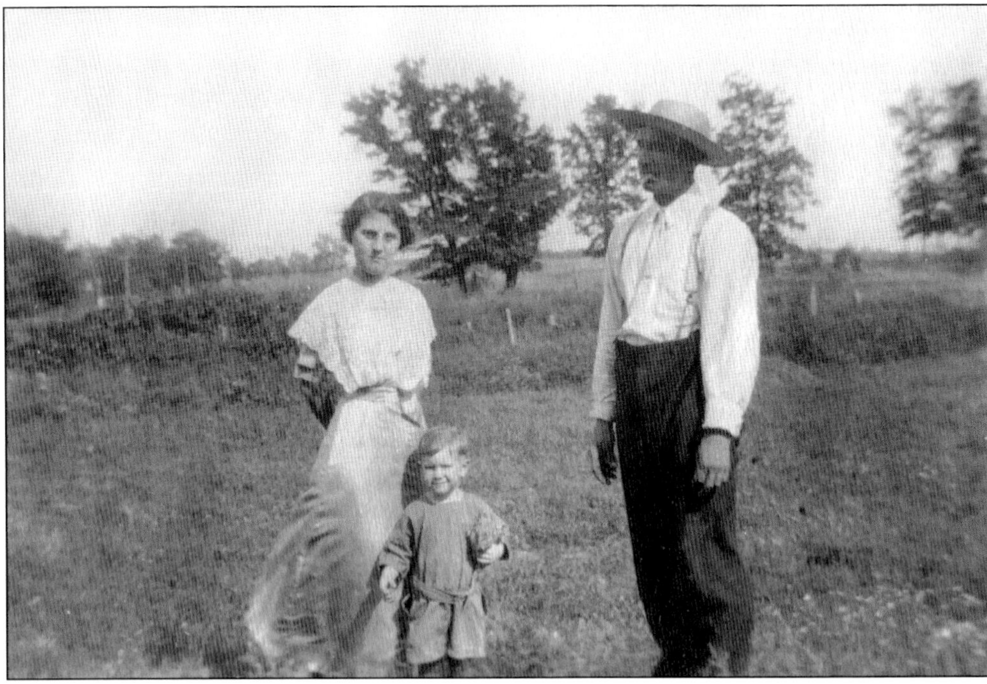

A teenage Anne M. Jeans (left in both images) enjoys moments of leisure with other relatives at the family farm around 1900. It would be William C. Jeans who, in 1910, led the way to start Byrneville School. That very school would be named Anne M. Jeans, as it remains today, in honor of her as its first teacher. (Both, AMJSCCS.)

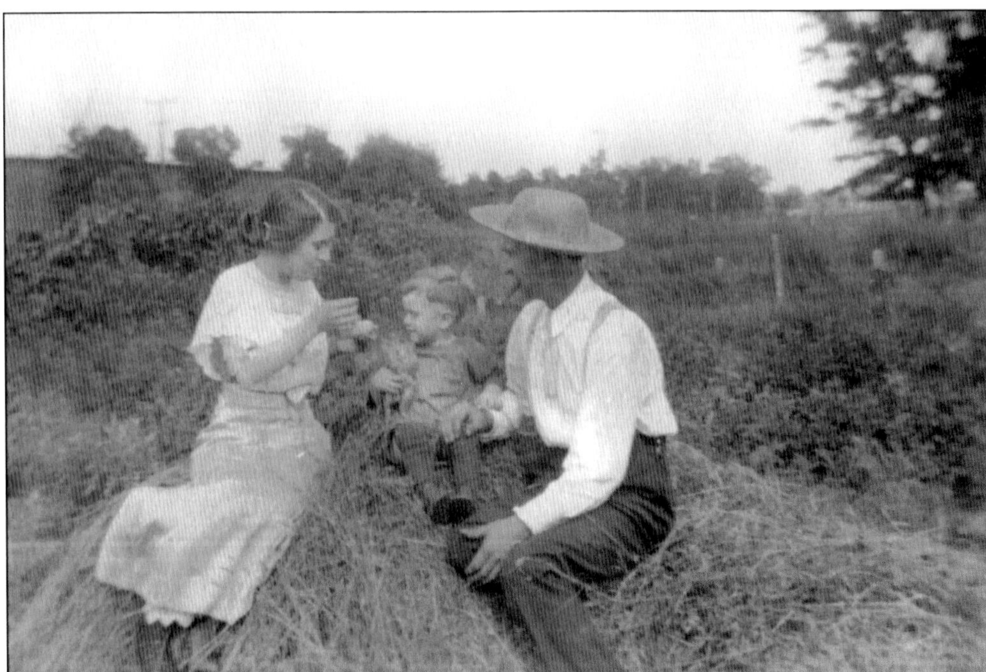

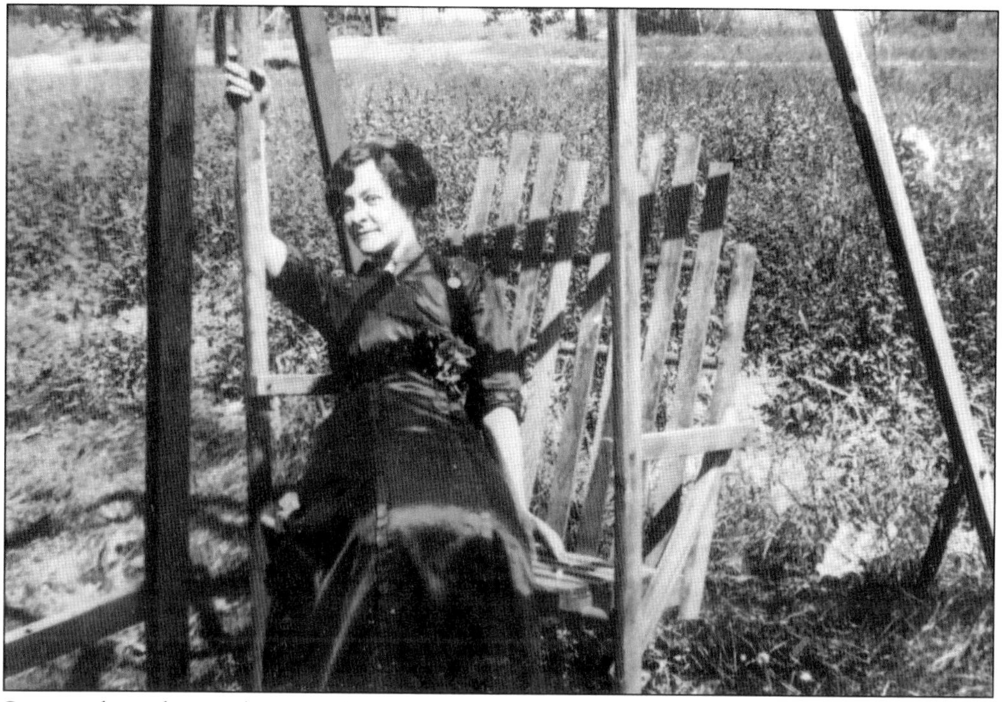

Summer heat during this period often meant sitting outside for the breezes when they were available and using a swing when they were not. A stylish dress did not necessarily mean a cool or comfortable one. A Jeans family member appears to be taking an elegant pause in the family home's backyard. (AMJSCCS.)

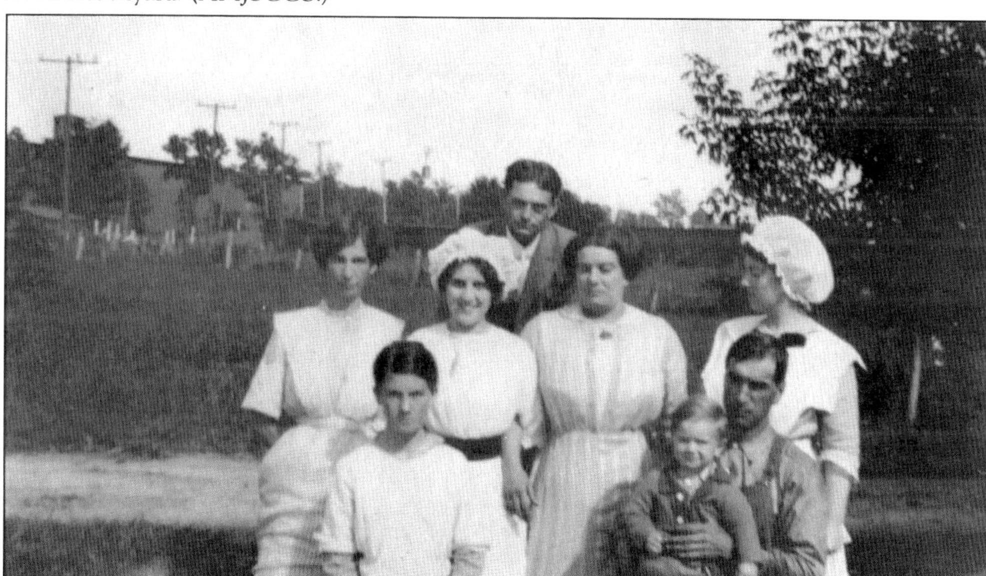

The Jeans extended family and neighbors pose—some apparently more willing than others—in the bright sun. The cap and white apron Anne wears appear to be very similar to those of a maid's uniform, but there is no record of her having done maid work. Women often protected their hair and dresses while doing housework, and the two women pictured dressed in this manner were likely pulled into the picture mid-task. (AMJSCCS.)

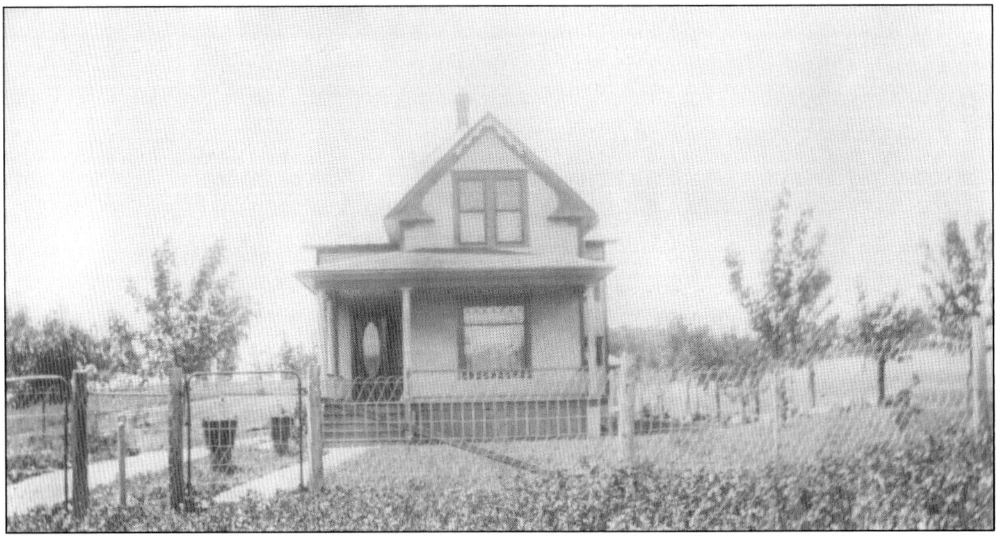

The Jeans family home stood at Madison and 91st Streets, an anchor at the beginning of the southern area known as the Palisades. The tiny "town" of Byrneville—and its train depot, where teachers and dairymen alike would catch the line—was quiet, it's been said, but for the sound of the steam train's whistle. (Both, AMJSCCS.)

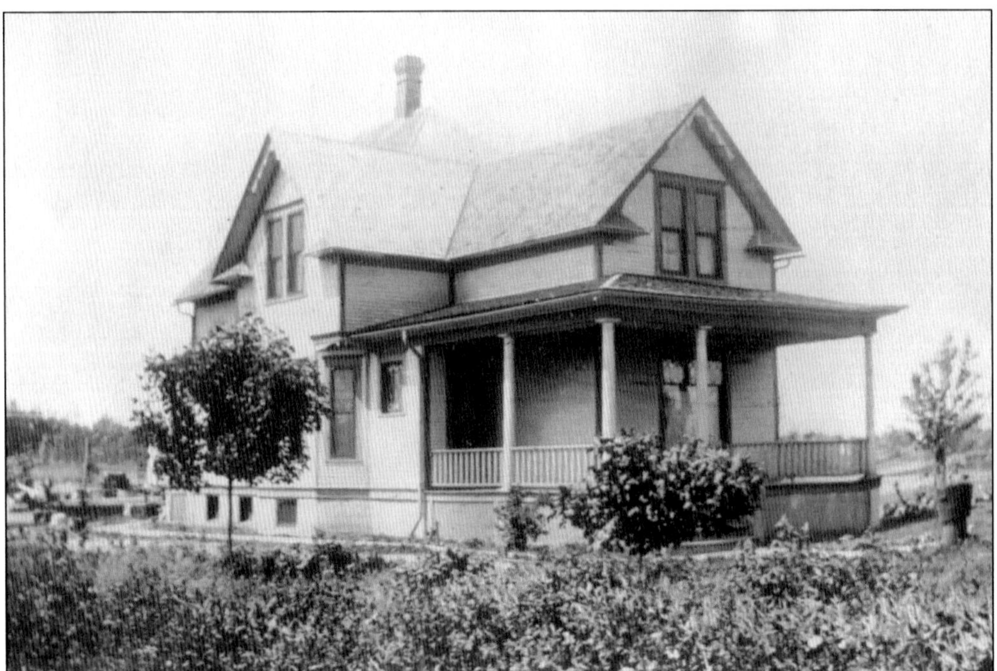

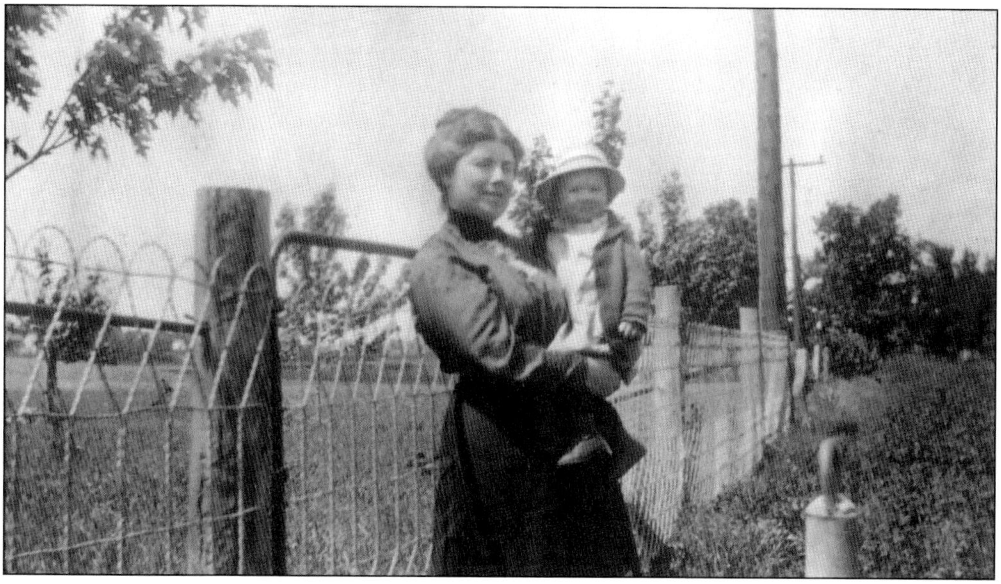

The gentle sloping and rolling landscape behind these Jeans family members reveals a topography that has changed little. Having such sturdy and heavy fencing was an absolute necessity: nearly every resident had, at the least, horses and often many dairy cows. Decorative fences were left for the "townies" in Hinsdale and La Grange. Families wanted to keep their lawns distinct from paddocks. (Both, AMJSCCS.)

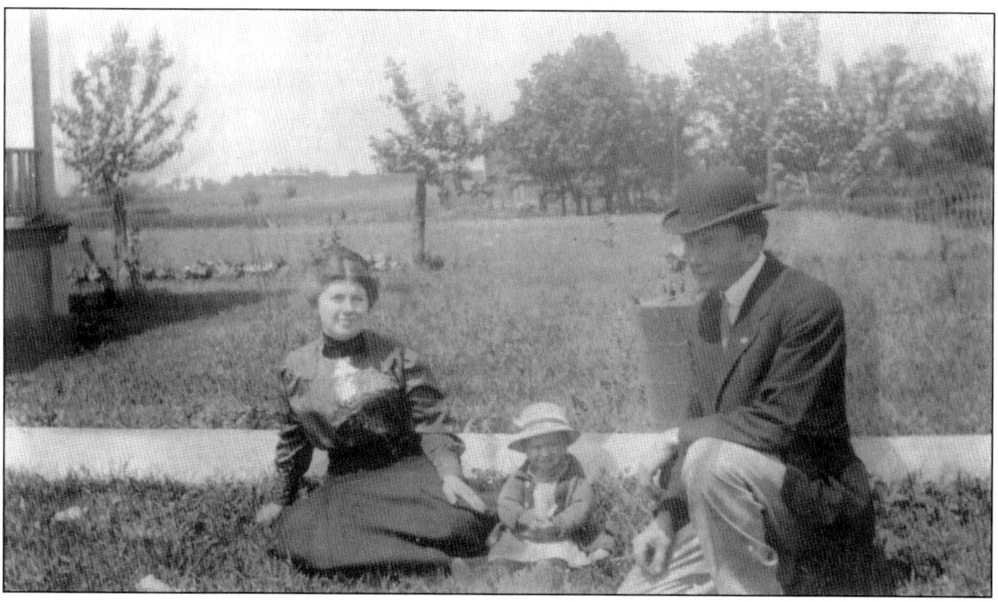

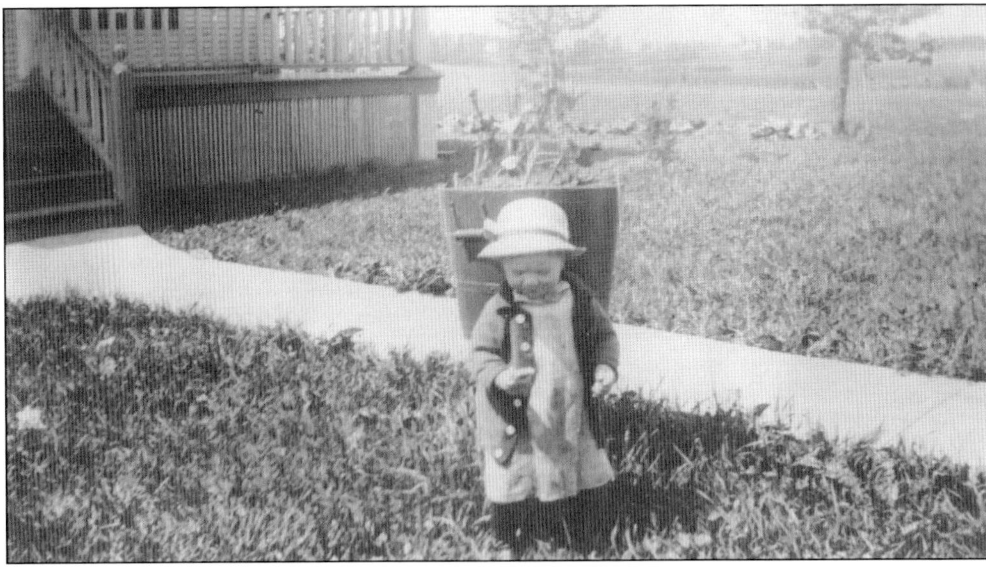

Yard work was a family affair. Clearly this Jeans family toddler (above) is blissfully unaware of the work his mother and family are doing around him while an older brother (below) appears to be taking a playful break. Women's work was in- and outside the home, and the Jeans were no different in their work ethic. (Both, AMJSCCS.)

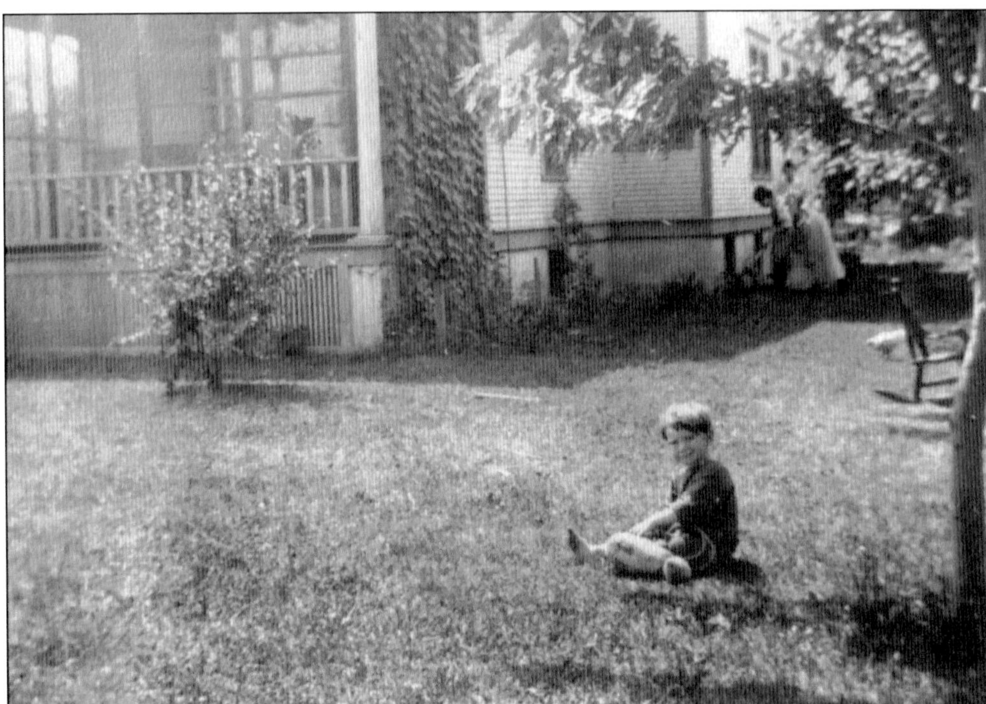

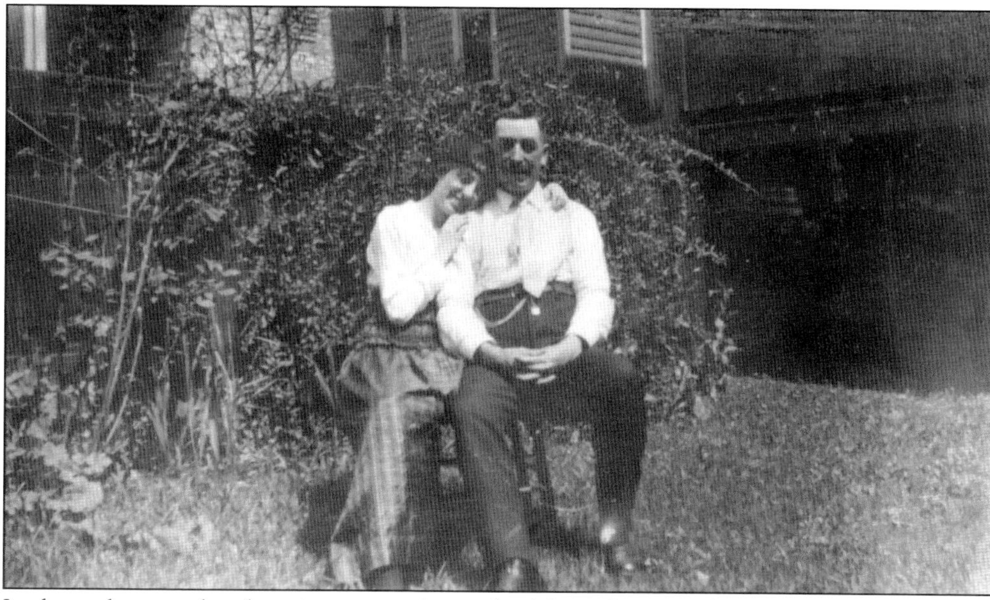

In these photographs, there is a sense of everyday life in the area: above, a Jeans family couple poses affectionately outside the home on a summer's day. Below, another glimpse shows just how far the next home is—across two paddocks and a yard, a smaller home is visible to the east. The man's confidence in his horsemanship shows. (Both, AMJSCCS.)

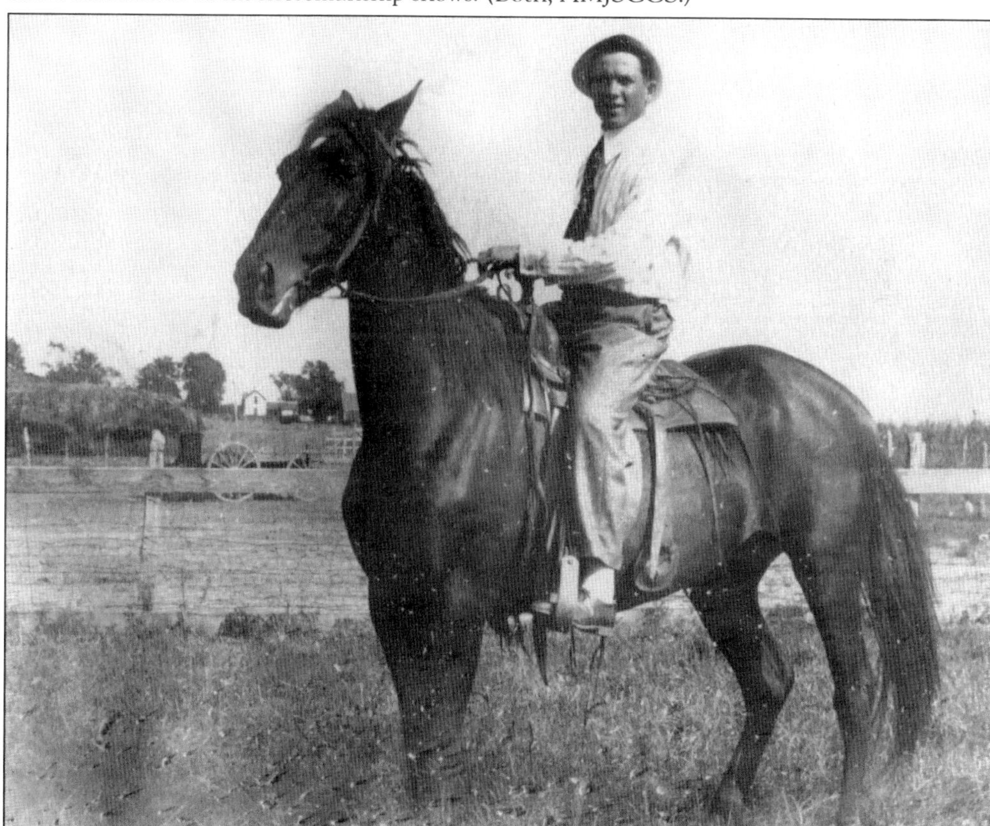

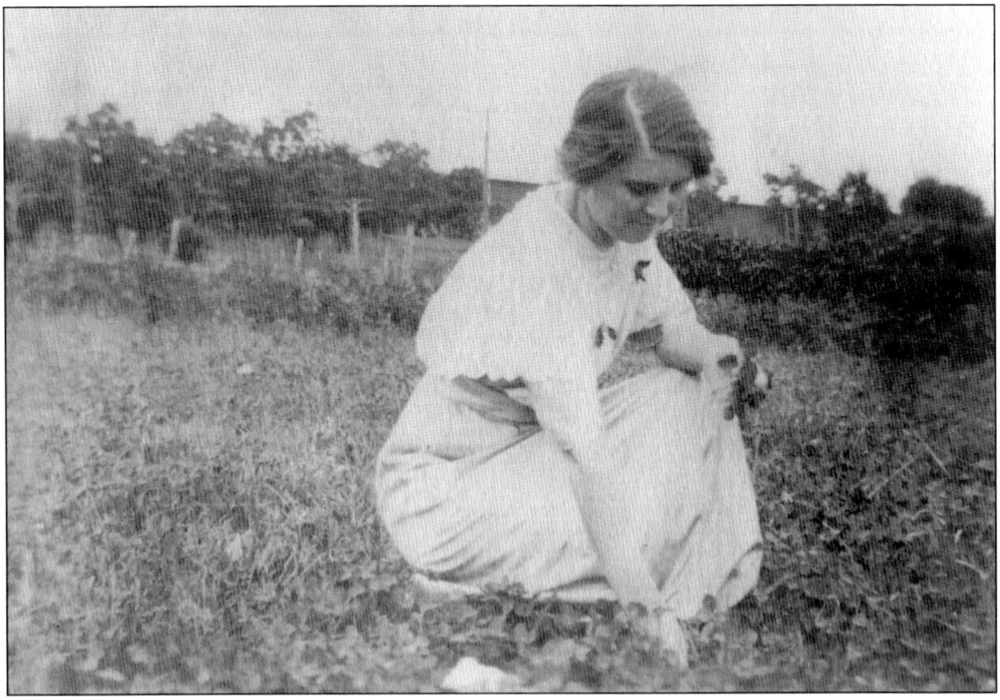

Here we see a young Anne in 1905, playful and silly at home. Picking flowers one day (above) and climbing the barn roof with friends the next (right) seems to convey a joyful (if dangerous) approach of hers that became well known and beloved later in her career as a teacher. (Both, AMJSCCS.)

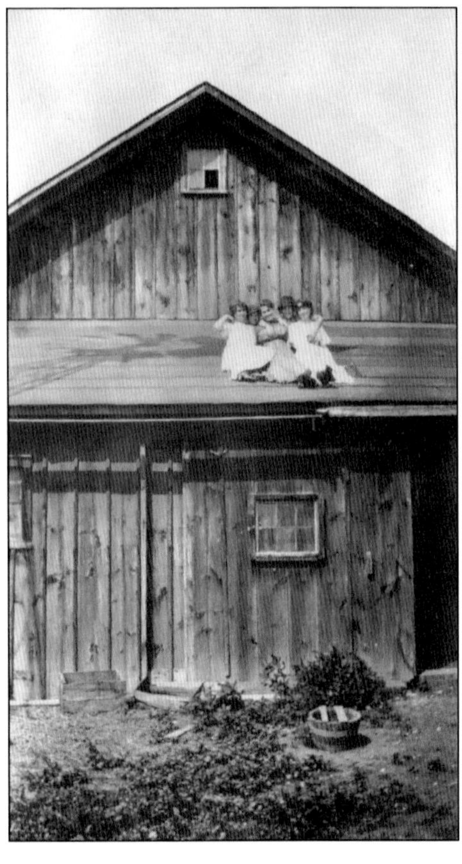

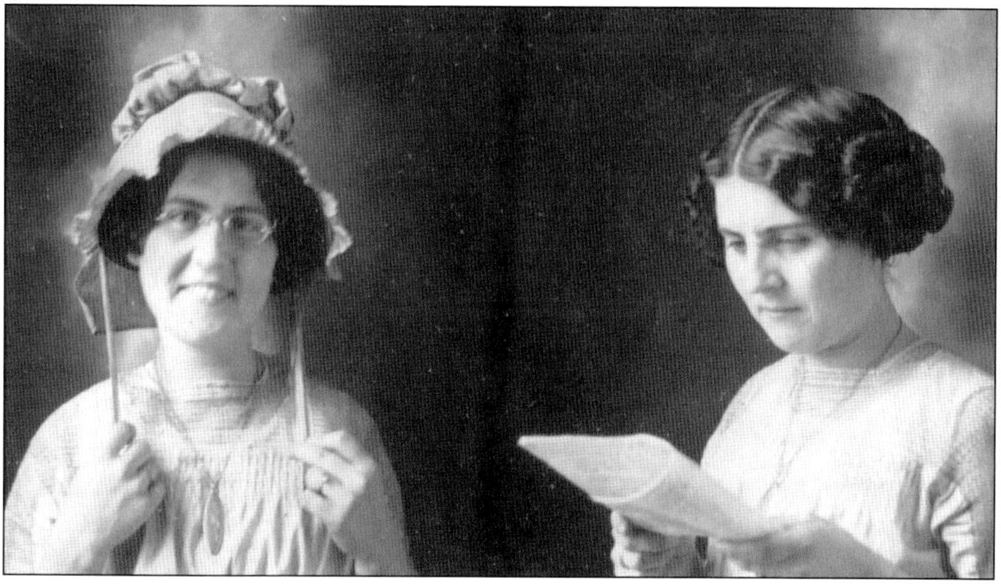

Anne's scrapbook from her life in college characterizes the period well. Women did enter higher education in rapidly increasing numbers after 1900, but statistically, it was still rare. Often, education was the most common profession for women at the time. While Anne was away at college in 1908, she (above) and her university friends (below) are shown taking a break for fun. (Both, AMJSCCS.)

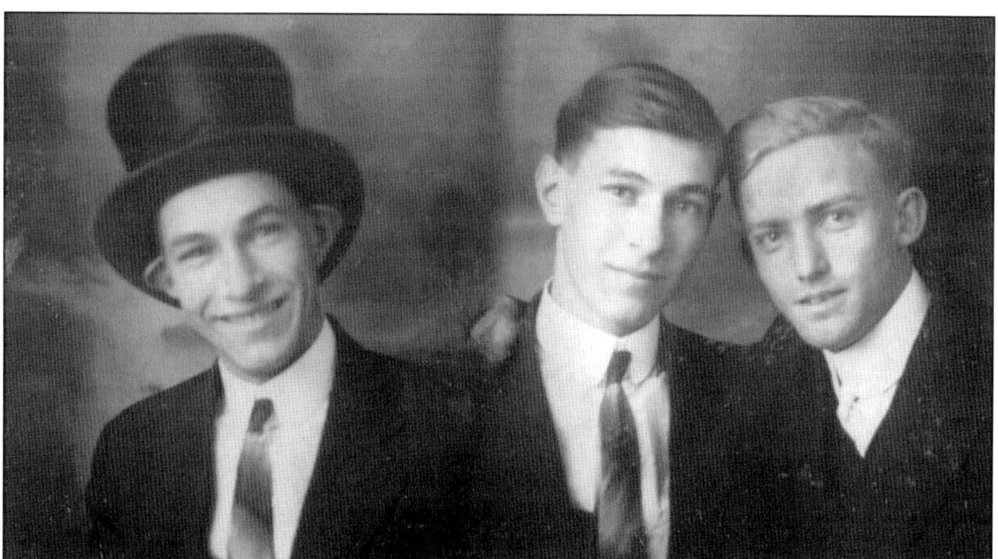

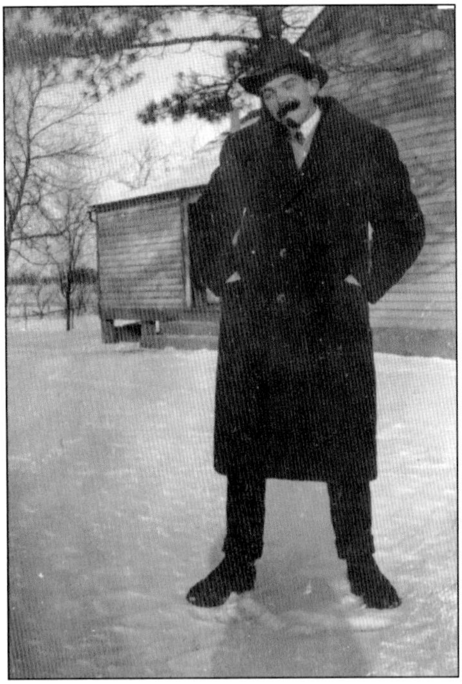

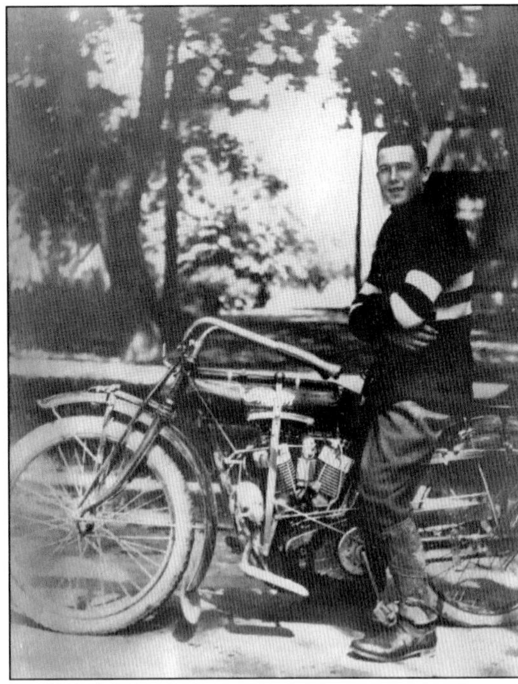

Anne returned to her home often during her college years. Her friends would visit, just as college students sometimes now bring home friends. It is fun to imagine that the young man pictured below with his motorbike may have brought it to Tiedtville. (Both, AMJSCCS.)

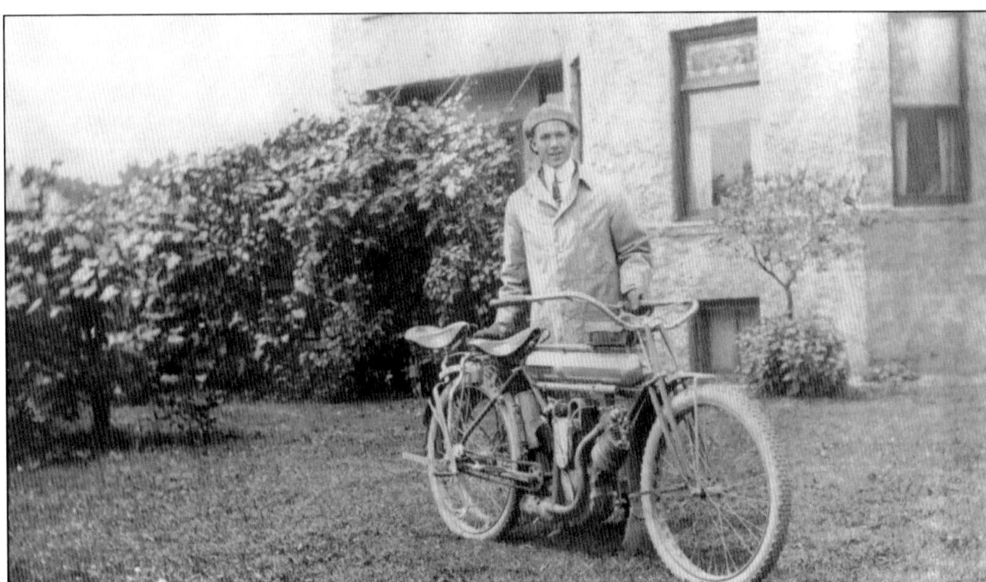

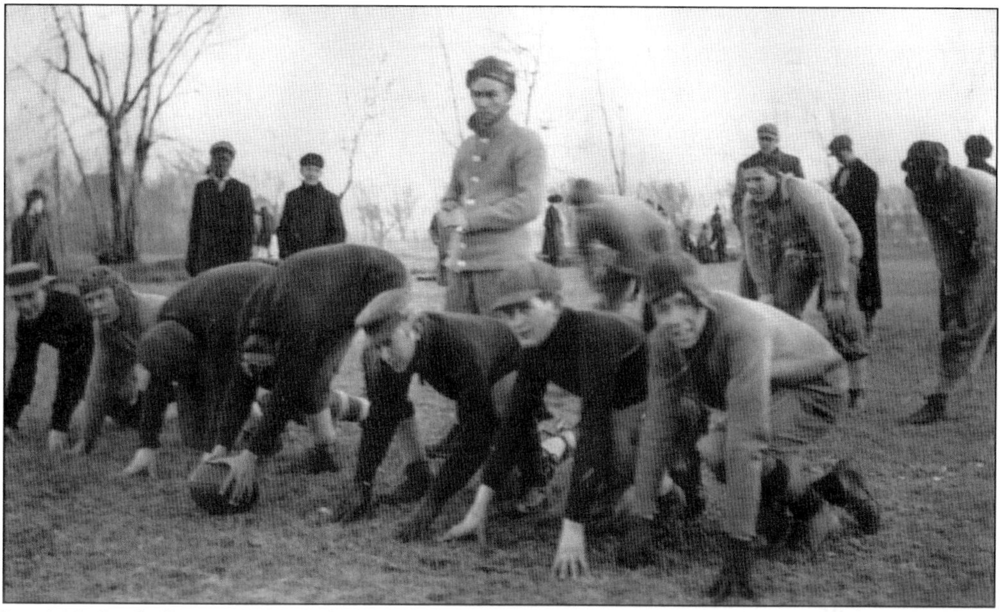

In 1908, football was very popular. One journalist wrote that year, "With the modernized plays that are being brought into the game, football is, in its present state, the national game in the fall the same as baseball [is] in the summer." Then, as now, local teens enjoy a pickup game as spectators look on. (AMJSCCS.)

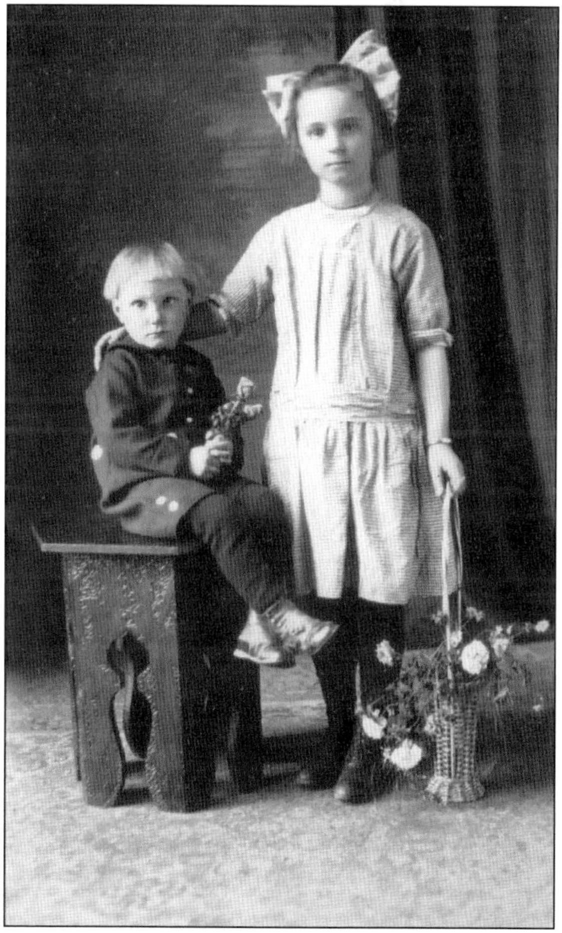

Two of the Jeans family children pose for a portrait in 1900. At the time, photographers would visit door to door with equipment and offer to take home portraits, which this appears to be. (AMJSCCS.)

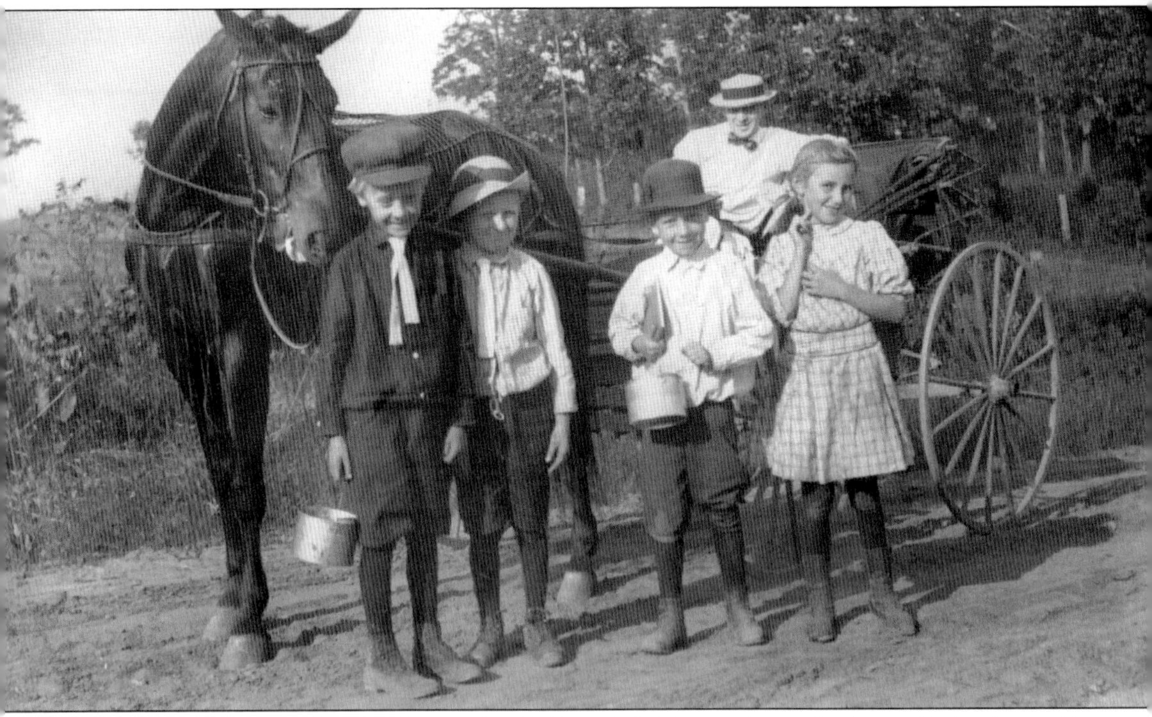

Finally, the Byrneville School opened in 1910, and children no longer had to walk the three miles to Cass School any longer. Lunch pails in hand, these schoolchildren prepare for the day under the watchful eye of a parent. These Tiedt children are believed to be among some of Anne's first students. (AMJSCCS.)

Four

Industrious Families

The Great War had come and gone, taking many with it. After the war, new mechanized technologies began to be applied to the working farms here. By the 1920s and 1930s, a way of life had pivoted away from the horse-drawn buggy and plow and toward increasing mechanical power and industry. Make no mistake, this was still the bread-and-butter, meat-and-potatoes folk who listened to WLS's (World's Largest Store) *The Prairie Farmer* radio broadcasts, made famous by the strategic purchase and promotion of *The Prairie Farmer* newspaper by Burridge D. Butler. International Harvester had, by now, invented—and perfected—the famous Farmall tractor, testing it at what was called the Hinsdale Farm on its lands on Plainfield Road. It had sold its land east of County Line Road and focused on perfecting crop mechanics to a degree that would change global food production. For the ordinary farming residents, the need for teams of horses diminished. The Chicago Worlds Fair, "A Century of Progress," in 1933–1934 even featured International Harvester as a symbol of progress and innovation. The 1920s to 1930s saw an even more modern generation—automobiles were now ordinary, and everyday life included radio, telephones, and modern conveniences like refrigeration. Schools such as Trinity Lutheran and Pleasantdale were built (or rebuilt) to accommodate growing student bodies. However, where the 1920s inspired a certain excitement and growth, the 1930s grew more sullen with the Great Depression. More than ever, families and churches became havens for many, safety nets in a time of uncertainty. "Making do" was simply what was done.

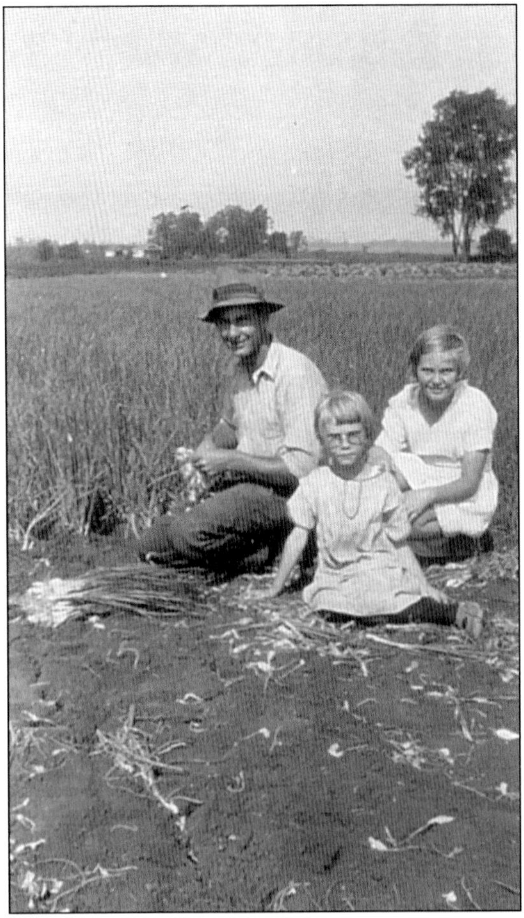

Newer families began arriving in the area, such as the Bulthuis family. They came to own the farm where the Flagg Creek Heritage Society stands today on Wolf Road. Father Hank Bulthuis with daughters Talena and Jenny are seen here on that land in 1928. (Courtesy of Sandy Bulthuis and Flagg Creek Heritage Society.)

Ed Sass works with a mechanical thresher in 1920. The farming techniques of even two decades earlier were more labor intensive and time consuming. (Courtesy of Flagg Creek Heritage Society.)

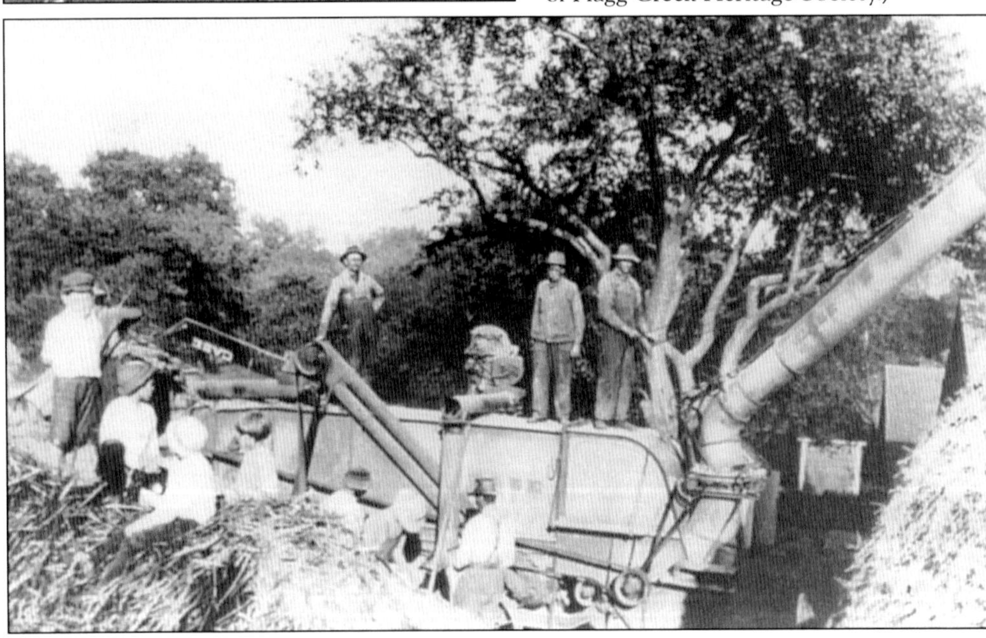

George Rufus Gear, who as a young man taught schoolchildren how to plant seed corn, poses with his cane in 1930. (Courtesy of Flagg Creek Heritage Society.)

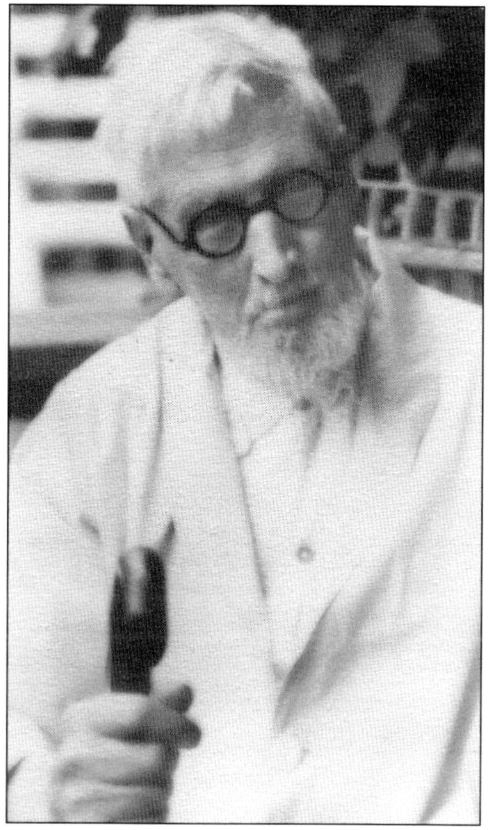

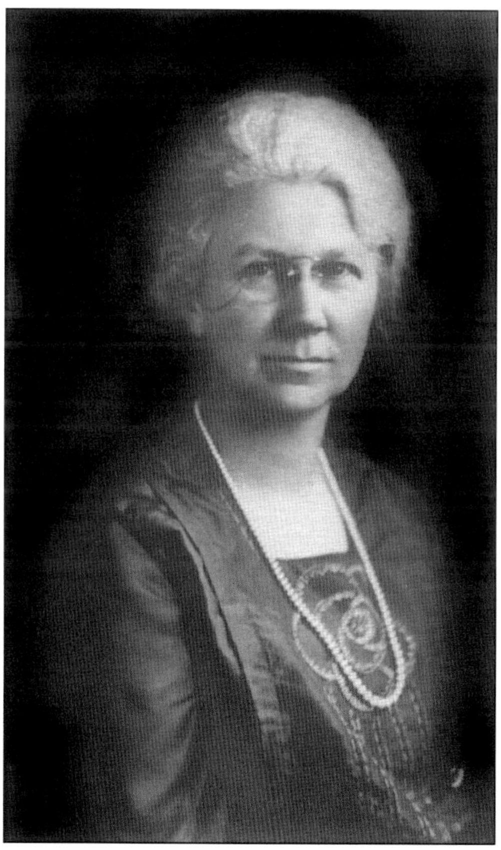

Esther A. Craigmile by 1929 had become a noted science educator, having returned to college at the University of Chicago to earn her master's in science. She taught science and nature study for her career in La Grange and River Forest. (Courtesy of Sandra Browning.)

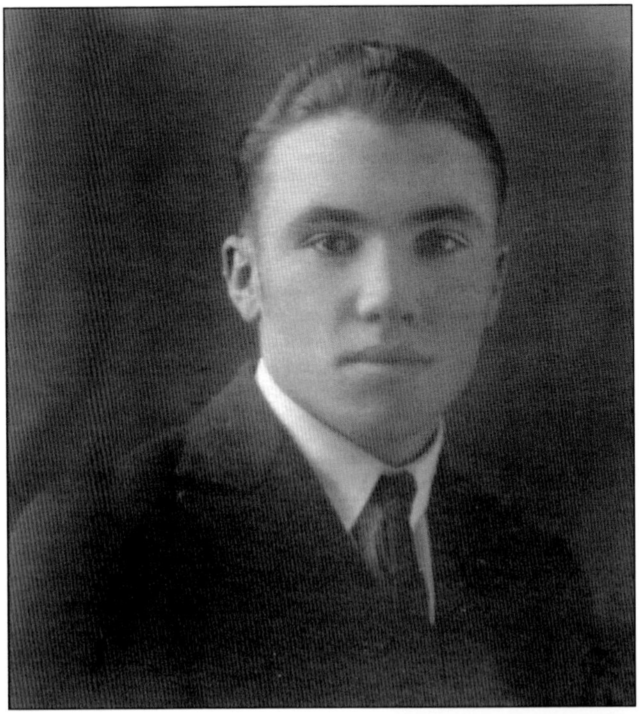

Leonard Comstock came to the area soon after his high school graduation in Comstock, Nebraska, in 1922 (when this photograph was taken). He joined the Young People's Club at Lyonsville Church, where he met his future wife, Harriet Hoyt. Work was difficult to find, and with his young wife and child to support, he made do as best he could, becoming a janitor at the Pleasantdale School, among other jobs. He was working the day the original school burned down in 1929 and, according to an oral history interview, "rescued his broom" since the children were all outside already. "Later, in the Lyonsville Church basement, the broom was put to very good use." (Courtesy of Sandra Browning.)

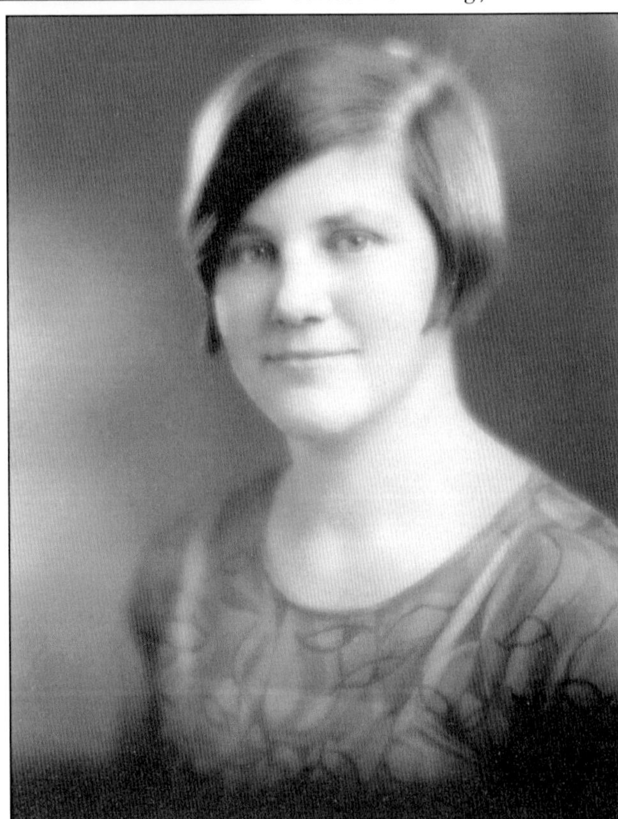

Harriet Hoyt, seen here in her 1924 high school graduation photograph, was the eldest daughter of Ruth and Howard Hoyt. She, too, recalled the Pleasantdale School burning, writing, "We were living at the Joe Bielby house on Seventy-second Street. We think it burned that January in '29. It was heated with a coal furnace. A teacher added more fuel at lunch time. They said there was a strong wind blowing; they also think there was a hole in the chimney and that sparks blew into the attic." (Courtesy of Sandra Browning.)

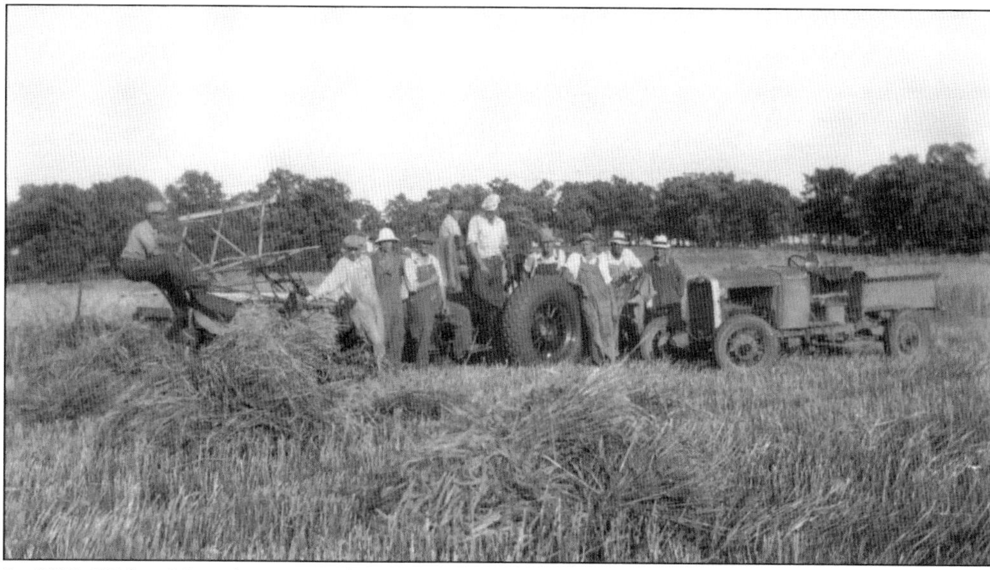

In 1935, Walter Hoyt (center, with foot on tire) used one of the era's "new mechanicals" to work the Vial land on Plainfield Road. One Vial niece recalled hearing the engine puffing and puttering loudly into the early evenings. Many early families' descendants worked on Vial lands. During the Depression, no work was too small. (Courtesy of the Flagg Creek Heritage Society.)

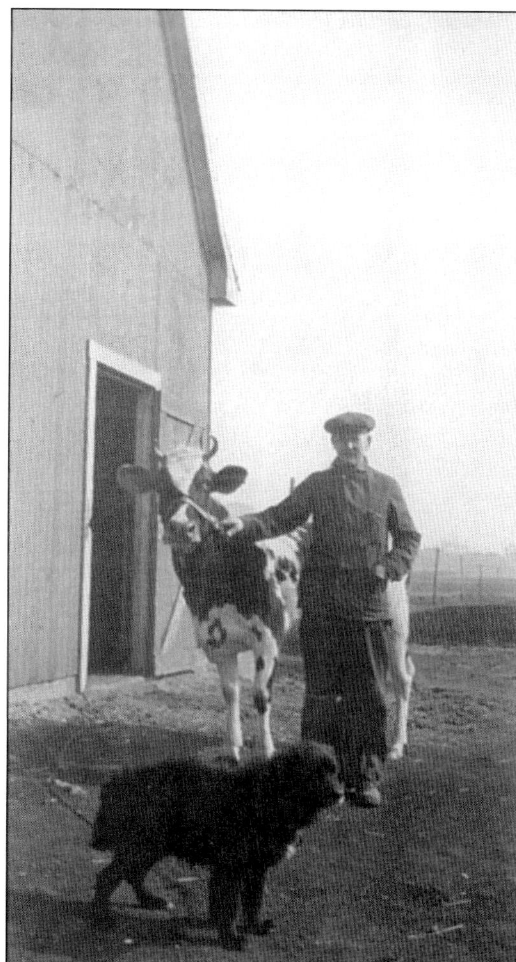

A point of pride was the quality of stock a family owned. And during the Depression, that did not mean "stock" as in the market. Family farms—as well as Sedgeley and Four Pines—took great care to secure and promote herds or, in this case, one "prized cow," pictured around 1938. (Courtesy of the Flagg Creek Heritage Society.)

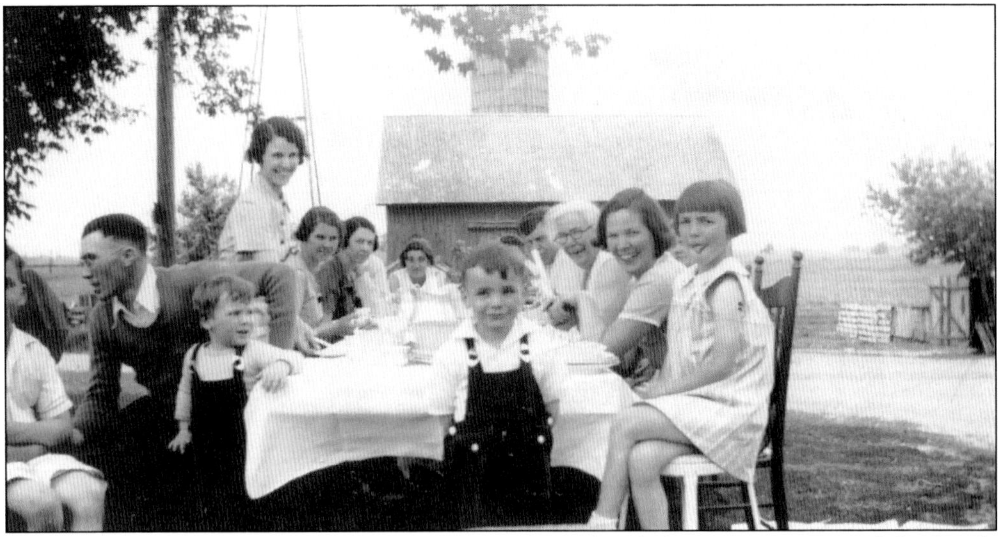

Typically, families gathered together on Sundays after church for picnics on one of the family farms. The Vials hosted quite often, and today we can know which farm is which by the silo: if there is a silo, it was likely a Vial farm because they had the first—and only for quite a number of years—family-owned working silo. The mix of families was from across the Burr Ridge area, typically from Lyonsville Church if it was a Vial event. Here, a hungry crew of adults and children laugh as they await a good supper and fellowship around 1933. (Courtesy of Sandra Browning.)

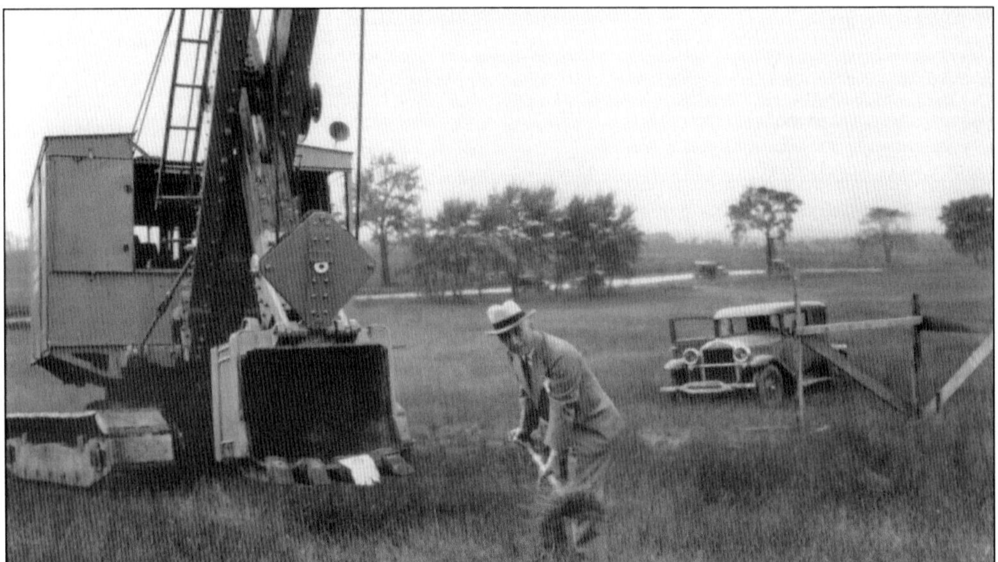

Some organizations met the Depression with compassion that extended to the larger needs of a growing community. One of these was the Godair Memorial Home for the Aged at 63rd and Madison Streets, funded initially by Mr. and Mrs. John Godair. At nearly the same time, in 1931, construction began on the King-Bruwaert House on County Line Road on the 35.5 acres formerly owned by Edward and Laura Carrington. Decades later, the Godair Memorial Retirement Home collaboratively merged with King-Bruwaert. William Bruckner, trustee, participated in both its groundbreaking and eventual merger. Bruckner is shown here at Godair's start in 1933. (Courtesy of King-Bruwaert House.)

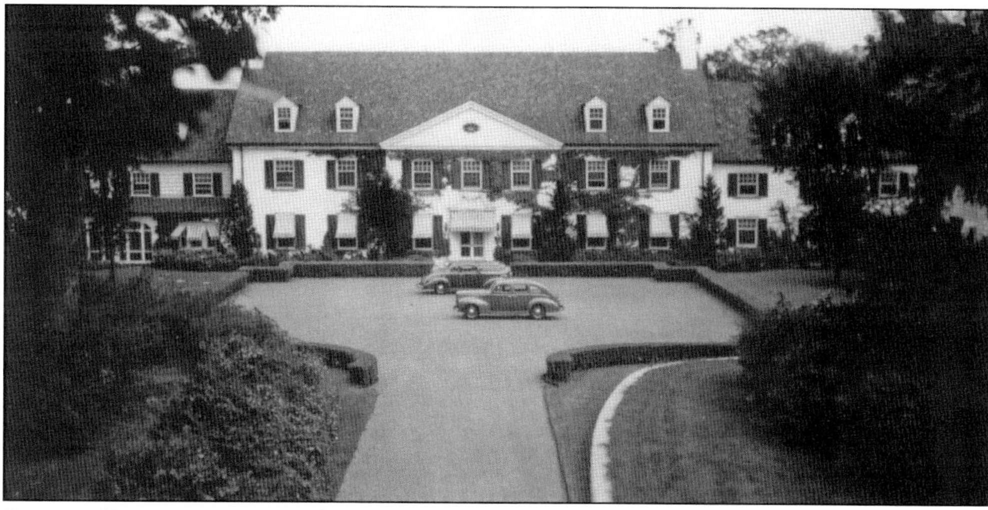

Suzanne King was a young Chicago socialite and Edmond Bruwaert was a French statesman recently appointed as the French commissioner for the 1893 World's Columbian Exposition in Chicago. It was in this capacity that he met her, and by 1894, they were married with romantic pomp that the *Chicago Tribune* called "one of the largest and most fashionable affairs of the week." After a storied and lifelong marriage, Suzanne King-Bruwaert lost her Edmond in 1927. In a year, she joined him. However, in her one year of widowhood, she noted that widowed women were often disadvantaged. She left in her will explicit directions to support and care for women "of gentle birth and breeding" with a residential home. In 1933, King-Bruewart (pictured here around 1938) opened its doors. (Courtesy of King-Bruwaert House.)

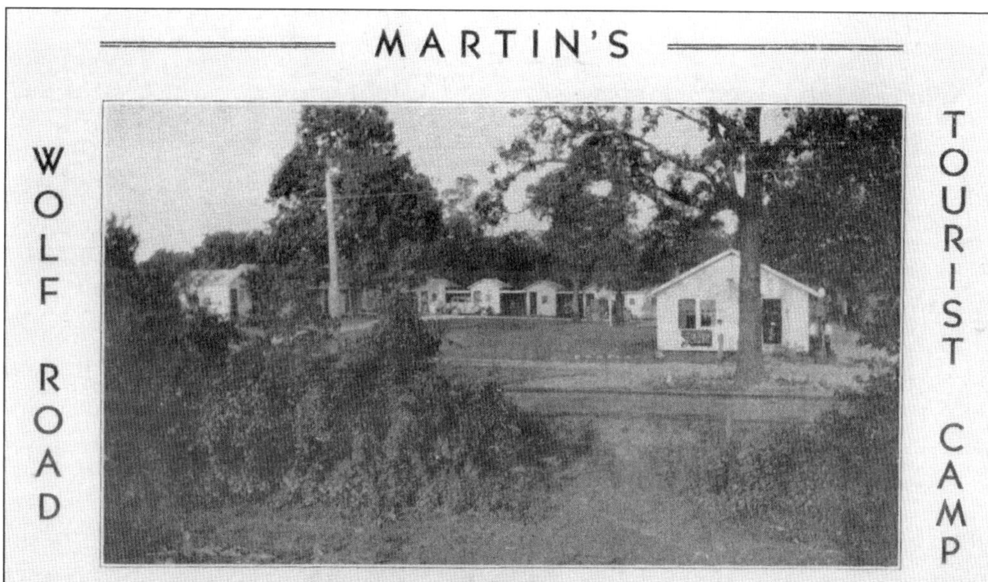

One aspect of Depression-era thinking is entrepreneurship. An example comes from when Martin's Tourist Camp opened. It stood on Vial land, within a mile of where Joseph Vial's Tavern stood almost 100 years prior. It too offered respite in the shady woods and peaceful cabins, providing not quite a Tiedtville-level of frolicking but rather time away from the cares of the day. Martin's Tourist Camp printed postcards for guests to send home, like any local attraction. This one is from around 1935. (Courtesy of Hazel Martin Sharp.)

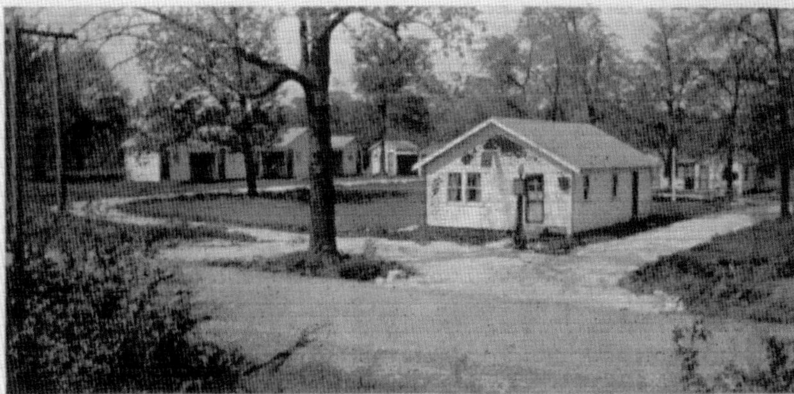

WOLF ROAD TOURIST CAMP,
LA GRANGE, ILL.
SHADE — QUIET — GOLFING

PLACE ______________________ DATE __________
DEAR ______________________________

HOW ARE YOU? I AM
- ENJOYING
- LONESOME
- BROKE
- REDUCING
- GETTING FAT
- HAPPY

PEOPLE HERE ARE
- CATTY
- DUMB
- POLITE
- WISE
- ACCOMMODATING
- INTERESTING

I NEED
- MONEY
- LOVING
- A DRINK
- SLEEP
- YOU
- SYMPATHY
- PEPPING UP
- $1.000.000.00

HERE I ENJOY
- GOLFING
- CROQUET
- TENNIS
- DANCING
- HORSEBACK RIDING
- MOVING PICTURES
- BATHING
- FISHING
- SIGHTSEEING
- THE MOONSHINE

I SPEND EVENINGS
- TALKING BUSINESS
- MAKING WHOOPEE
- STEPPING OUT
- PETTING
- DANCING
- SPOONING
- THINKING OF YOU
- WITH THE BOYS
- WITH THE GIRLS
- NOVELTY SHOPPING
- WRITING POST CARDS

I DON'T FISH MUCH, BUT LANDED
- A SUCKER
- A BEAUTY
- IN A PRETTY MESS
- SOME GAME ONES
- BOTTLE BASS

MY NEXT STOP IS ______________

EXPECT ME HOME ______________

HERE IT IS
- HOT
- COLD
- DELIGHTFUL
- BONE DRY
- WET

BUSINESS IS
- GOOD
- PUNK
- PICKING UP

YOURS
- SINCERELY
- LOVINGLY

SAVE TIME—CHECK ITEMS EXPRESSING YOUR SENTIMENTS

Travelers—often businessmen and salesmen—from Chicago would drive up the Joliet or Plainfield Roads on their way to International Harvester or to make calls on local farmers in the South Hinsdale area. There were no hotels nearby. The traveler's lodge fit the need these travelers had. Martin's Tourist Camp even took it upon itself to suggest notes guests might send to the folks back home. Another key aspect of the era was maintaining a good sense of humor when the economy offered little to smile (or write home) about. This clever time-saving card was produced around 1935. (Courtesy of Hazel Martin Sharp.)

Five

Church Life

Churches were more than institutions. They created bonds that afforded natural supports during difficult times. They also gave early settlers in the area an immediate sense of belonging and companionship.

Some, like those German families who settled the southern edge of Burr Ridge, came with only faith and their most treasured possession from their faraway homeland: the family Bible. Families with names such as Bachman, Boness, Schlichting, and Tiedt came for the same reasons many immigrant families sought the United States in the 1800s: religious tolerance and opportunity. These German settlers began arriving at least as early as 1839, bringing with them their families to start new lives. And start they did, founding (and finally building) Trinity Lutheran Church in 1865.

So, too, was it with Congregationalism. A faith rooted in that of the early Puritans, by the 19th century, Congregationalism was steeped in principles of democracy, participation, and institution building. Some early families attended the First Presbyterian Church in Chicago, but that was difficult for even the hardiest and most faithful. So on May 14, 1843, a meeting was held at the first schoolhouse in the area, a log home near the corner of Joliet and Plainfield Roads, to found Lyonsville Congregational Church.

Both would be anchor institutions in the 19th and early 20th centuries, leading the way for a rich diversity of faiths to take root in the decades following.

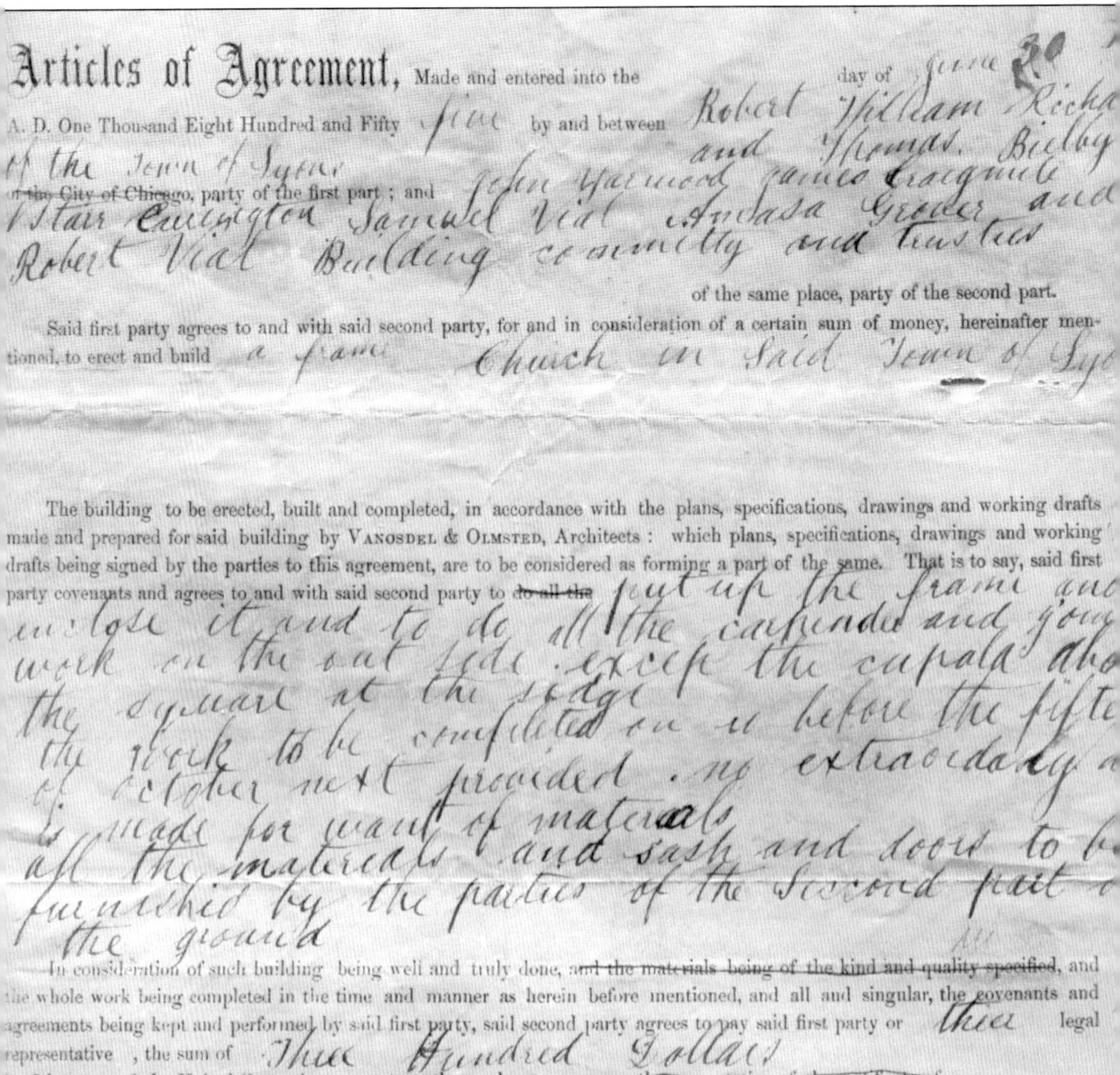
Articles of Agreement, Made and entered into the 30 day of June A. D. One Thousand Eight Hundred and Fifty five by and between Robert William Ricka and Thomas Bielby of the Town of Lyons ~~or the City of Chicago~~, party of the first part; and John Yarwood James Craigmile Stair Carrington Samuel Vial Amasa Greeler and Robert Vial Building committy and trustees of the same place, party of the second part.

Said first party agrees to and with said second party, for and in consideration of a certain sum of money, hereinafter mentioned, to erect and build a frame Church in Said Town of Lyo

The building to be erected, built and completed, in accordance with the plans, specifications, drawings and working drafts made and prepared for said building by VANOSDEL & OLMSTED, Architects: which plans, specifications, drawings and working drafts being signed by the parties to this agreement, are to be considered as forming a part of the same. That is to say, said first party covenants and agrees to and with said second party to ~~do all the~~ put up the frame and enclose it and to do all the carpender and joiner work on the out side except the cupala above the square at the ridge the work to be completed on or before the fifte of October next provided no extraordinary is made for want of materials all the materials and sash and doors to be furnished by the parties of the Second part on the ground

In consideration of such building being well and truly done, ~~and the materials being of the kind and quality specified~~, and the whole work being completed in the time and manner as herein before mentioned, and all and singular, the covenants and agreements being kept and performed by said first party, said second party agrees to pay said first party or their legal representative, the sum of Three Hundred Dollars lawful money of the United States, in payments as the work progresses, ~~on the presentation of the certificate of~~

After Lyonsville Church was founded in 1843, members began to look for an appropriate location. A committee chose a site near County Line Road on Joliet Road. Though some disagreements were had over that particular location, $693 was pledged. Finally, in 1855, Wolf Road at Joliet Road was chosen, and articles of agreement were drawn. The building was completed in 1858 for $1,800. (Courtesy of Lyonsville Congregational Church.)

Rev. Robert McCord served Lyonsville Congregational Church from 1882 to 1886. (Courtesy of Lyonsville Congregational Church.)

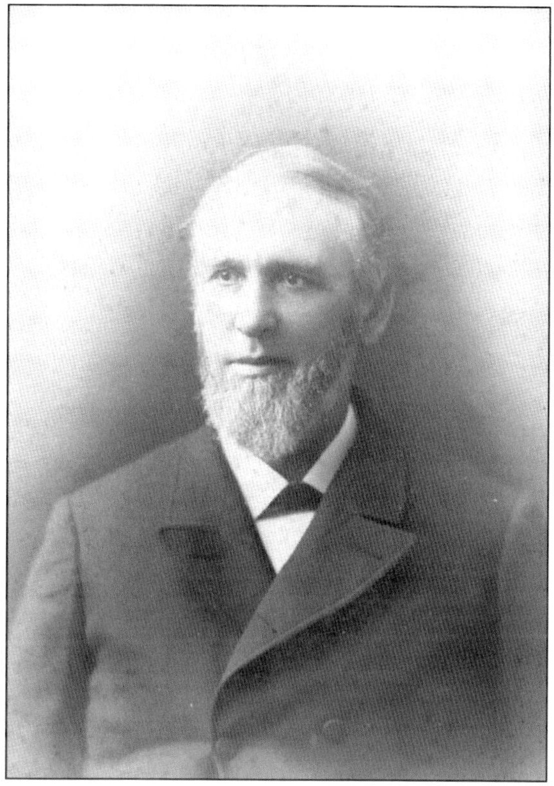

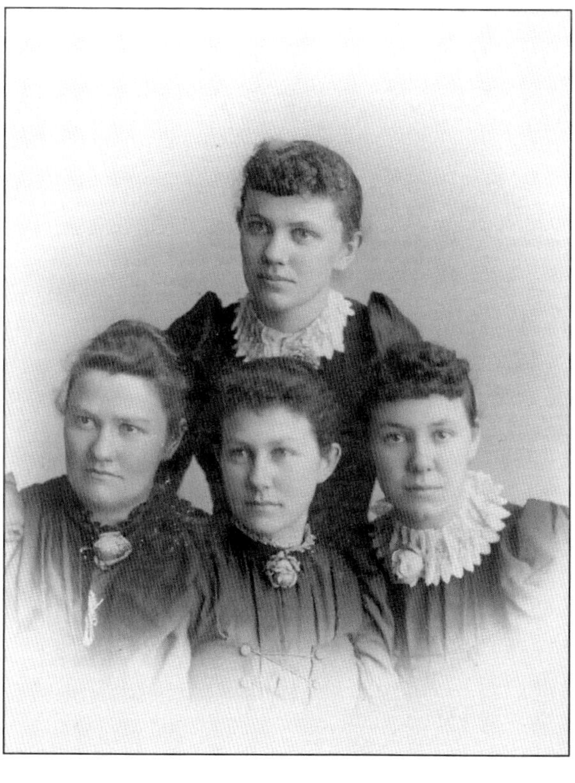

The Craigmile brothers all attended Lyonsville as soon as it was formed. David's daughters—Nellie, Sarah, Esther, and Ruth, seen here in the 1890s—would carry the tradition forward in their own lives and those of their families. Generations were baptized, married, and laid to rest within a few miles of the church. The Lyonsville Cemetery behind it is considered one of the oldest Congregational cemeteries in Cook County and is the resting place of members of founding families Vial, Bielby, Craigmile, Yarwood, and others, including noted Civil War captain Hiram McClintock. (Courtesy of Lyonsville Congregational Church.)

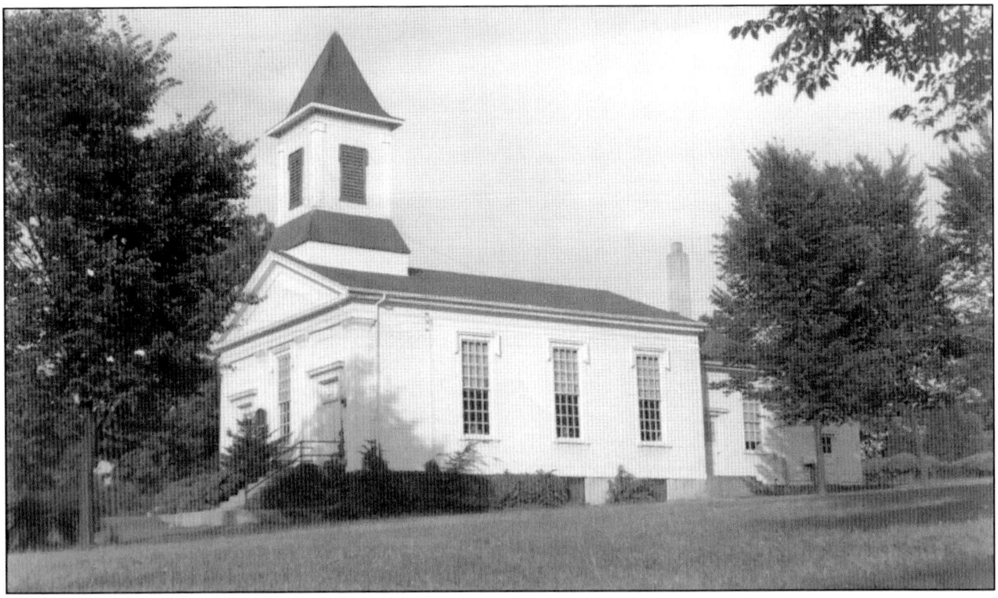

The original spire atop the 1858 structure was blown down in a storm in 1916. The steeple pictured around 1947 was considered a temporary replacement. Lyonsville has been described as nurturing daughter Congregational churches that would later form in the downtowns of La Grange and Hinsdale. The United Church of Christ in Burr Ridge shares services even today. (Courtesy of Lyonsville Congregational Church.)

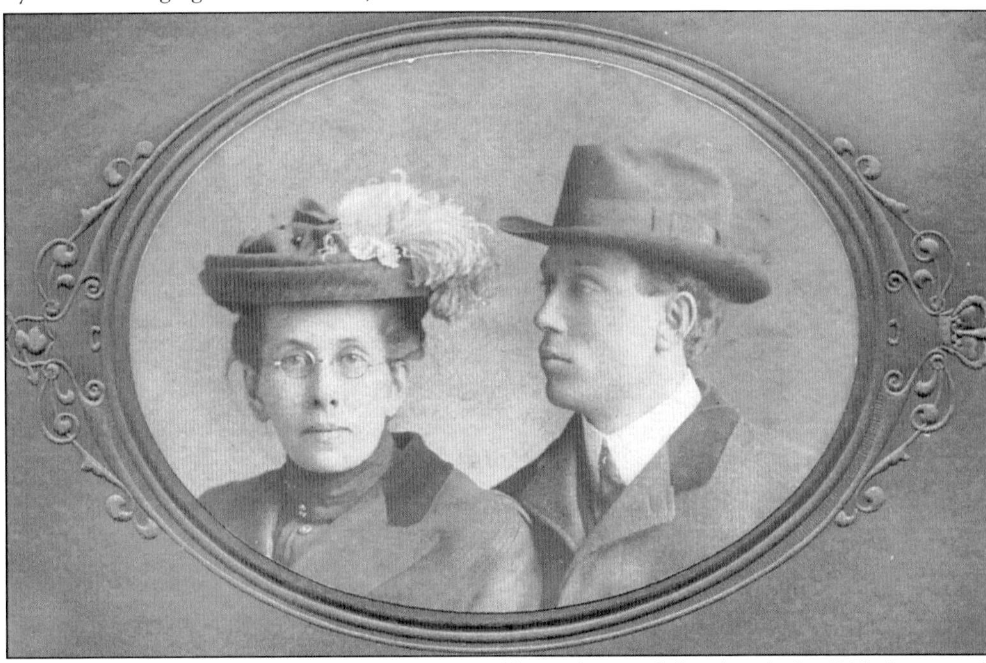

At the turn of the 20th century, a new pastor and his wife served the church. In 1915, the growth of the congregation necessitated new spaces be added. A basement was built with plows, shovels, picks, and scrapers. Heating had been two wood-burning stoves, with occasional mishaps resulting in a room filled with soot and smoke. A furnace was a modern necessity for the growing church. (Courtesy of Lyonsville Congregational Church.)

Lyonsville was still a landmark in the 1940s. It wasn't uncommon for passersby to stop and take photographs of the church, known to locals as the Church on the Corner, as this tourist did in 1947. (Courtesy of Reynolds Chadwick family.)

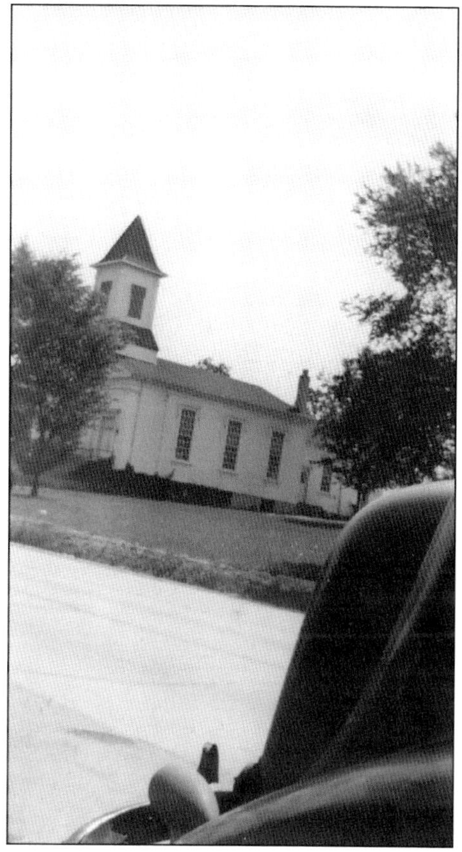

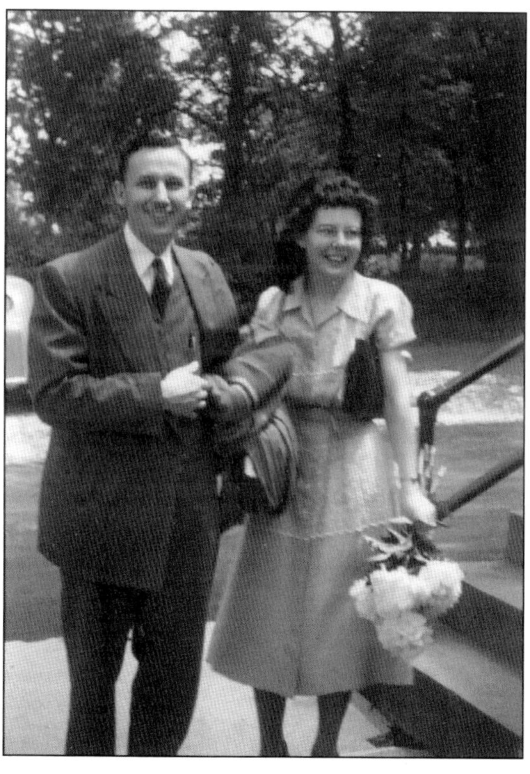

Lyonsville Congregational Church's Rev. Norman Brooks and his wife, Blanche, are all smiles after Reverend Brooks officiated a wedding in 1948. (Courtesy of Lyonsville Congregational Church.)

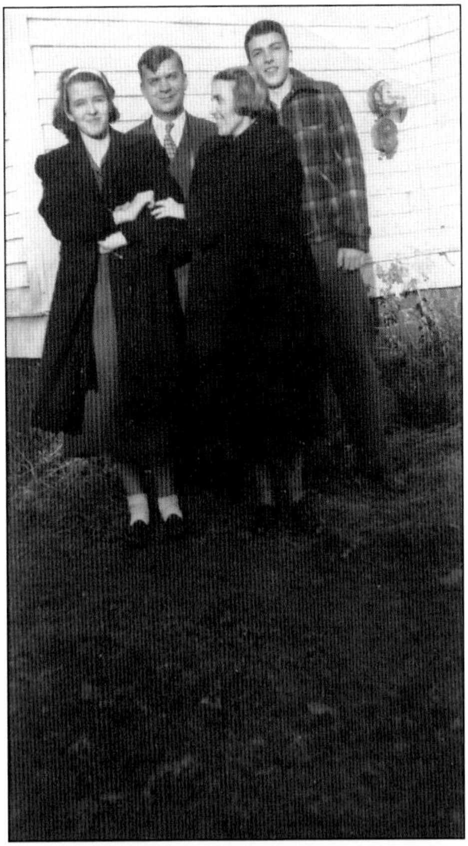

The church was a hub of social life well into the 1940s as third- and fourth-generation families grew up together, celebrating 100 years. (Courtesy of Lyonsville Congregational Church.)

That the church had grown was a point of quiet joy for the earlier generations. Attending a dedication on the anniversary of the church, Alice Vial and Mary Francis Bielby listen to Rev. Calvin Bremer in this c. 1965 photograph. Vial would write of the church on its anniversary, "Surely its strength and holiness of the past years will continue to provide courage and reverence for the years ahead." (Courtesy of Lyonsville Congregational Church.)

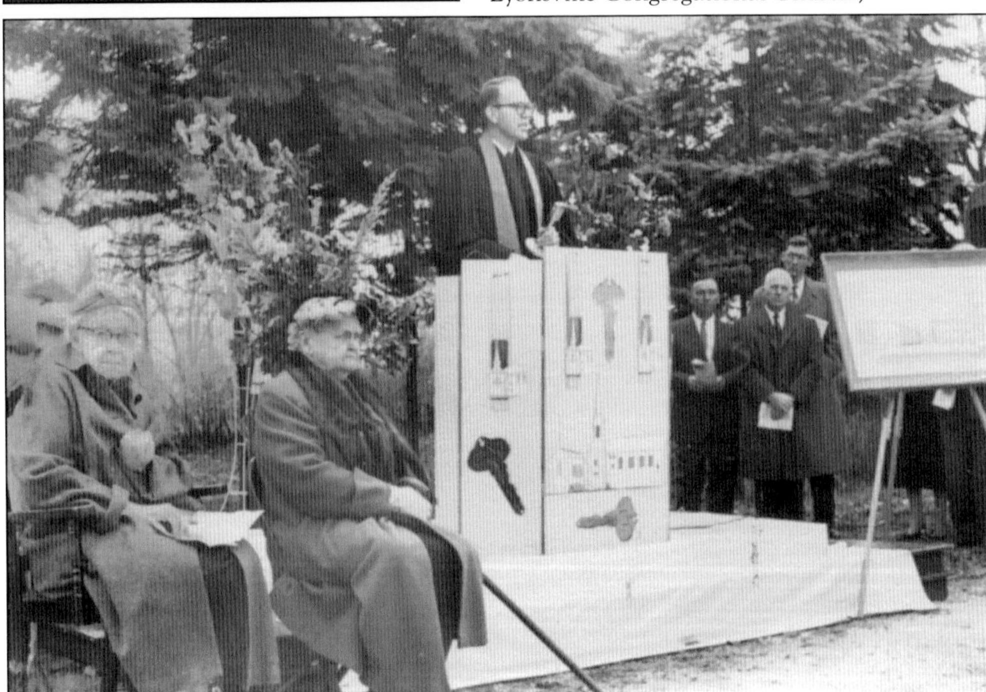

Lyonsville Church appeared stately prior to 1915, with its steeple still intact. (Courtesy of Lyonsville Congregational Church.)

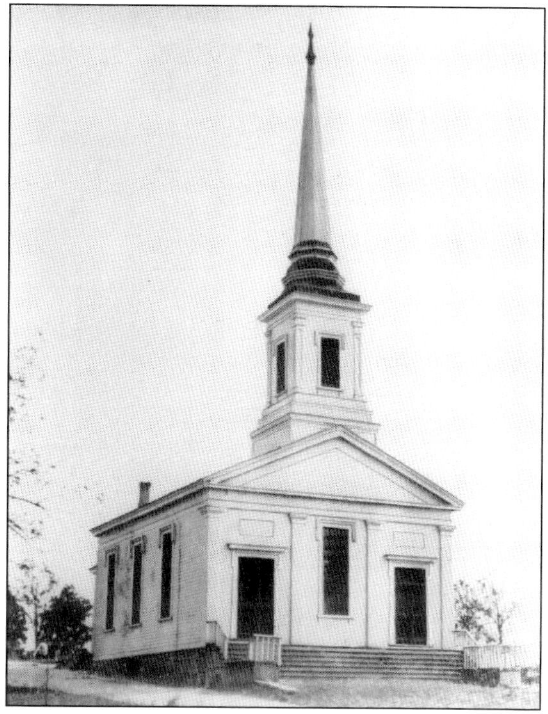

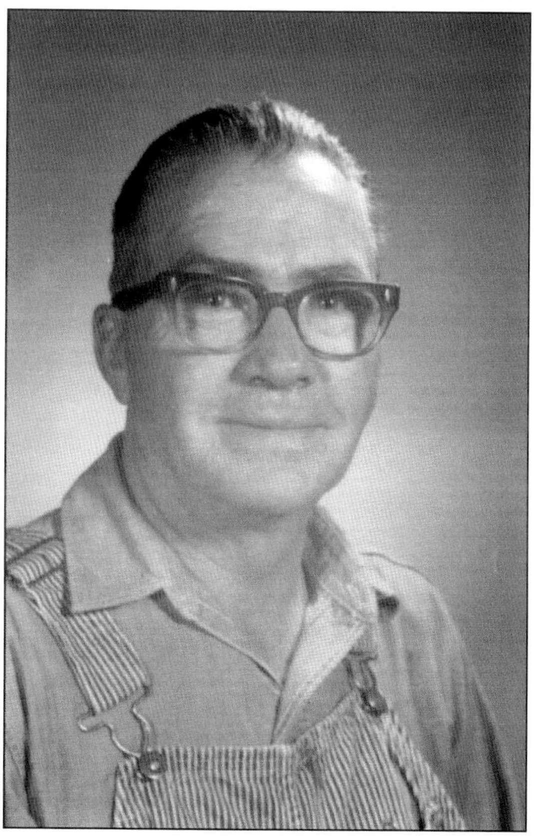

Leonard Comstock, shown in 1968, served the church in a variety of ways, but he was most noted for his years as the longest-serving janitor, a job he also held for Pleasantdale School. Years of Harvest Dinners, hosted annually as a Lyonsville tradition, would be cooked and served by the women; but it was his duty to make sure the church was spotless for services afterward. (Courtesy of Sandra Browning.)

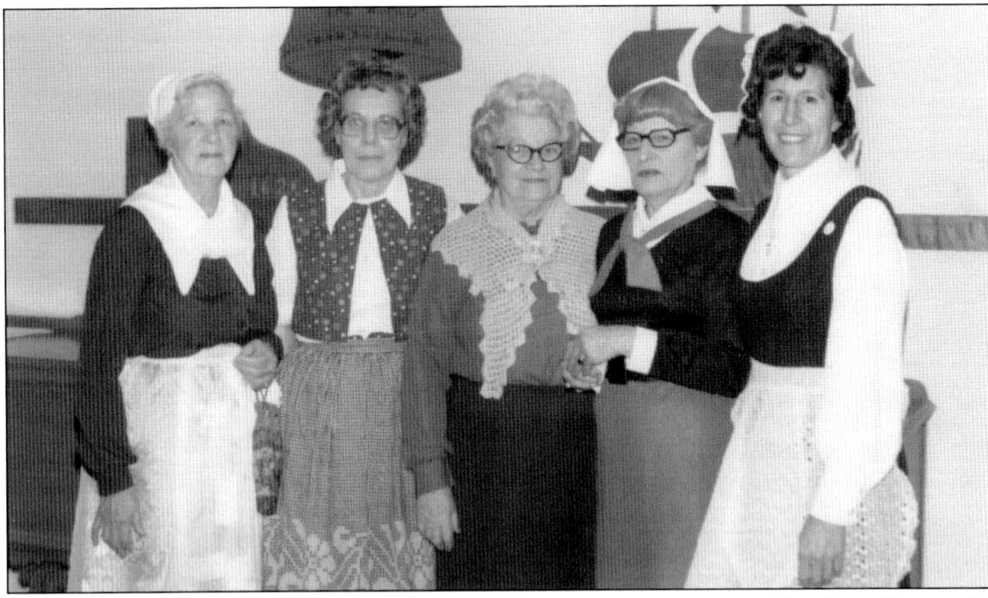

The women of Lyonsville, like those in most church communities, were considered excellent cooks. The basement kitchen is described as the scene for many a dinner, post-service fellowship tea, or luncheon prep. Over many years, there has developed a folklore of founding-family recipes. Such things as Nutty Spice Cake and Strawberry Pie are noted as original mothers' and "grannys' " in church archives. These women pose for a photo—in costume, no less—at a Harvest Dinner in 1978. (Courtesy of Sandra Browning.)

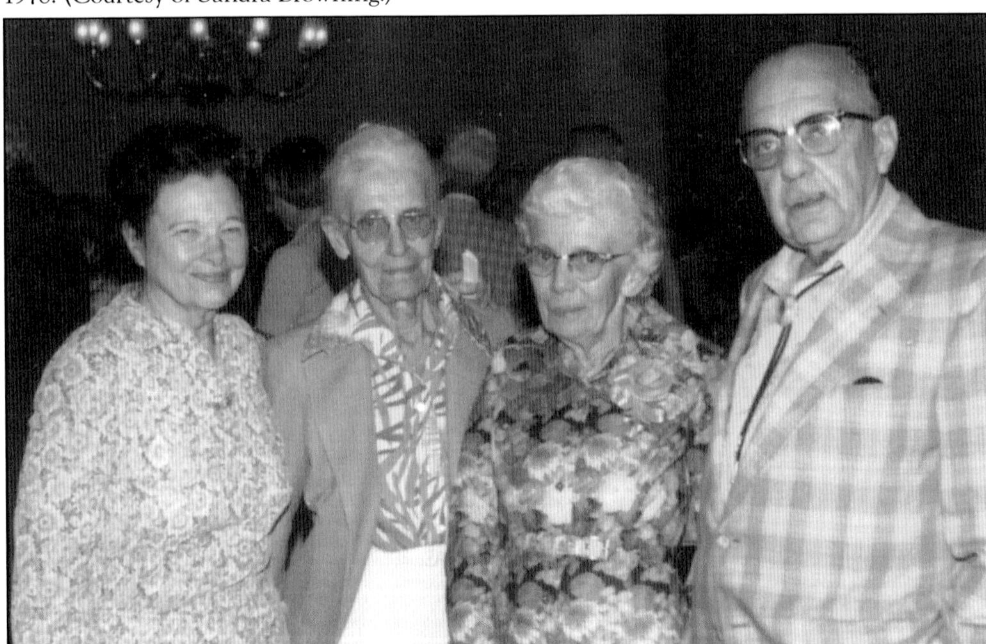

By the early 1980s, living memory of church history was kept by this generation: (from left to right) Sarah Craigmile Baumrucker, Mary Delight Craigmile, Ruth Vial Martin, and George Baumrucker. Ruth Vial Martin would be instrumental in saving the Robert Vial home, which was made into a museum of the Flagg Creek Heritage Society. (Courtesy of Lyonsville Congregational Church.)

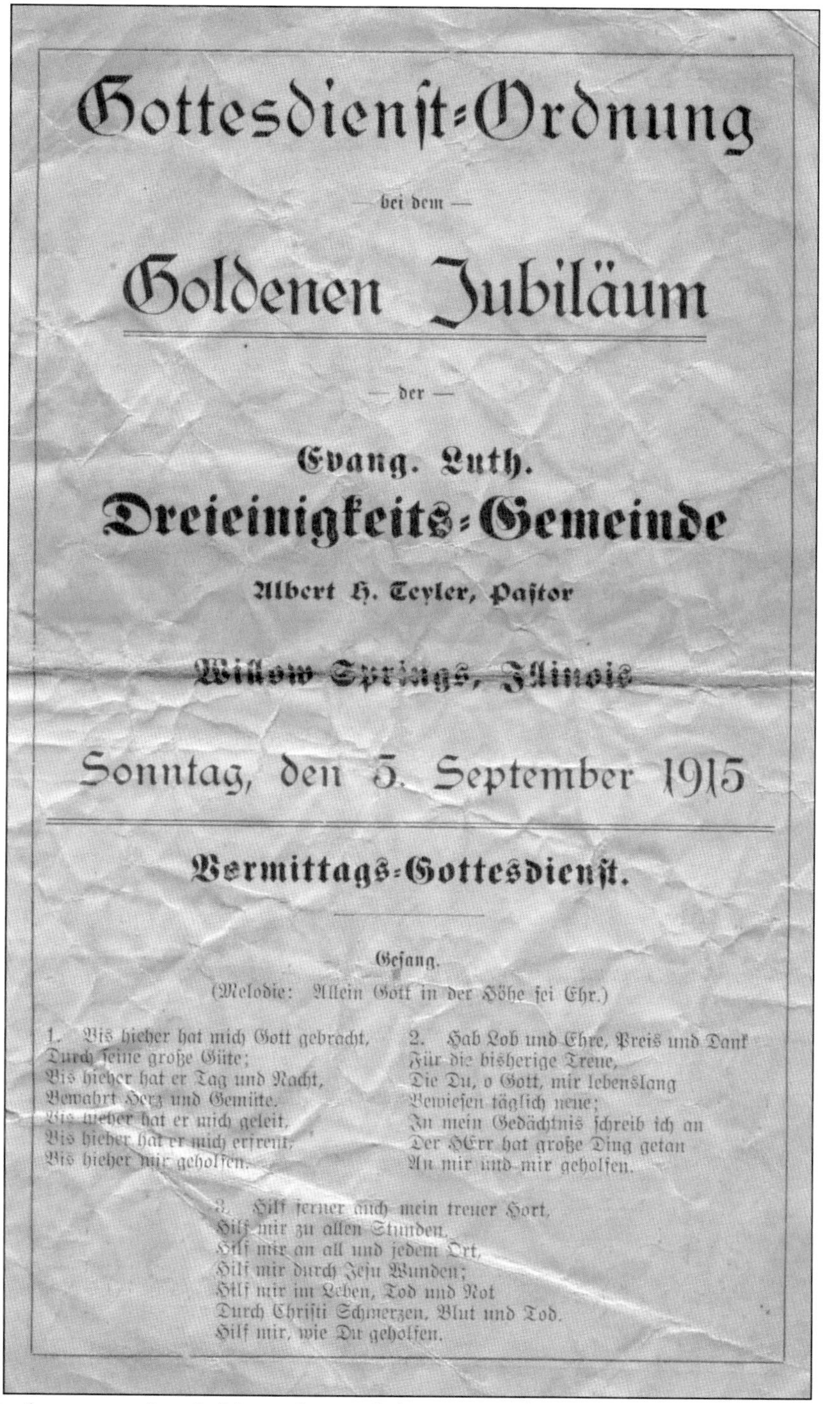

Gottesdienst-Ordnung

— bei dem —

Goldenen Jubiläum

— der —

Evang. Luth.

Dreieinigkeits-Gemeinde

Albert H. Teyler, Pastor

Willow Springs, Illinois

Sonntag, den 5. September 1915

Vormittags-Gottesdienst.

Gesang.

(Melodie: Allein Gott in der Höhe sei Ehr.)

1. Bis hieher hat mich Gott gebracht,
Durch seine große Güte;
Bis hieher hat er Tag und Nacht,
Bewahrt Herz und Gemüte.
Bis hieher hat er mich geleit,
Bis hieher hat er mich erfreut,
Bis hieher mir geholfen.

2. Hab Lob und Ehre, Preis und Dank
Für die bisherige Treue,
Die Du, o Gott, mir lebenslang
Bewiesen täglich neue;
In mein Gedächtnis schreib ich an
Der HErr hat große Ding getan
An mir und mir geholfen.

3. Hilf ferner auch mein treuer Hort,
Hilf mir zu allen Stunden,
Hilf mir an all und jedem Ort,
Hilf mir durch Jesu Wunden;
Hilf mir im Leben, Tod und Not
Durch Christi Schmerzen, Blut und Tod.
Hilf mir, wie Du geholfen.

Trinity Lutheran was founded by and served the German-born and German-speaking families along what would come to be called "German Church Road." Founding families include Boedecker, Bachmann, Harders, Hamm, Pantke, and Sternitzke. Next-generation early families included Eggert, Hess, Marwitze, Sass, and Tiedt. The earliest sermons and hymns, like this one from 1915, were in German. (Courtesy of Trinity Lutheran Church.)

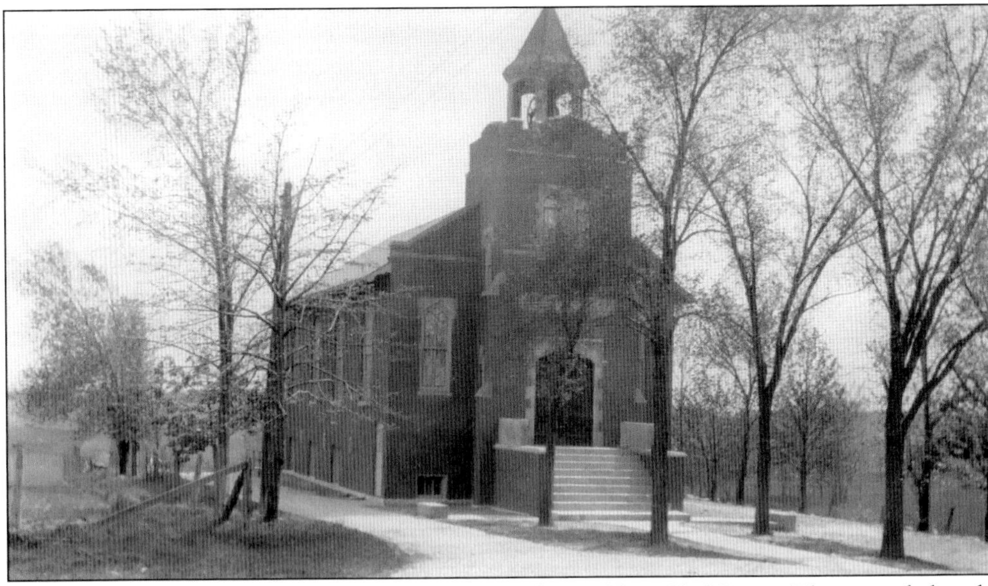

Trinity Lutheran Church's first building was erected in 1865 on 83rd Street. The second church, built in 1893 with a tall steeple, was struck by lightning and burned to the ground in 1924. A new church was constructed and dedicated in 1926. (Courtesy of Trinity Lutheran Church.)

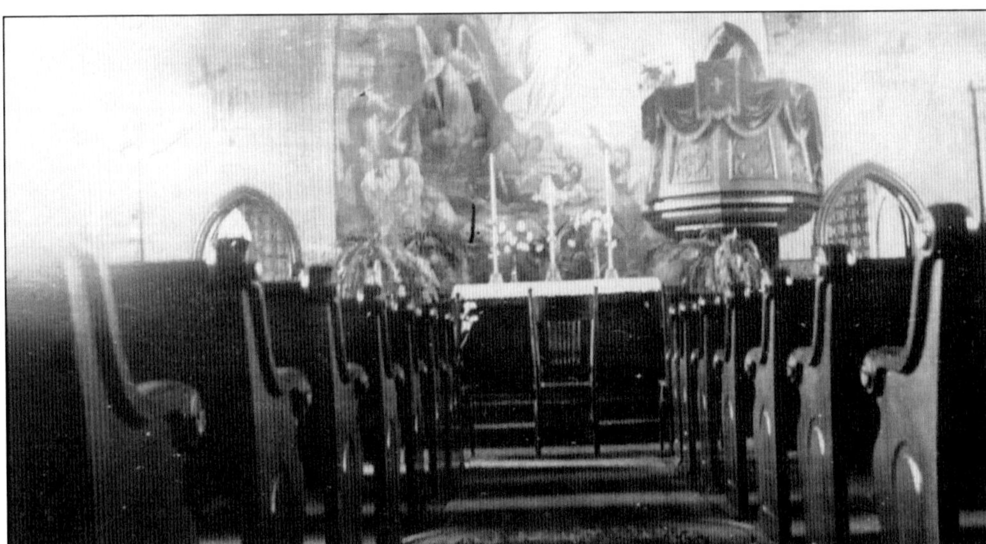

This early photograph of the interior of the church was taken in 1922 on confirmation Sunday from what appears to be a child's viewpoint. One of the early church members, Viola Tiedt, recalled in 1984 that when she attended the first wooden church, she and other Sunday school students took turns getting water from a pump near the parsonage. (Courtesy of Trinity Lutheran Church.)

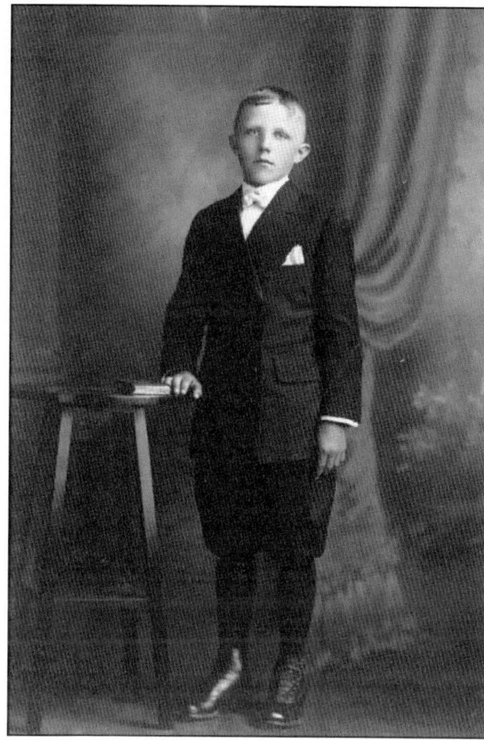

Confirmation Sunday, then as now, represented a point in spiritual maturation, a commitment taken with seriousness as well as celebration. Young William Tiedt and Ella Tiedt (Marwitz) reflect these traits in their formal confirmation photographs. (Both, courtesy of Trinity Lutheran Church.)

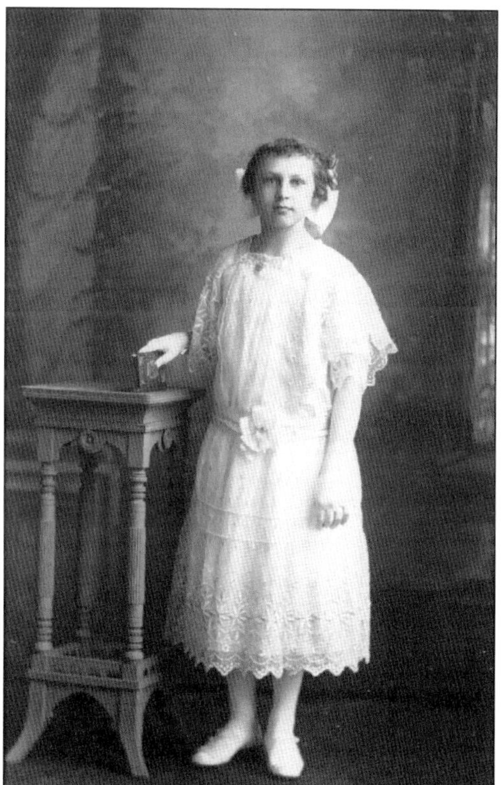

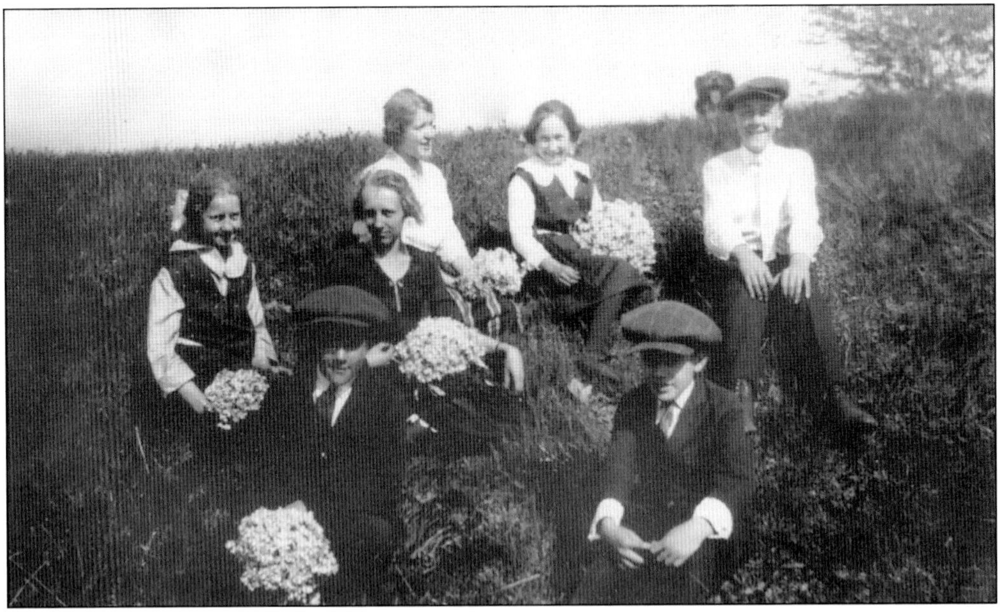

Picnics near the church were common, especially after a wedding, christening, or other celebration. The freedom and joy of the moment shines in the faces of Irma Tyler, Lou Knapp, Ralph Tiedt, and others on this sunny day in the 1920s. (Courtesy of Trinity Lutheran Church.)

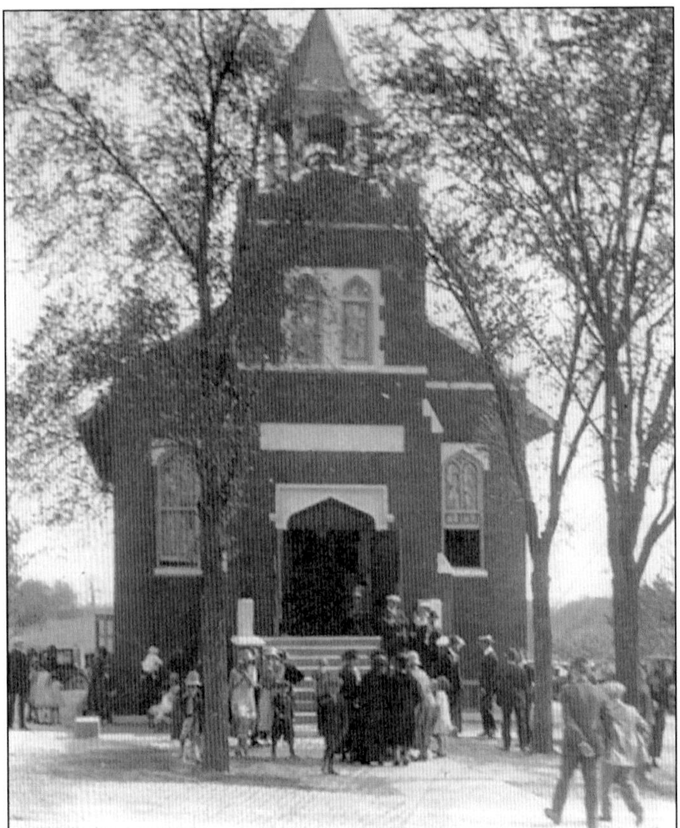

The energy in the steps of those pictured belies the possibility of being late to church on this 1926 Sunday morning. (Courtesy of Trinity Lutheran Church.)

The Knapps were among the many active families from the early years of the church. Pictured is Louise Knapp in the 1930s. (Courtesy of Trinity Lutheran Church.)

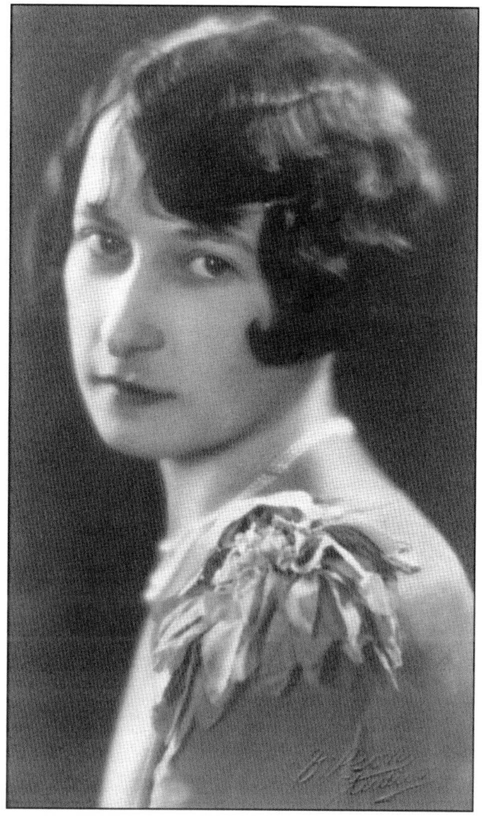

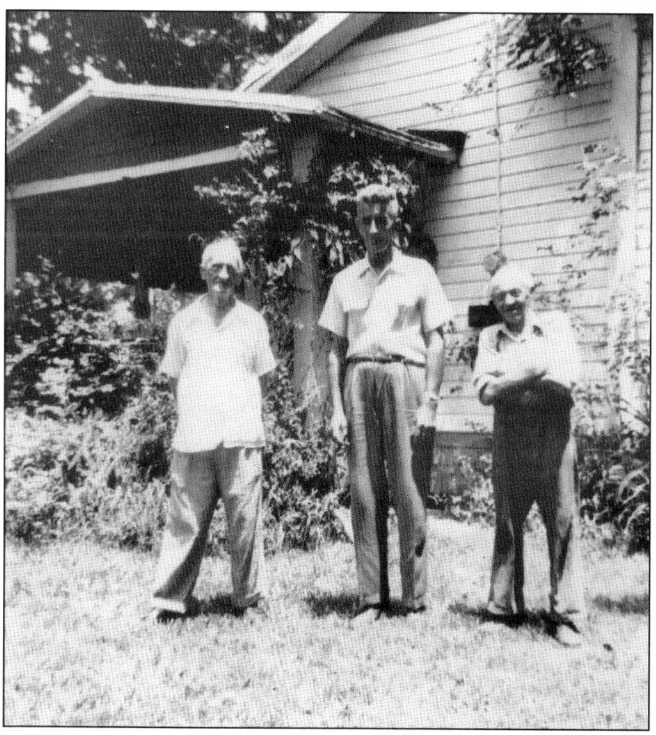

Trinity Lutheran members (from left to right) Charlie Bodecker, Al Marwitz, and Albert Bodecker stand nearly at attention at one of the original family homes still left in the German Church Road area in the 1950s. (Courtesy of Trinity Lutheran Church.)

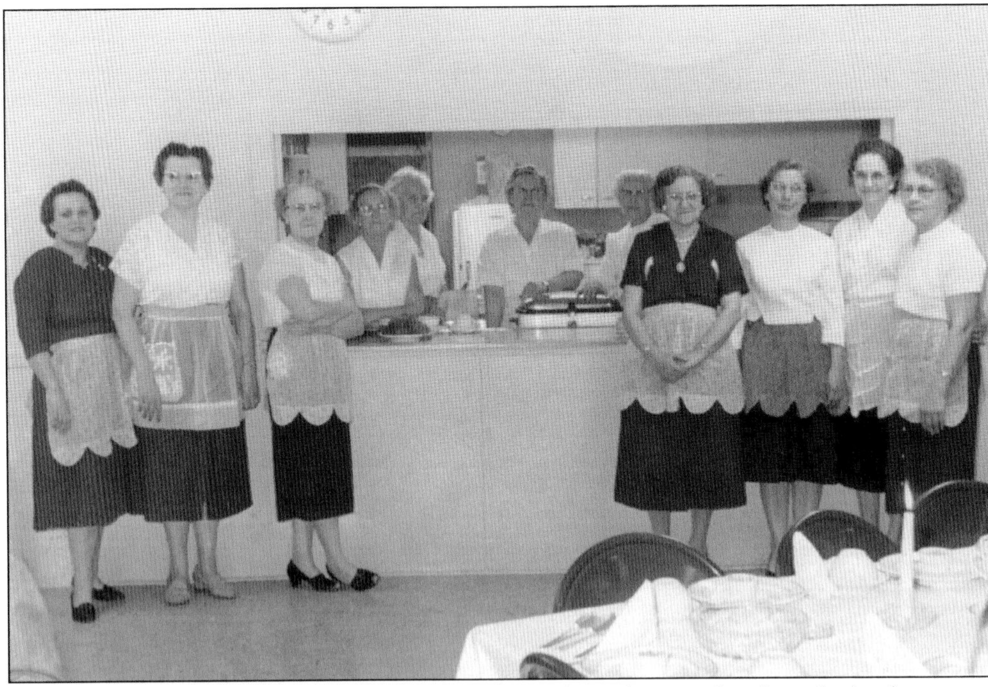

As with most churches, the kitchens hum with the busy activity of female volunteers, such as these members in the 1950s. (Courtesy of Trinity Lutheran Church.)

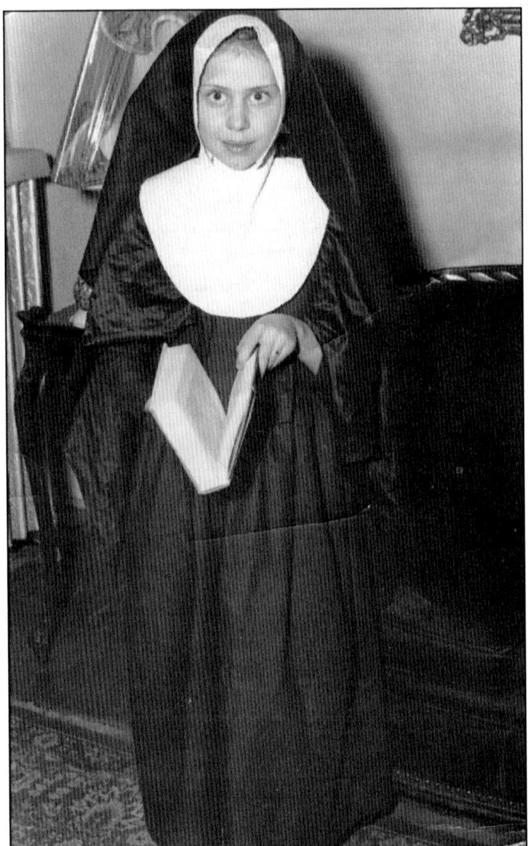

While the oldest churches in the immediate area were Lyonsville and Trinity, Catholic churches included St. James Church (at Cal Sag Bridge) and St Patrick Church, both in Lemont, and St. Isaac Jogues in Hinsdale. Our Lady of Peace in Darien opened over a decade later. Many churches were eventually embraced by the area's families as these early churches were. (Courtesy of Pat J. McHugh.)

Six

Plainview and Pleasantdale Schools

Is it Plainview or Pleasantdale? And what of Flagg Creek School? The history of the area's earliest schools' names is often confusing to many who have lived in—or even attended schools in—said districts. The schools share the same history to a point and then diverge.

The first school was built in 1843 near the corner of Joliet and Wolf Roads, and it is not apocryphal to say it was a one-room schoolhouse. In fact, it was a log cabin that also served as the Lyonsville Church in its earliest years. This log cabin was sold and converted into a blacksmith shop.

In 1861, a new one-room schoolhouse was built, and local families came to call it Flagg Creek School. It was in what then was called District No. 3. Source documentation indicates that on August 19, 1901, it changed to District No. 107. Between these two district number changes, it came to be known as "Pleasant Dale" School. Alice Vial, Robert Vial's daughter, taught at the school after becoming one of the earliest graduates from Lyons Township High School.

In 1927, the unthinkable occurred: the wooden timbers caught fire during the school day. Quietly, with remarkable calm and quick wits, Pleasant Dale School teacher Miss Marie Derby called for recess, and the children "evacuated" safely and watched as their school burned down.

Much to the children's chagrin, one can imagine, classes continued to be held over the many months it took for a new building to be erected. They met in Edgewood Valley Country Club and Lyonsville Church until 1928. The new brick building stands today, although it is significantly renovated and has grown.

What of Plainview? That also grew from the original log cabin schoolhouse. In 1867, a school was built on Plainfield Road nearer to Willow Springs Road, and about that time, it was called District 106. It wasn't until 1948, however, that District 107 and what had become District 106 officially became distinct schools.

Shared heritage informs our look back at the districts, as does reflecting on the experience of students. Some working families moved back and forth down Plainfield and Joliet Roads and up and down Wolf and County Line Roads. Some of these school children would attend one, and then the other, back and forth. Be it Plain or Pleasant, View or Dale: education was a core value.

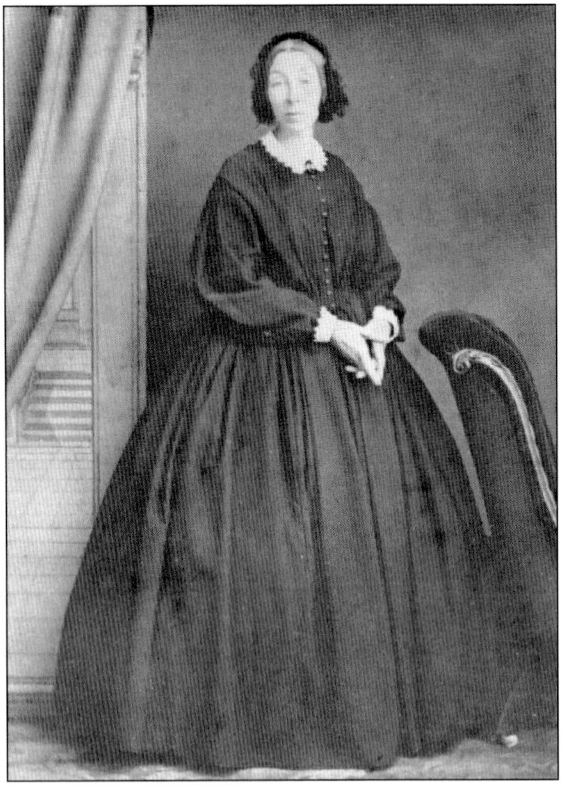

In 1843, the area's first schoolhouse, a one-room log cabin where the Lyonsville Church also held services, opened with Mary McNaughton as its first schoolteacher. This small school was located close to the intersection of Wolf and Joliet Roads. (Courtesy of Lyonsville Church.)

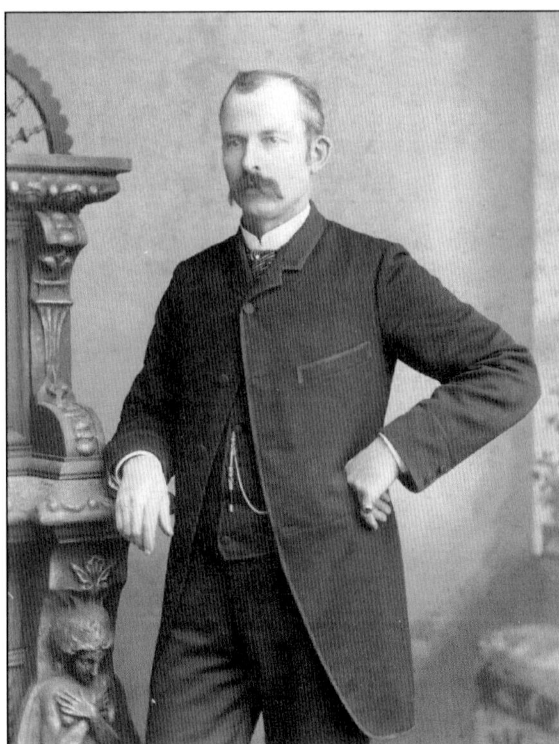

An offshoot of the original log cabin schoolhouse was Plainview School, which was completed in 1867. Located on Plainfield Road near Willow Springs Road, Plainview was part of the then-new District 106. W.E. Jayne, shown here in 1871, served as Plainview's first headmaster. (Courtesy of Flagg Creek Heritage Society.)

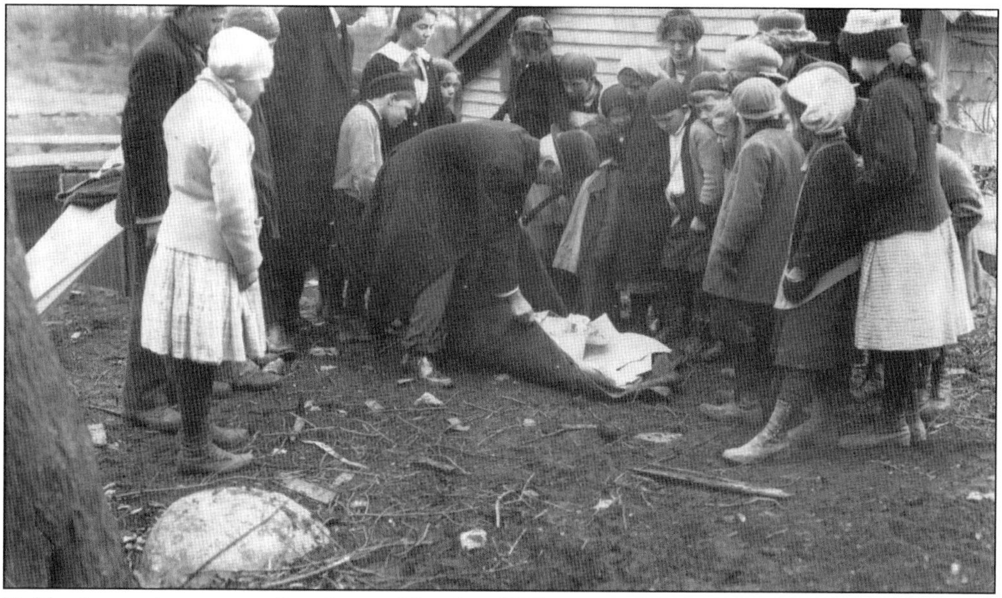

Field trips to the surrounding farms, like this 1915 visit to the Gear property, gave Plainview students firsthand experience with the area's agriculture industry. (Courtesy of Flagg Creek Heritage Society.)

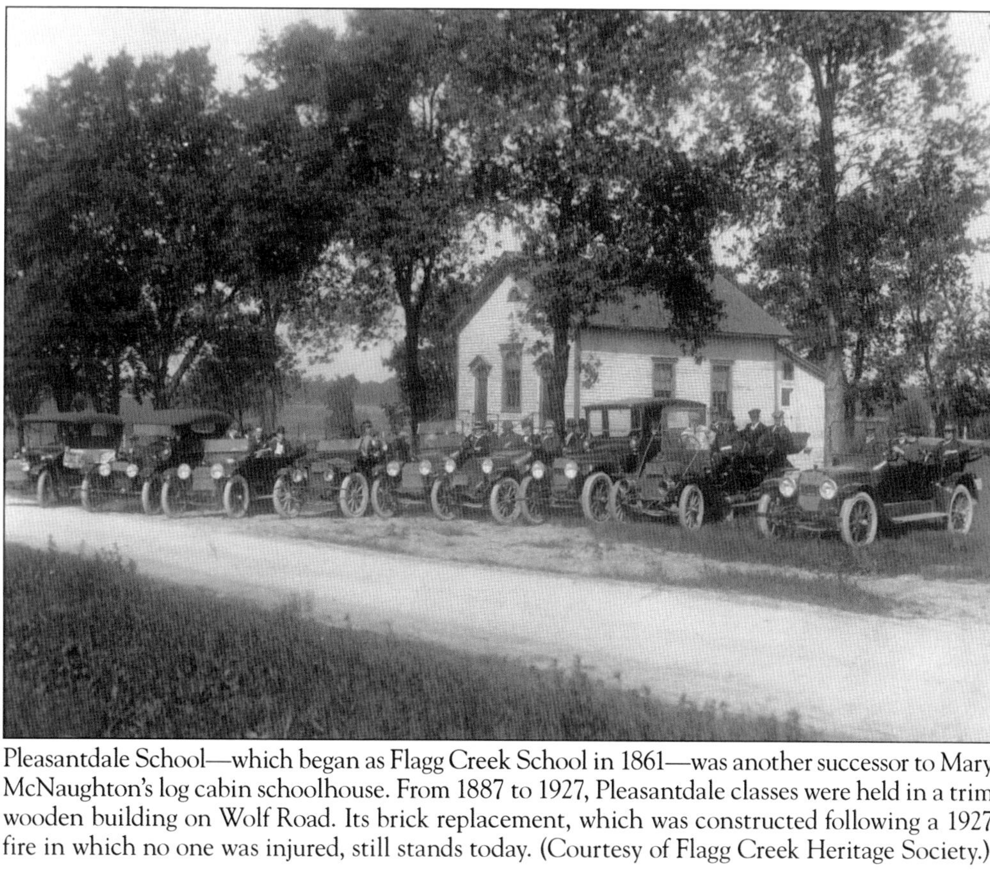

Pleasantdale School—which began as Flagg Creek School in 1861—was another successor to Mary McNaughton's log cabin schoolhouse. From 1887 to 1927, Pleasantdale classes were held in a trim wooden building on Wolf Road. Its brick replacement, which was constructed following a 1927 fire in which no one was injured, still stands today. (Courtesy of Flagg Creek Heritage Society.)

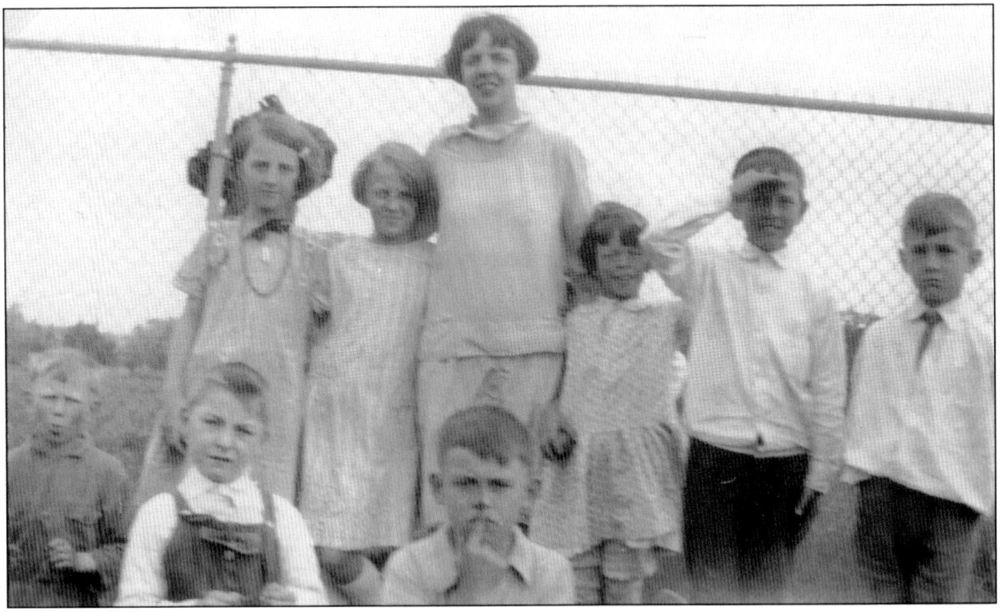

Plainview students stand at the edge of the school's grounds during the 1920s. Several years after its founding, Plainview moved to its present location: the modern-day La Grange Highlands school site. (Both, courtesy of Flagg Creek Heritage Society.)

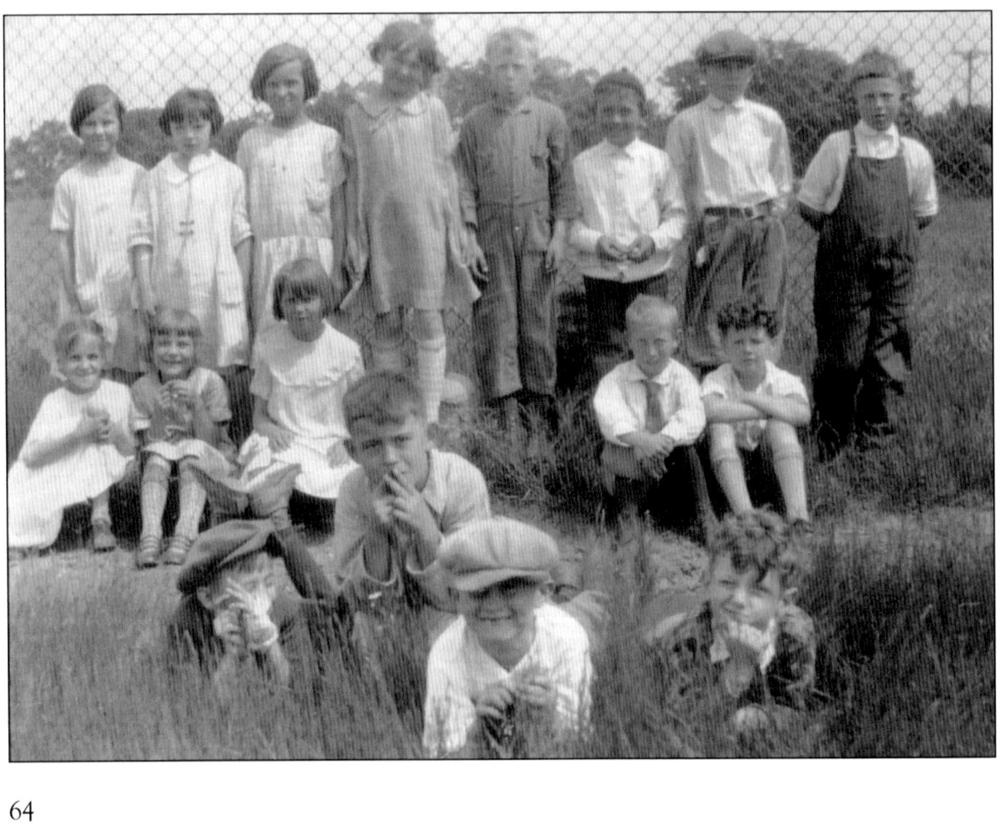

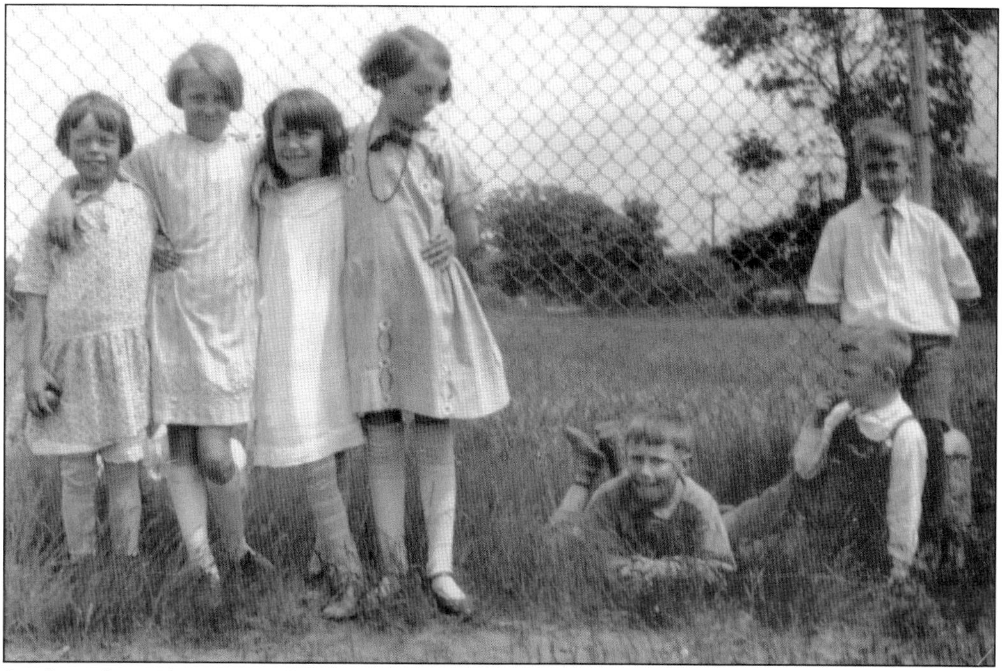

Students from Plainview School in the 1920s seem to exhibit the age-old girls versus boys stance; note the girl standing looking at the boys, who seem utterly carefree in the moment. (Courtesy of Flagg Creek Heritage Society.)

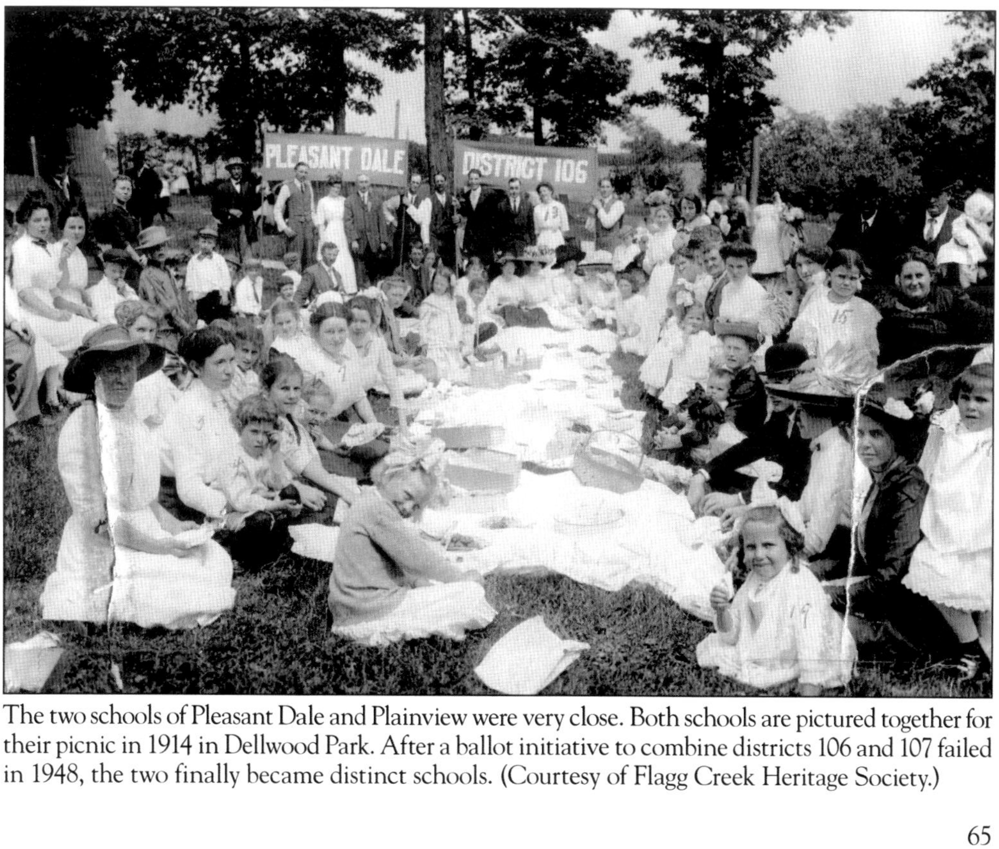

The two schools of Pleasant Dale and Plainview were very close. Both schools are pictured together for their picnic in 1914 in Dellwood Park. After a ballot initiative to combine districts 106 and 107 failed in 1948, the two finally became distinct schools. (Courtesy of Flagg Creek Heritage Society.)

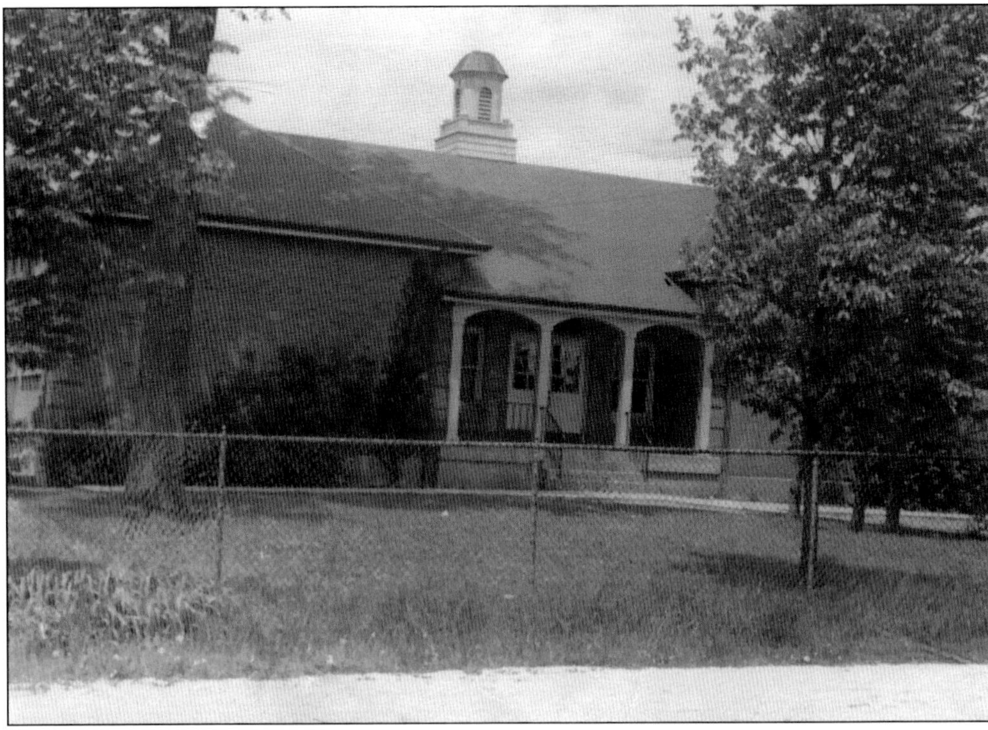

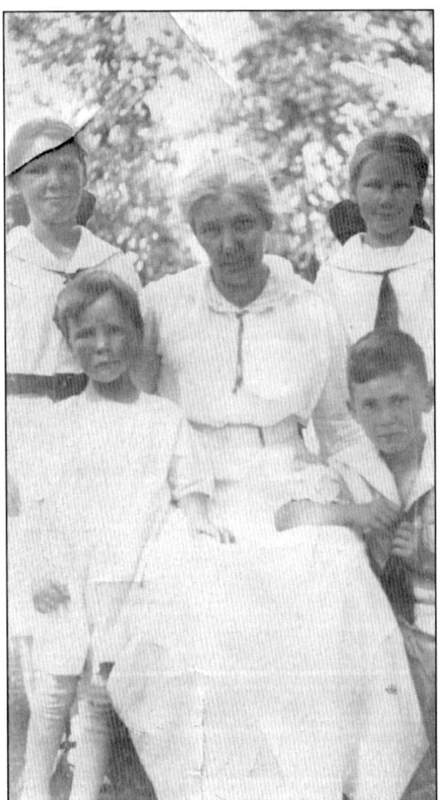

Plainview School's building was enlarged in 1941; it is seen here as it appeared a few years after the renovations, in 1946. It would expand once more, in 1949, as the student population increased further. (Courtesy of Flagg Creek Heritage Society.)

Ruth (Craigmile) Hoyt lost her husband, Howard, to the flu epidemic and watched her family land—and even its dairy herd—auctioned off. She raised her children alone and never married again. To make ends meet, she became the janitor at Plainview School and lived across the street. Her children stood by her throughout those hard years. (Courtesy of Sandra Browning.)

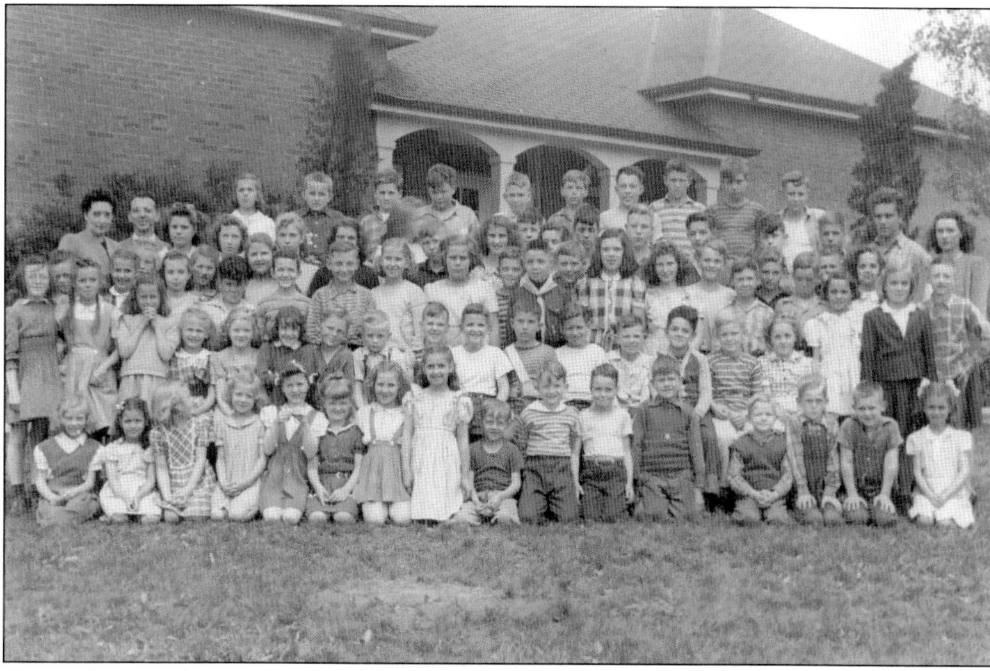

The students in this 1944 photograph still knew their school as Plainview, but it would change its name to La Grange Highlands in late 1955. (Courtesy of Flagg Creek Heritage Society.)

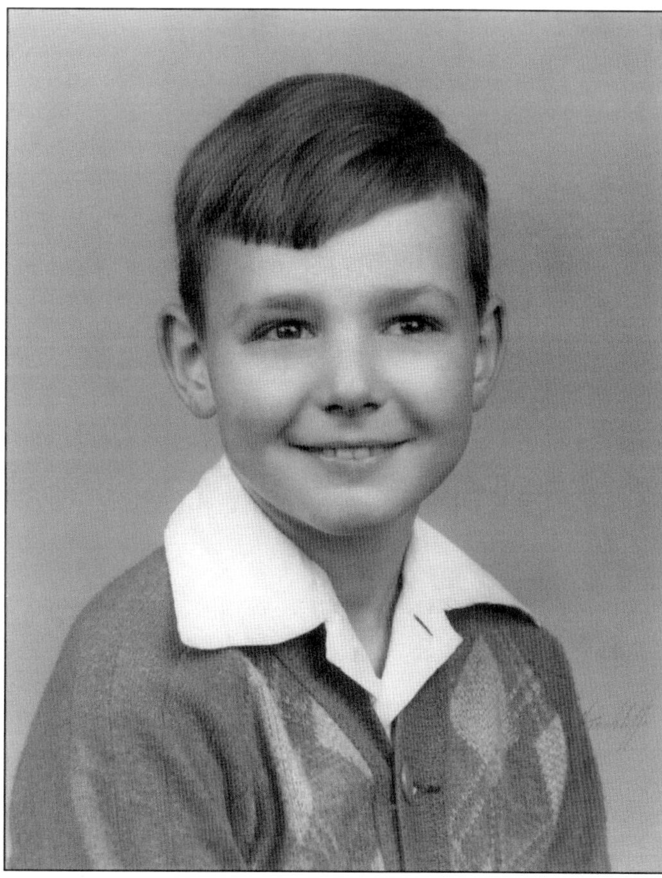

During the many years that Ruth Hoyt served as a janitor, there were still light moments. One day when she came into the classroom to empty a bin, the teacher asked the students to say thanks. All but one said in unison, "Thank you, Mrs. Hoyt." Her young grandson, seated in the classroom, instead blurted out, "Thank you, Grandma!" While his teacher was stunned, his grandmother told the story for years afterward with good humor. (Courtesy of David Comstock.)

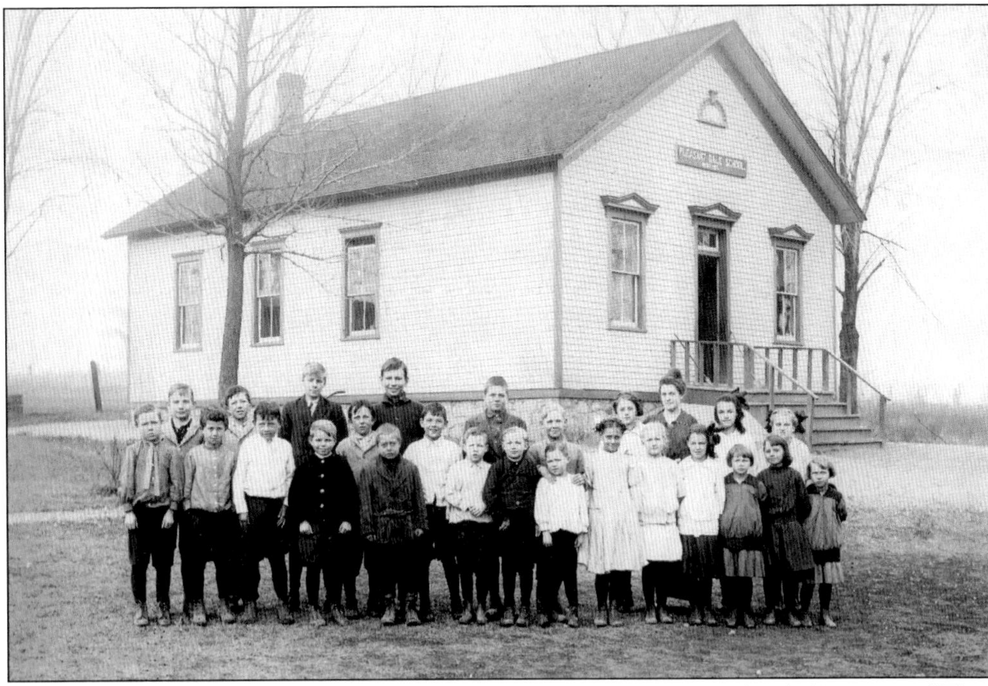

Miss Foran stands with her students outside the early Pleasant Dale School. (Courtesy of Flagg Creek Heritage Society.)

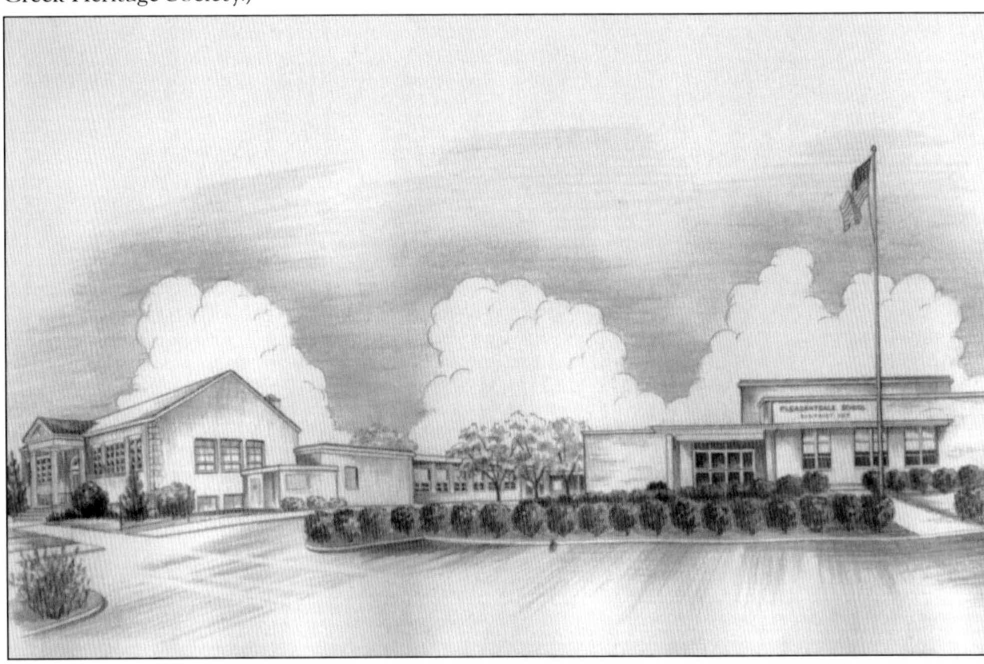

Just like Plainview, Pleasantdale School also had to expand to meet the needs of the community. Architectural plans were drafted and implemented in the 1950s to accommodate additional students; the new buildings were paid for by successive building bond issues. As populations boomed in the 1950s–1960s, additional schools such as Elm School District 181 would join to serve students. (Courtesy of Pleasantdale School.)

Seven

Gower and Anne M. Jeans Schools

Gower, Illinois, was its own town; like Tiedtville and Byrneville, it no longer exists. However, Gower had its own post office from 1870 to 1885 and again from 1886 to 1895, and had small businesses like the blacksmith shop in 1870 owned by George Huxhold and a general store tended by Mr. Hohlhuler. There was even a dance hall run by the Langkafel family where raffles, meetings, and—of course—dances were held. St. John's Church and Cemetery, originally built in 1859, served these early Gower residents (and would later be rebuilt at Lace, farther west, in 1899). Family farms play a large part in Gower School's history, as shown by the handwritten notes on photographs, such as "school picnic on the John Behm Farm" and "Jacob Jeans House." Others like Gauger, Redichs, Tameling, Marwitz, Wachter, Sass, Eggert, and Bolt are those families who also owned land in the immediate vicinity in what roughly is considered the "historical reach" of Gower School. Taking Madison Street south toward where the Byrneville Railroad station once served the local dairy farmers, one would have seen the architecture of the period: American vernacular homes, with broad porches and sturdy rooflines. These were the same families, especially the Kearneys, whom Anne M. Jeans befriended over the course of her life.

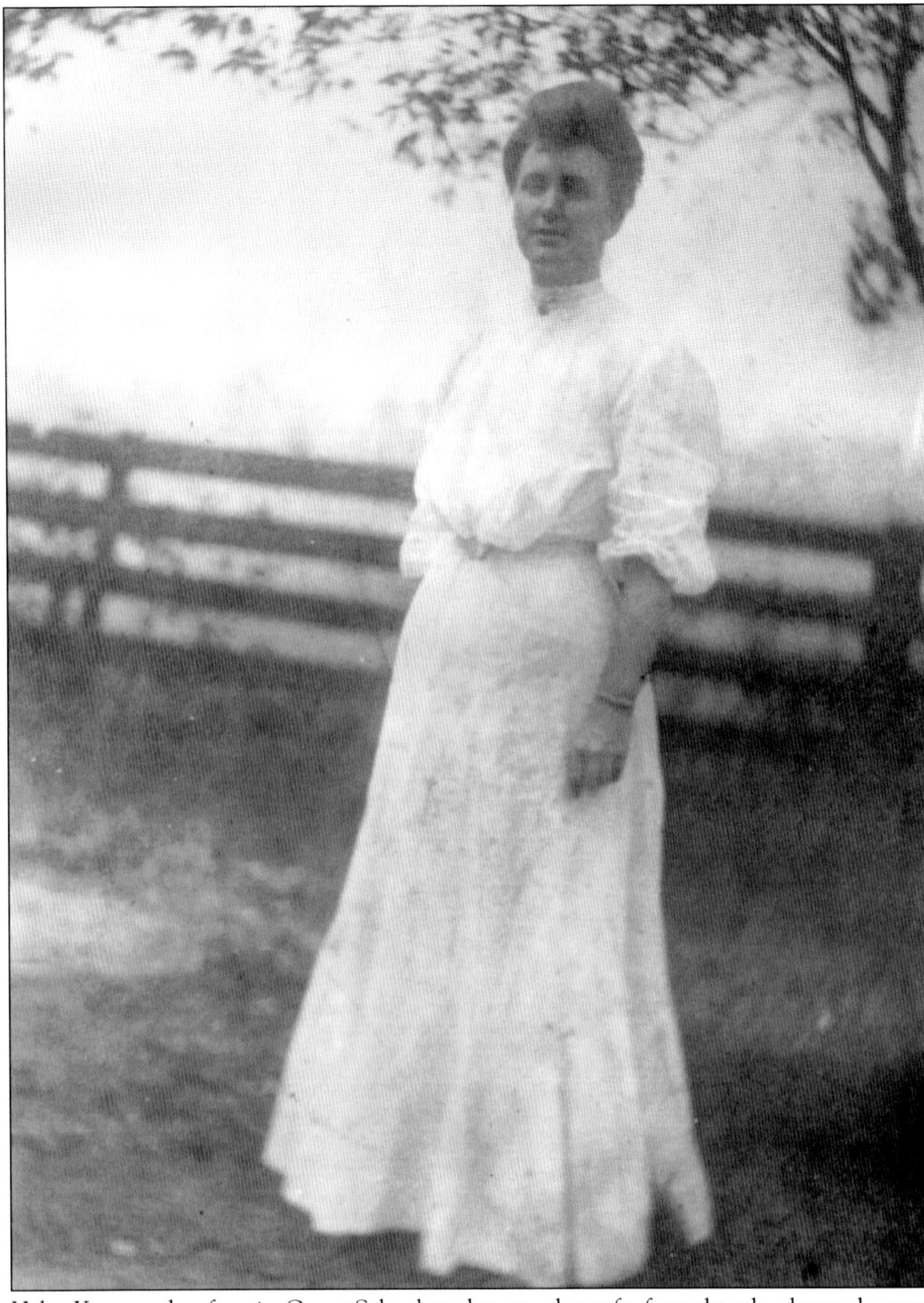

Helen Kavanaugh, a favorite Gower School teacher, stands not far from the schoolroom doorway in 1905. Over 40 years prior to Kavanaugh's tenure, Gower School was District 7, but it changed to District 62 in 1900. According to a Downers Grove Township, DuPage County tax collector's roll from 1861, total taxes collected in that year for the school amounted to $192.86. (Courtesy of Gower School.)

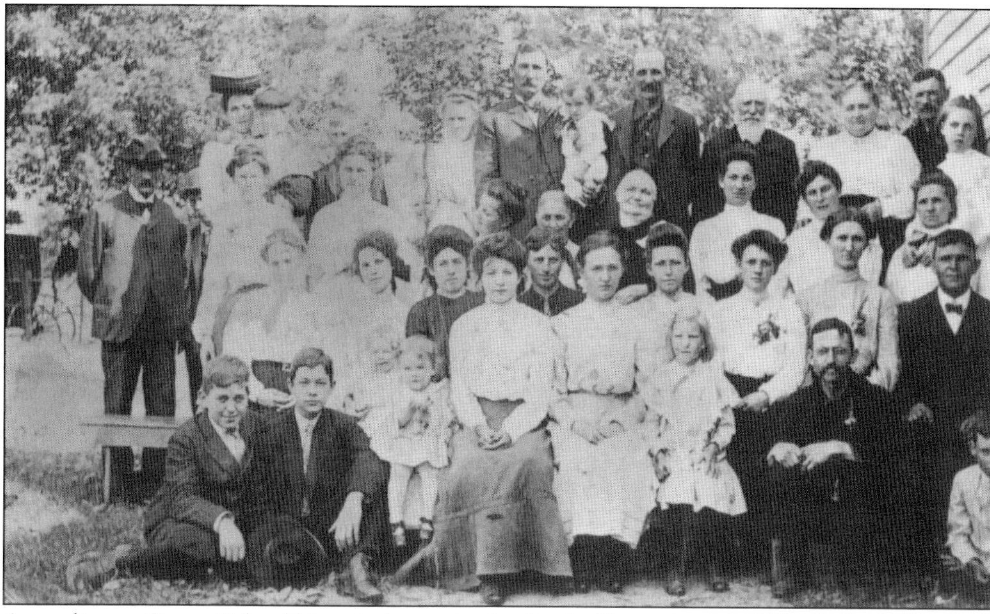

According to Gower School historical records, the first half acre that would be Gower School was donated by the French and Belgian family of Louis and Ann Fortmann in 1873. Since the school was located in what by then was a growing community with educational needs for their children, it is not surprising that records state that "the early years of the school were not easy ones." Total enrollment was approximately 20 for all of the eight grades until past the turn of the 20th century. Gower faculty and students pose for this c. 1905 class photo. (Courtesy of Gower School.)

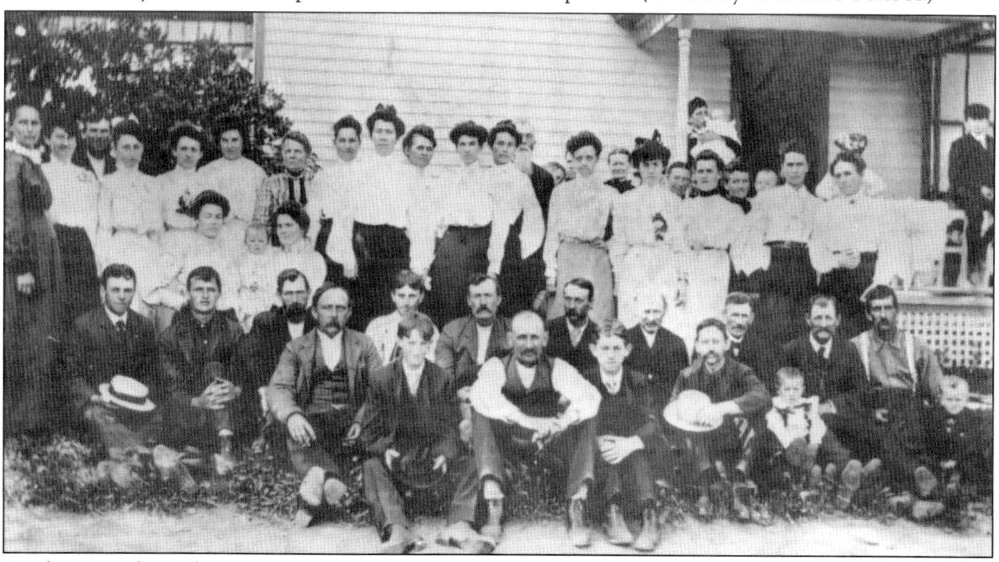

Students and teachers from Gower visit the John Behm farm in 1904 for a picnic. The Behm home would serve the Gower School children over many years and stood across from the school for easy recesses. A game noted in records was called "Drop the Handkerchief." Children would stand in a circle, and one child would run around and drop a handkerchief behind one of them. Whoever got the handkerchief dropped behind him or her would chase the child who dropped it, and a game of tag would ensue. But woe (or joy) to the child who was caught: some rules required not just a tag but also a kiss. (Courtesy of Gower School.)

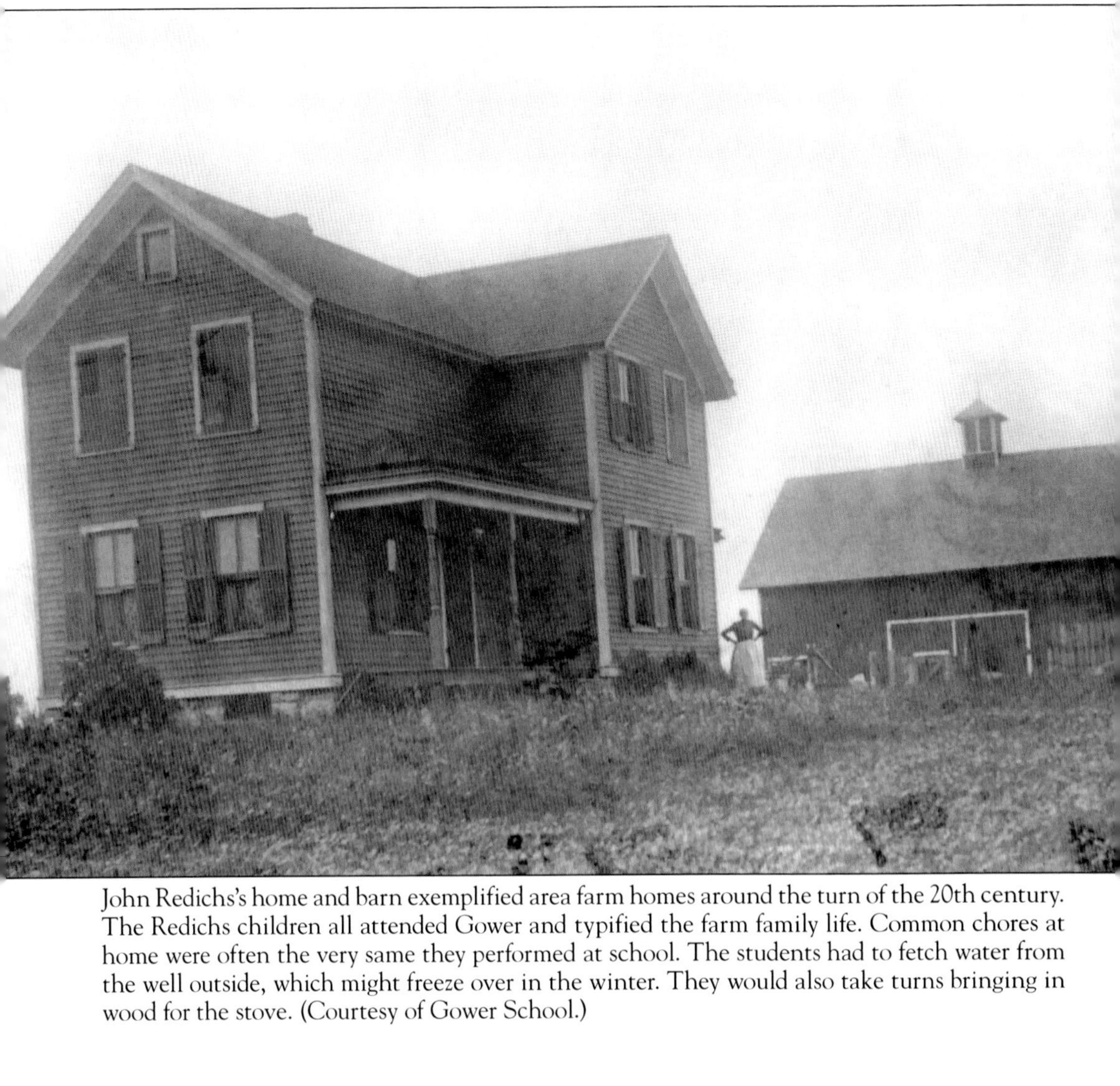

John Redichs's home and barn exemplified area farm homes around the turn of the 20th century. The Redichs children all attended Gower and typified the farm family life. Common chores at home were often the very same they performed at school. The students had to fetch water from the well outside, which might freeze over in the winter. They would also take turns bringing in wood for the stove. (Courtesy of Gower School.)

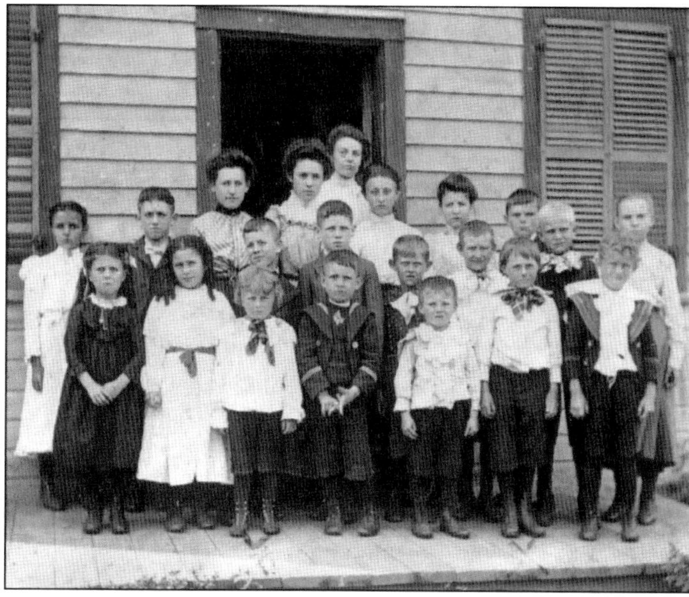

School discipline was quite different from modern sensibilities. One Gower School student from the time recalled, "The teacher rang a big school bell, and when that bell stopped jangling, we were in our seats. If you were naughty, you might get slapped by a ruler. But if a teacher told your parents on you, watch out!" Some of Gower School's younger students (seemingly with much self-restraint) stand still for this class photo in 1901. (Courtesy of Gower School.)

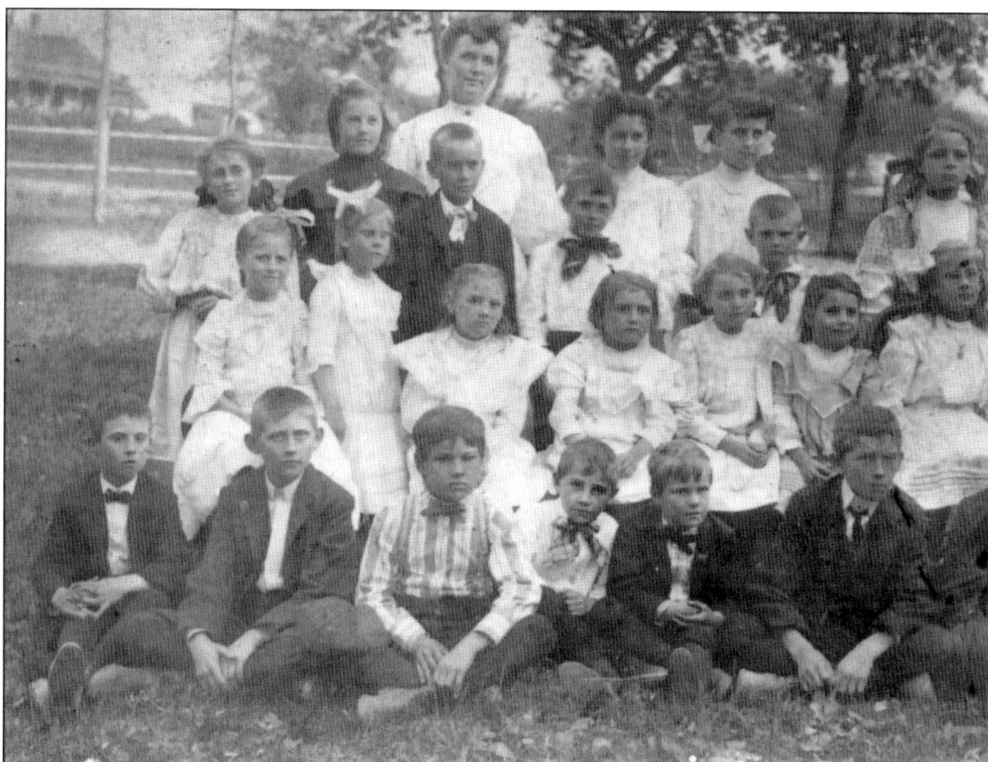

In an early report, a 1907 Gower graduate, Otto Dallner, recalled the school as a wood-frame, one-room structure. He said he was one of only 17 graduates that year. Not surprisingly, he recalled walking to school most days and that sometimes the snow was so deep in the winter farm fields that students would have to take "the longer way" to reach its doors. Helen Kavanaugh and her class pose for a snowless photograph in 1907. (Courtesy of Gower School.)

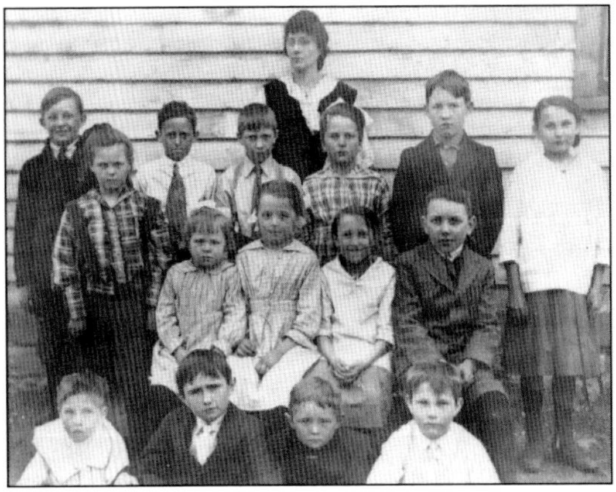

Teachers who did not live in the immediate area would board in local homes close to Gower School in order to be available. Country schools required that the teachers take care of their charges, as well as many "comforts" for the students. One Langkafel family member who attended the school recalled that during the holidays, his teacher would bring popcorn balls, an orange, or a piece of candy to spread holiday cheer. Lucia Kearney taught at Gower from 1911 to 1917. Her sister would follow in her footsteps. (Courtesy of Gower School.)

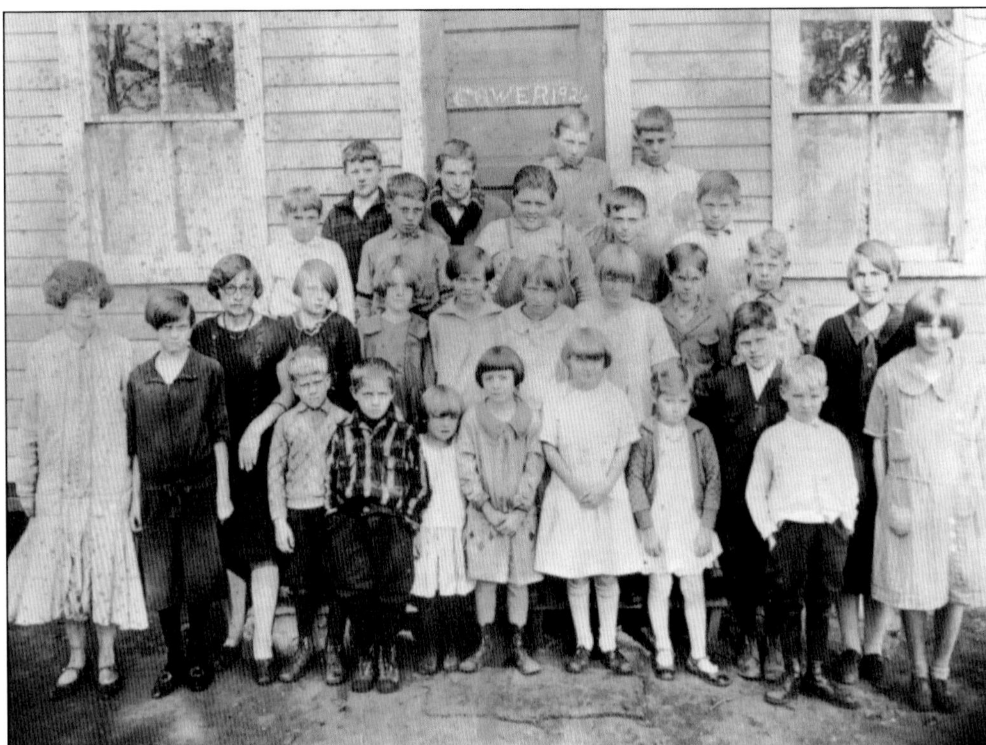

Anna Kearney was the longest-serving teacher of the era, staying there from 1914 to 1928. She and Anne M. Jeans were close friends, sharing both professional and church bonds. Kearney dutifully fulfilled many roles at the school, with one of her contracts dating from 1928 stating explicitly that her responsibilities would be to "teach, govern, and conduct;" "keep a register of daily attendance and studies of each (student)" and "make the report required;" and "endeavor to preserve, in good condition and order the school house, grounds, furniture, apparatus, and district property." Handwritten is an additional duty of "janitor work . . . of said school"—all for a princely monthly sum of $160. Kearney is shown here with her students in 1926. (Courtesy of Gower School.)

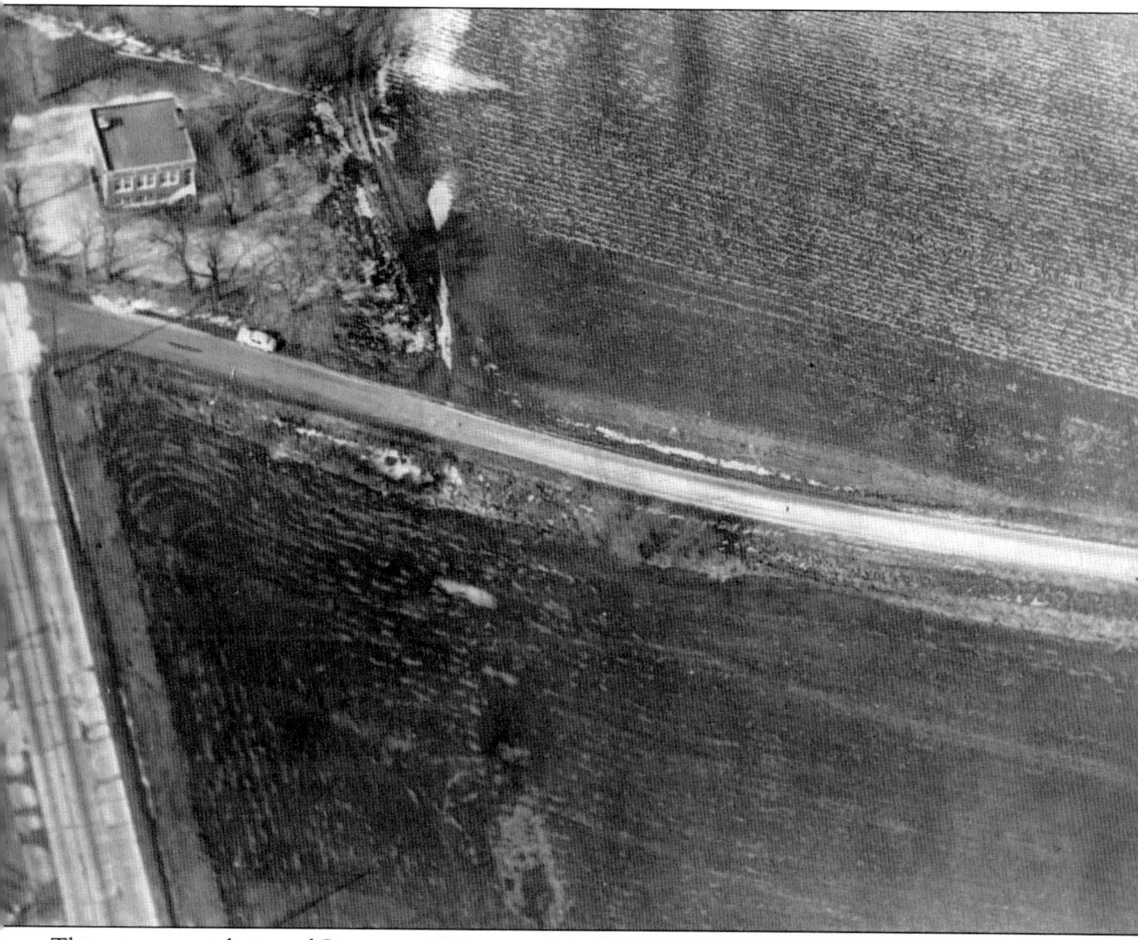

This winter aerial view of Gower in 1927 is revealing for just how much of the area was farmland. It was in that year that Mary Sajvera is noted as the grantor of .28 acres at a cost of $300 to the school. There was room to grow, and in that year, it did. According to an article celebrating a school anniversary, "In 1927 it was obvious a new school house was needed. A referendum was passed, plans drawn up, and bids accepted. The old school was moved to the corner of Madison and Rt. 66." While remaining a one-room schoolhouse, it was built with brick and given modern updates, which were welcomed by teachers, parents, and students alike. (Courtesy of Gower School.)

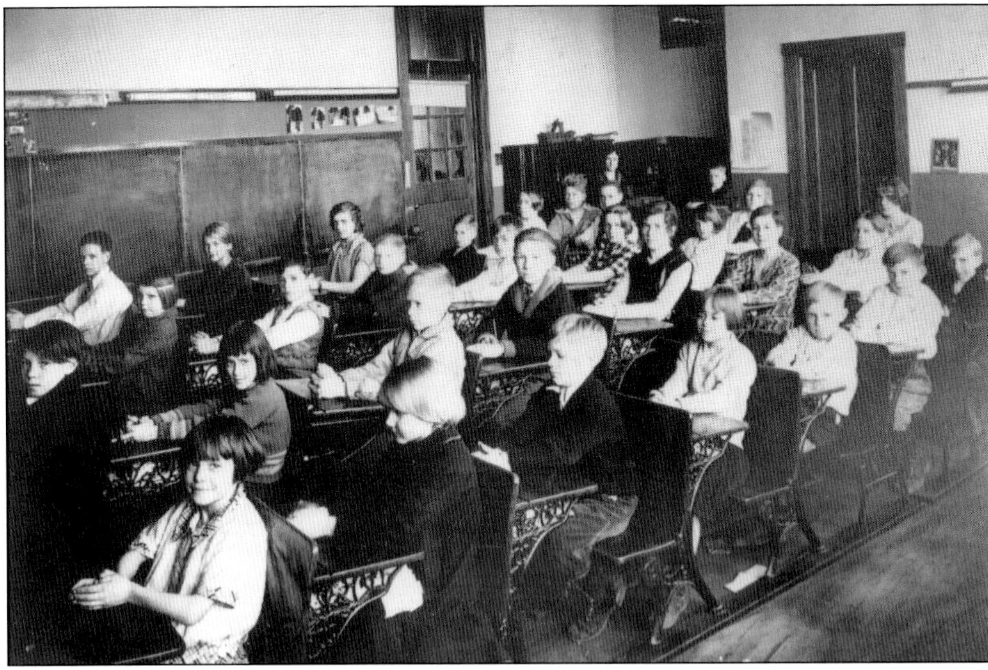

In the handwritten Proceedings of the Board of Directors, 1928, it was noted, "The president, clerk, and director agreed on the following: To install one set of Compton's Picture Encyclopedia in the School" along with "1 complete set of Illinois Pupils' Reading Circle Books" and "1 book case." Perhaps most welcomed was this detail: "We also agreed to install indoor toilets." Additionally, they agreed "to have green placed above the blackboard for the purpose of exhibiting drawings, specimen papers, and test papers." In this 1930 image, student artwork hangs above the blackboard just as stated. (Courtesy of Gower School.)

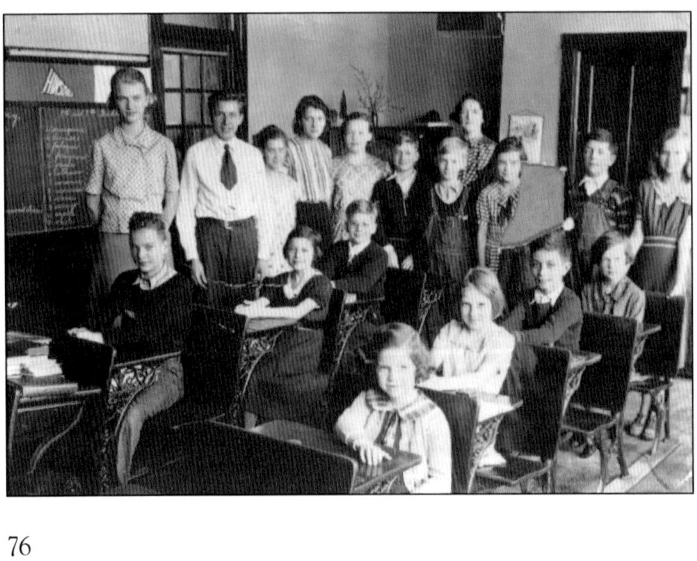

By 1935, the area was becoming increasingly developed, but the population was remaining consistent, with Gower School enrollment still hovering around 50. At the school's Golden Gala anniversary, one student recalled watching Joliet Road being paved and thinking it was something thoroughly modern and new. (Courtesy of Gower School.)

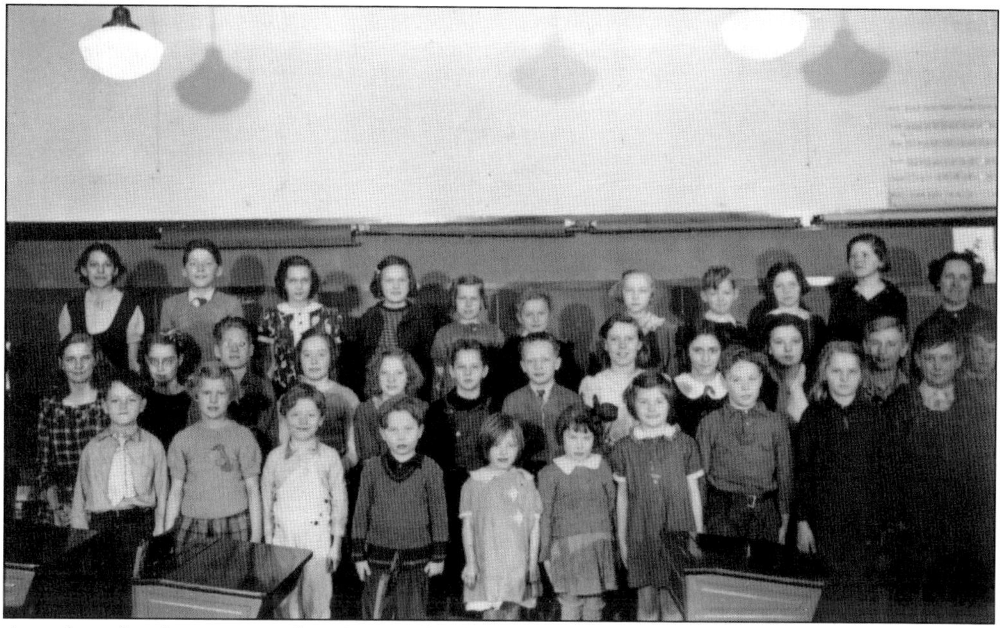

Area farm families remained as Gower slowly saw newer names and faces arrive. But one name still seen today is Tameling. Pictured in Gower's class photo from 1938 in the middle row are Sadie Tameling (far left), Stephen Tameling (seventh from left), and Henry Tameling (far right). The Tameling Nursery is still on Madison Street in what is now Willowbrook. (Courtesy of Gower School.)

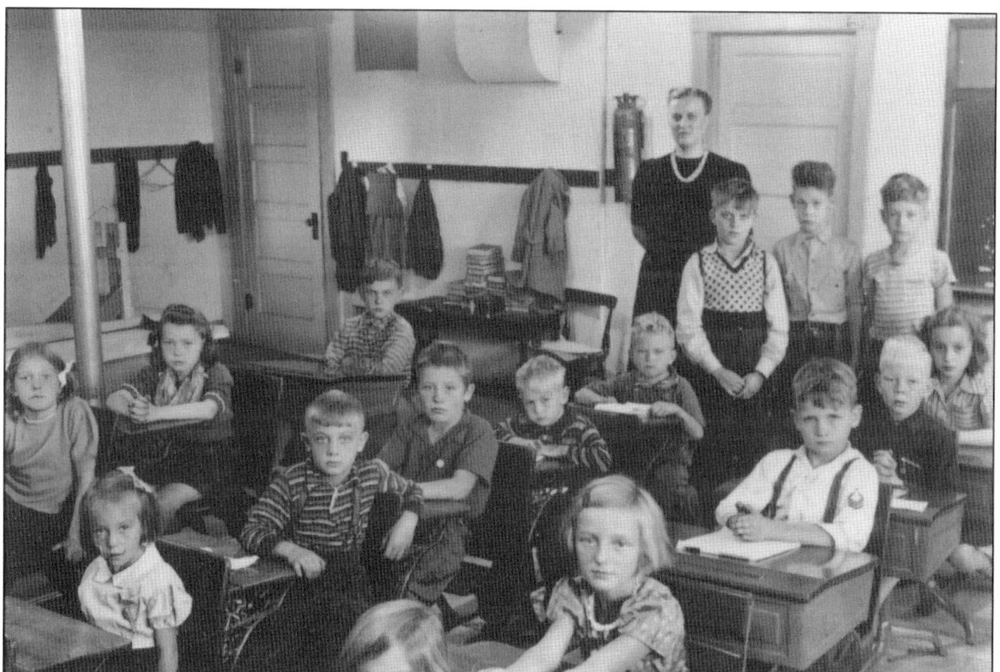

The basement classroom was remembered fondly by one past student, who noted that on some winter school days in the 1940s, the owner of Del Rhea's Chicken Basket on Route 66/Joliet Road would bring hot lunches. (Courtesy of Gower School.)

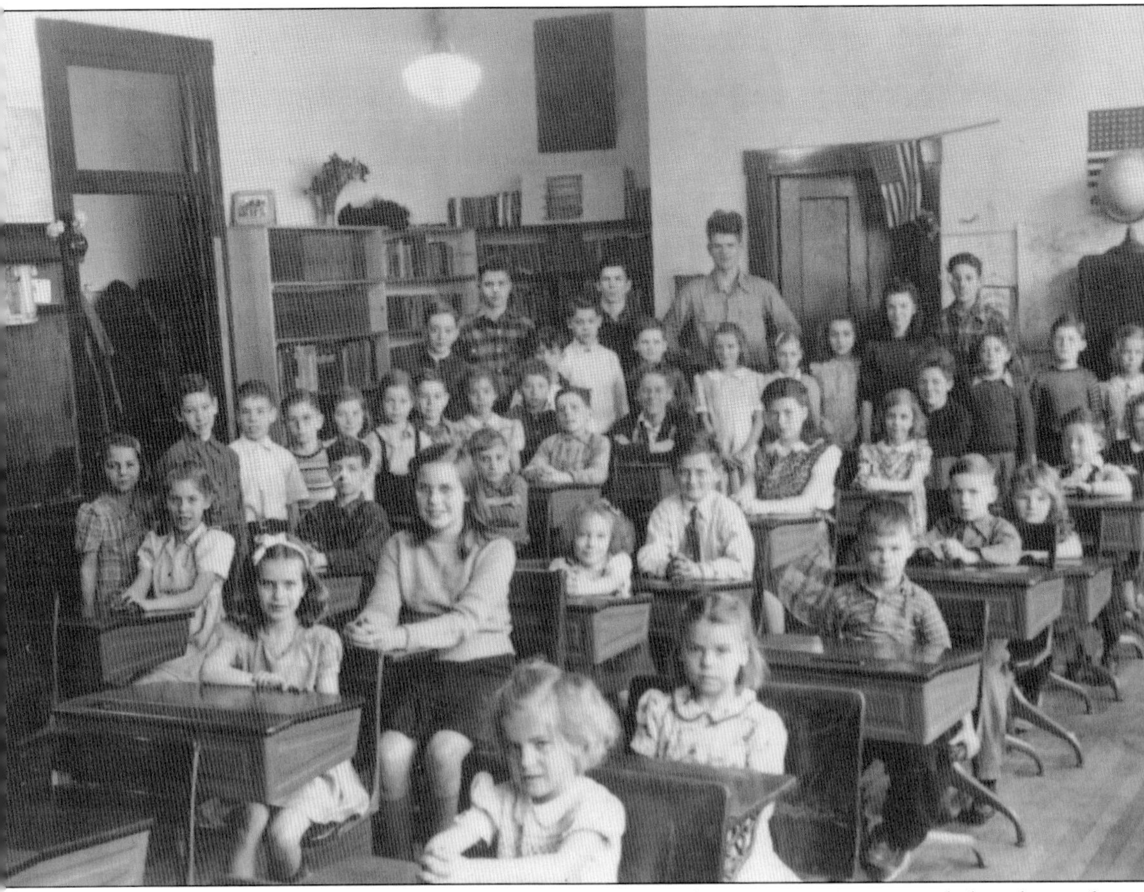

The American flags hanging on the wall of this Gower classroom in 1944 reminded students of the nation's ongoing sacrifices in World War II: patriotism was at an all-time high. (Courtesy of Gower School.)

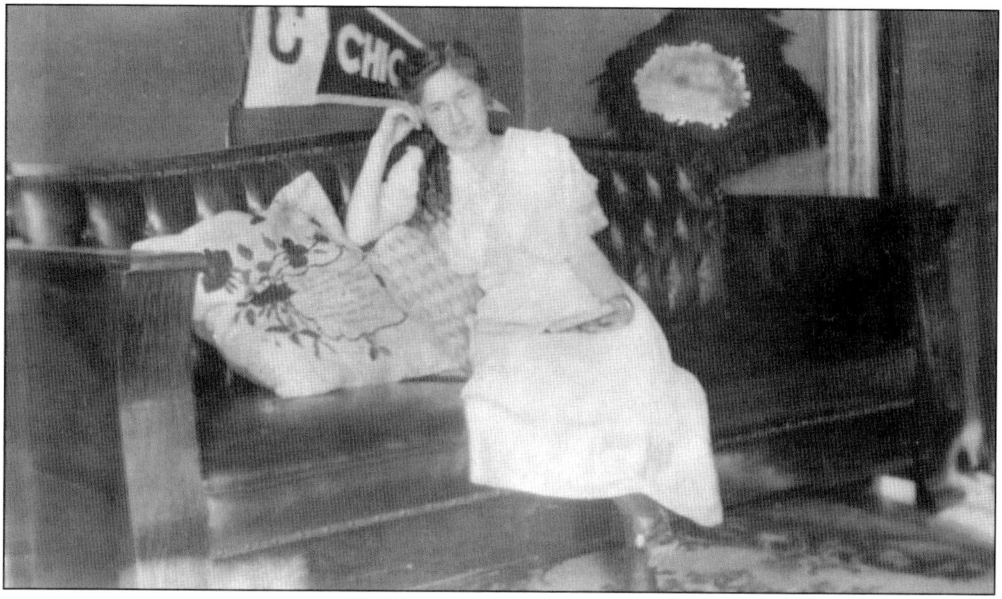

Growing up at Madison and 91st Streets, Anne M. Jeans remained dedicated to the children from her "neighborhood." After her college days, of which this 1908 photograph is a memento, she began her career in teaching. Known as playful and inspirational, she befriended Gower School teacher Anna Kearney, and they remained lifelong friends. (Courtesy of AMJSCCS.)

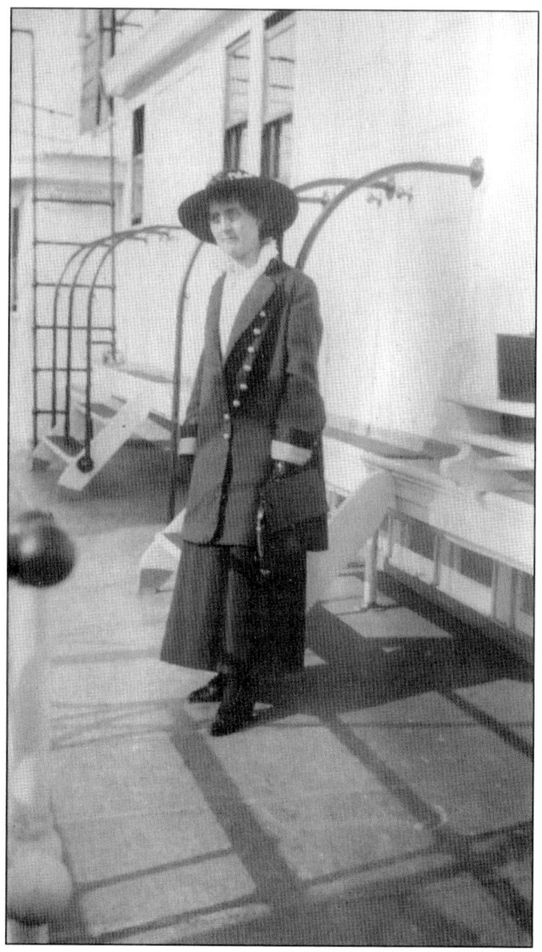

Jeans taught her first class in 1910, the same year this photograph was taken. Her first students included several Tiedts and other multigenerational families of Burr Ridge. (Courtesy of AMJSCCS.)

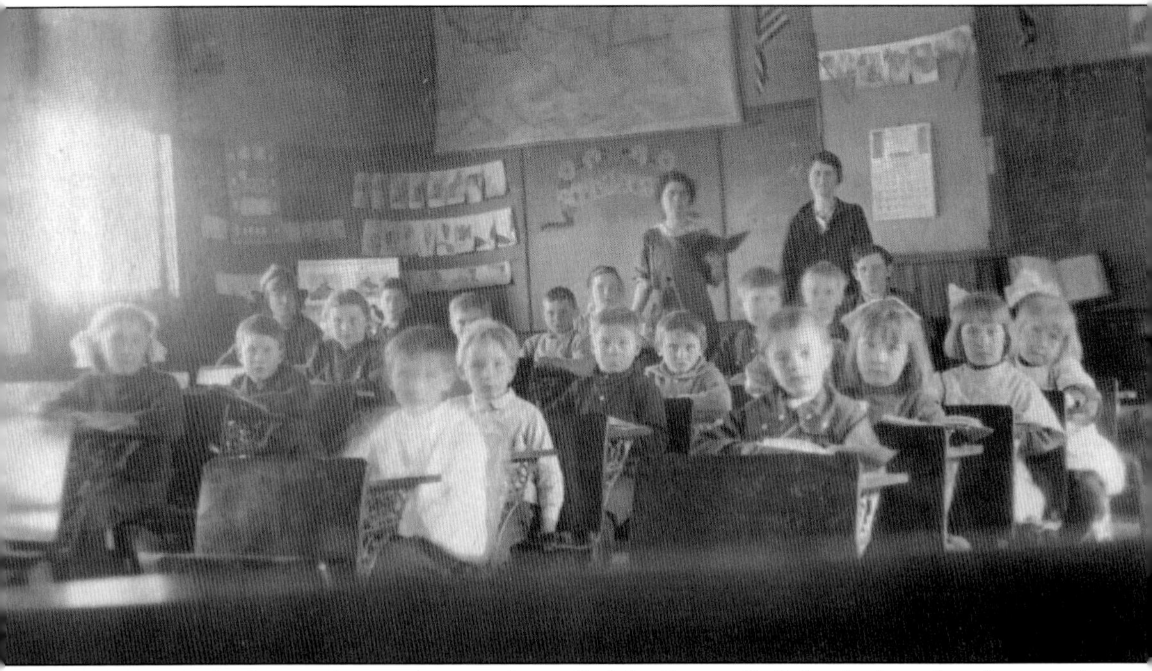

Jeans was the first teacher in what was then called the Byrneville School, where this photograph was taken in 1910, and she remained its only teacher until 1947. It was she who recommended that the name be changed to Palisades School, given the natural land's character. Ultimately, the school would be named in her honor. (Courtesy of AMJSCCS.)

Eight

High School Spirit

The Burr Ridge area, crossing the county line as it does, is served by two public high school districts. This has been true historically as well. The boundaries of Lyons Township District 204 extend to County Line Road on its farthest western border, where it meets Hinsdale District 86. Hinsdale High School and Lyons Township High School were founded nearly in tandem. Lyons Township opened its doors in September 1889, when 39 pupils made up its first class. Hinsdale High School's first graduating class was in 1893, but it would not officially be Hinsdale Township High School until 1925. In the earliest years, it was still not considered necessary to attend secondary school. That was certainly soon to change as the community itself was shifting from primarily agrarian to industrial work. Some of the success of Chicago's growth had no little influence: business required educated employees, and high school education was one avenue toward financial security. Business leaders themselves took care to support education as well. Marshall Field himself even donated a 500-pound bell to Lyons Township's new bell tower in 1889. Hinsdale High School would grow with the village of Hinsdale proper but would swell with the increased population after World War II–era parents settled into the area and had children coming of age. Hinsdale Central High School opened its doors in 1950, and Hinsdale South followed in 1965. Much has changed, but the rivalry among the Lions, Red Devils, and Hornets has not.

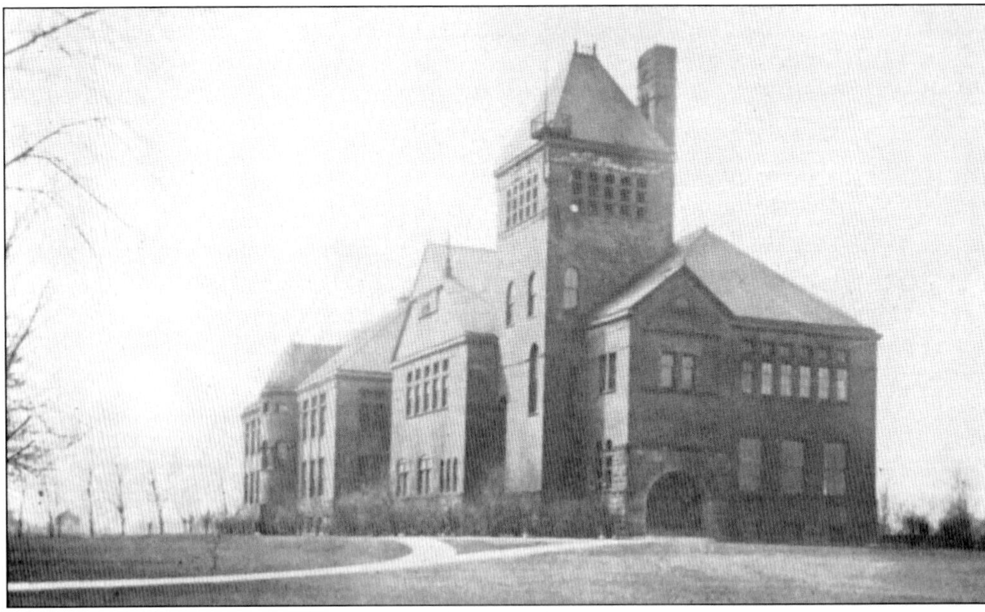

Lyons Township High School opened in the fall of 1888. This 1899 photograph of the school does not include Emmond Field, which did not open until 1914. (Courtesy of Lyons Township High School.)

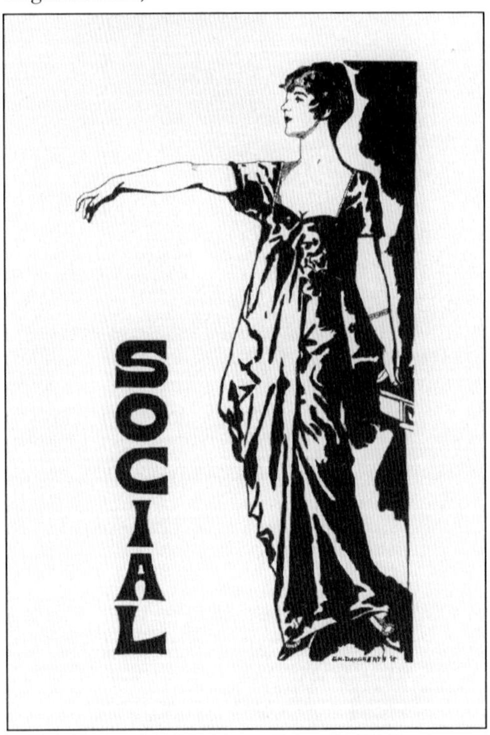

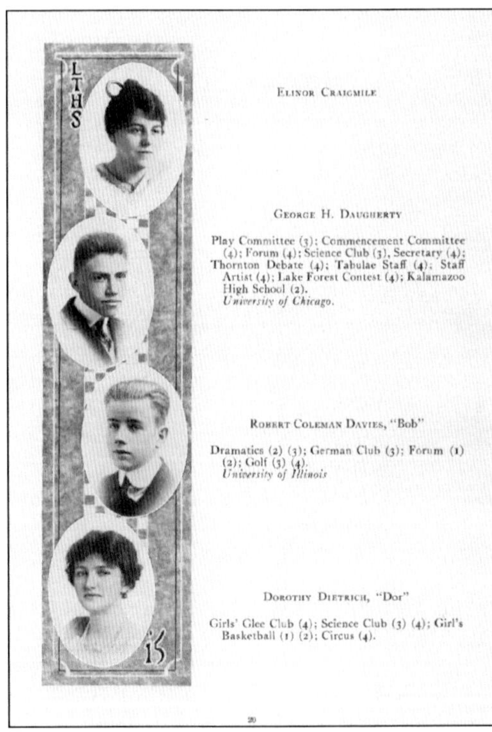

LTHS

15

ELINOR CRAIGMILE

GEORGE H. DAUGHERTY

Play Committee (3); Commencement Committee (4); Forum (4); Science Club (3), Secretary (4); Thornton Debate (4); Tabulae Staff (4); Staff Artist (4); Lake Forest Contest (4); Kalamazoo High School (2).
University of Chicago.

ROBERT COLEMAN DAVIES, "Bob"

Dramatics (2) (3); German Club (3); Forum (1) (2); Golf (3) (4).
University of Illinois

DOROTHY DIETRICH, "Dor"

Girls' Glee Club (4); Science Club (3) (4); Girl's Basketball (1) (2); Circus (4).

20

George H. Daugherty, a talented LTHS senior, drew the illustration at left for the 1915 yearbook cover. The class of 1915 (right) had diverse talents. Dorothy Dietrich belonged to the science and glee clubs as well as the basketball team. Her classmate Robert Coleman Davies enjoyed German Club, dramatics, forum, and golf. (Both, courtesy of Lyons Township High School.)

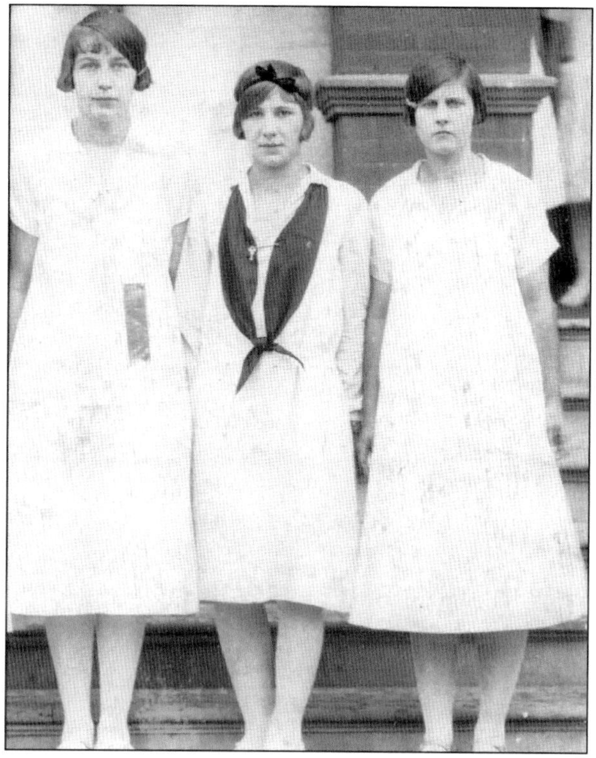

These three LTHS students won a statewide award for domestic science in 1920. They went to Springfield to receive the award. (Courtesy of Lyons Township High School.)

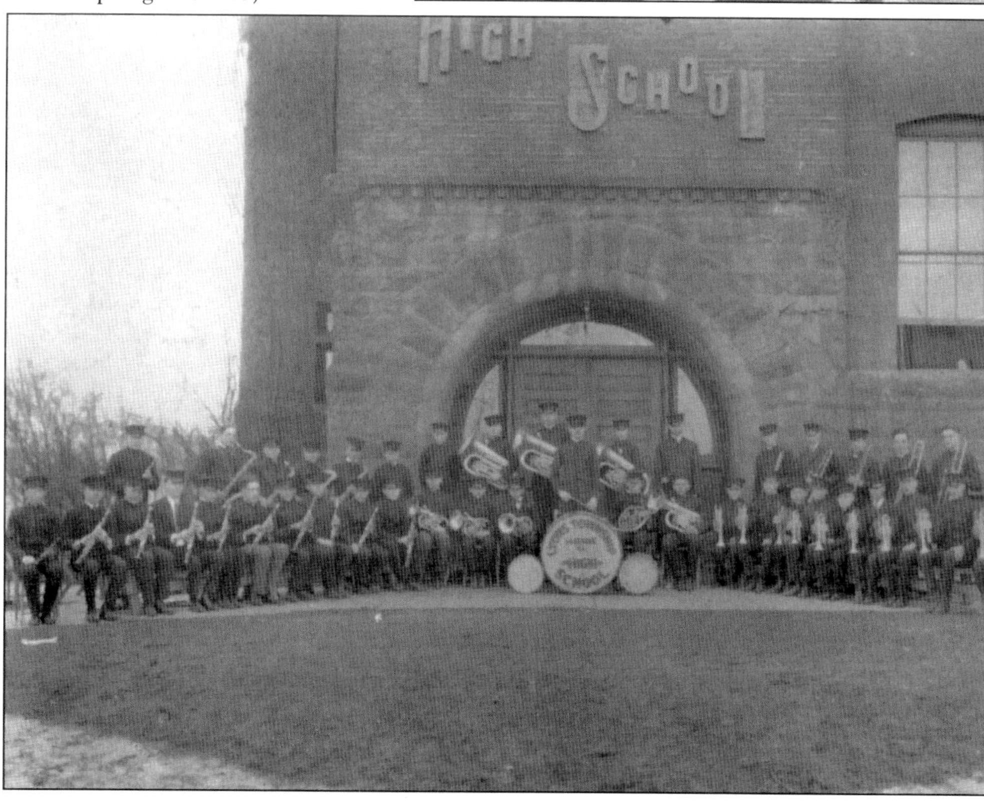

Musically inclined students could join LTHS's band, shown here around 1923 in front of the main building. (Courtesy of Lyons Township High School.)

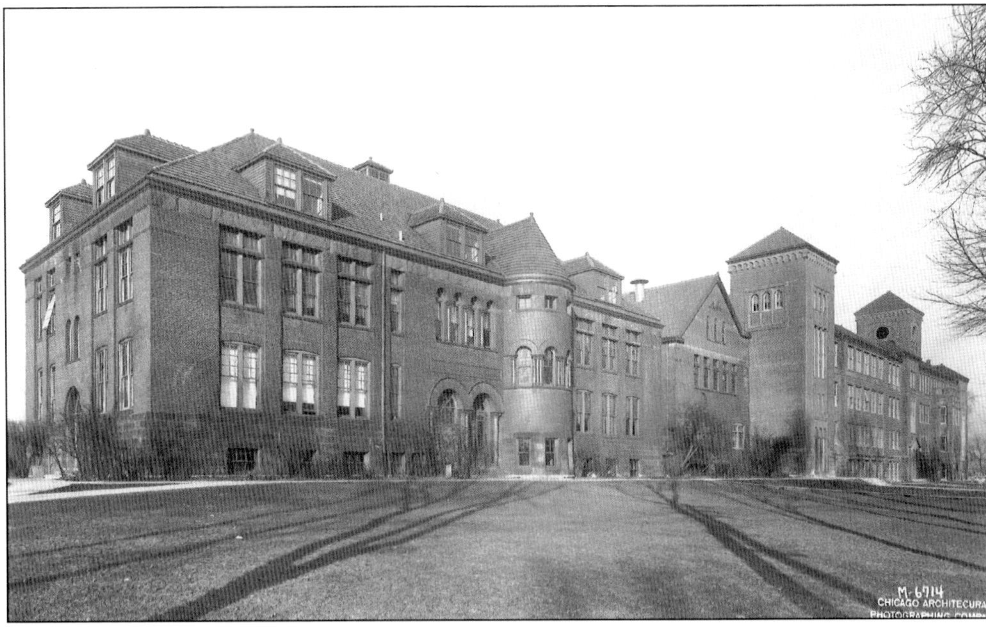

The high school's famous clock tower, which was part of a series of renovations that began in 1926, is already visible in this photograph, taken in the spring of 1928. These renovations would not be completed until the following year: note that the clock faces have not yet been installed. (Courtesy of Llewellyn Boardman.)

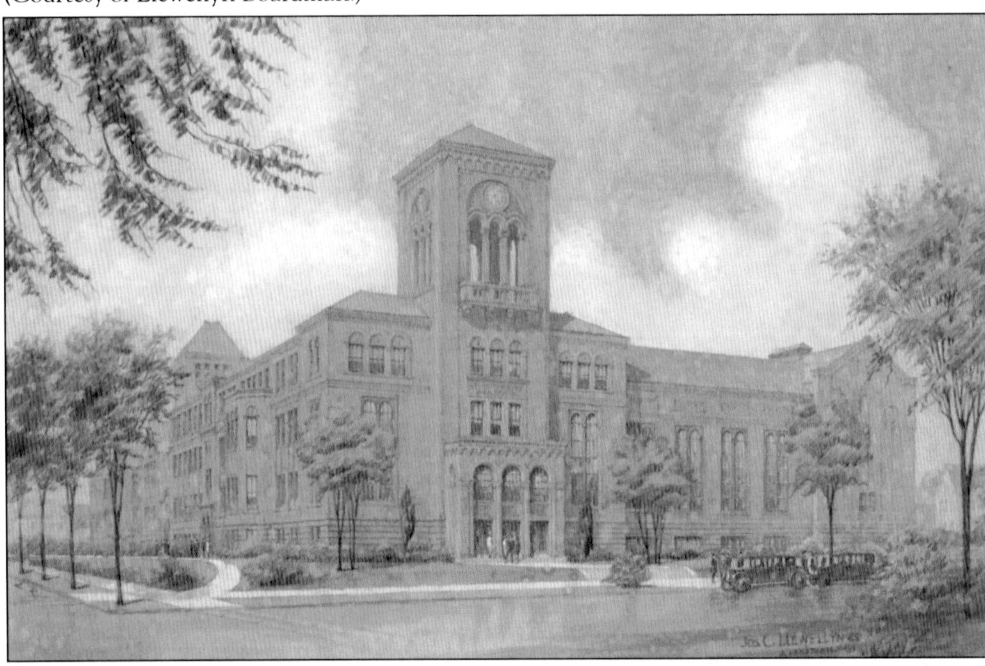

The Joseph C. Llewellyn Company was an established Midwestern architectural firm, most known for creating distinctive institutional designs. Architecture in Chicago's early 20th century was synonymous with such names as Louis Sullivan and Frank Lloyd Wright. However, Joseph Corson Llewellyn's reputation rested in creating iconic school designs, such as this drawing of the new clock tower in 1928. (Courtesy of Llewellyn Boardman.)

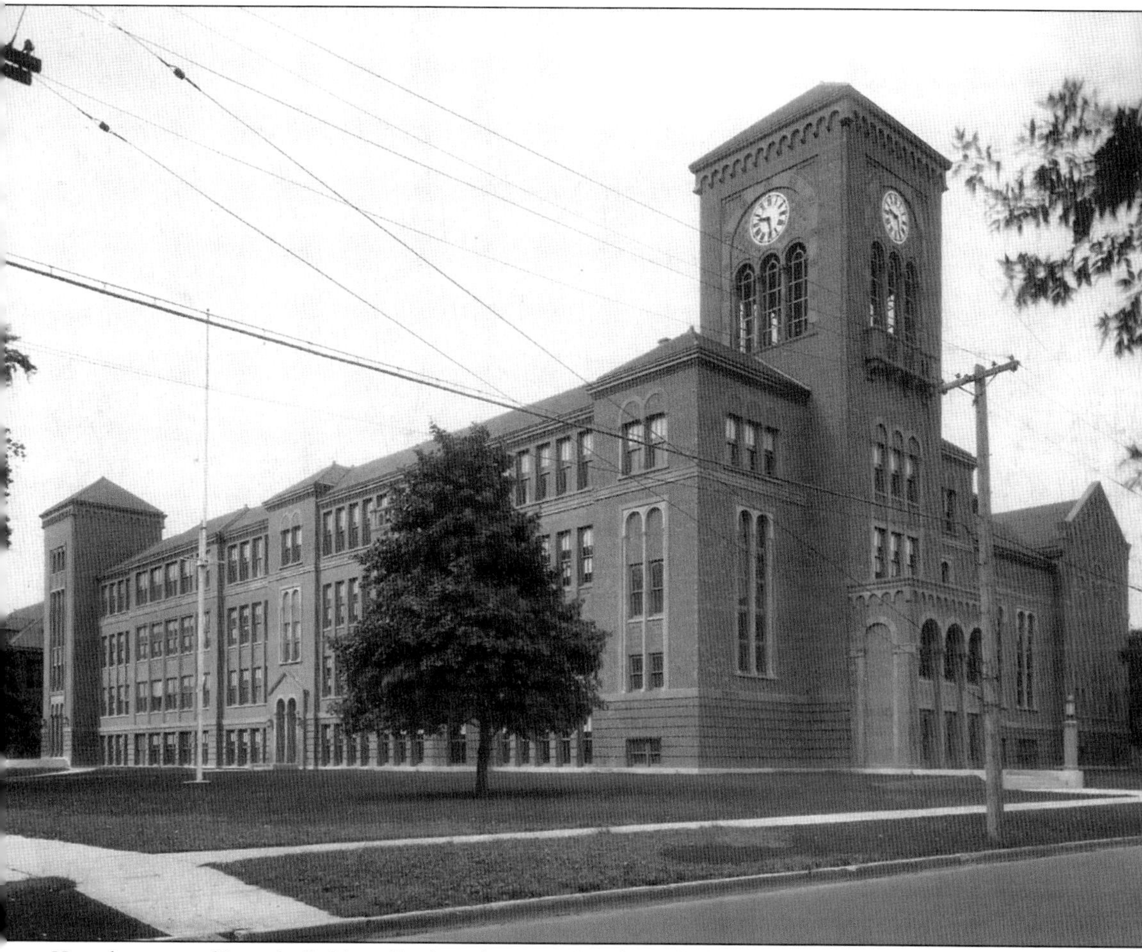

Key elements of Joseph C. Llewellyn's architectural style included LTHS's post-renovation front entrance, which still exists in its original form. Llewellyn's designs garnered many honors, and he was inducted as a fellow of the American Institute of Architects. His reputation as an innovator of public spaces in the field of architecture remains. Many of the firm's drawings, photographs, and papers were donated to the Art Institute of Chicago Ryerson and Burnham Library when the firm closed its doors in 1992. (Courtesy of Llewellyn Boardman.)

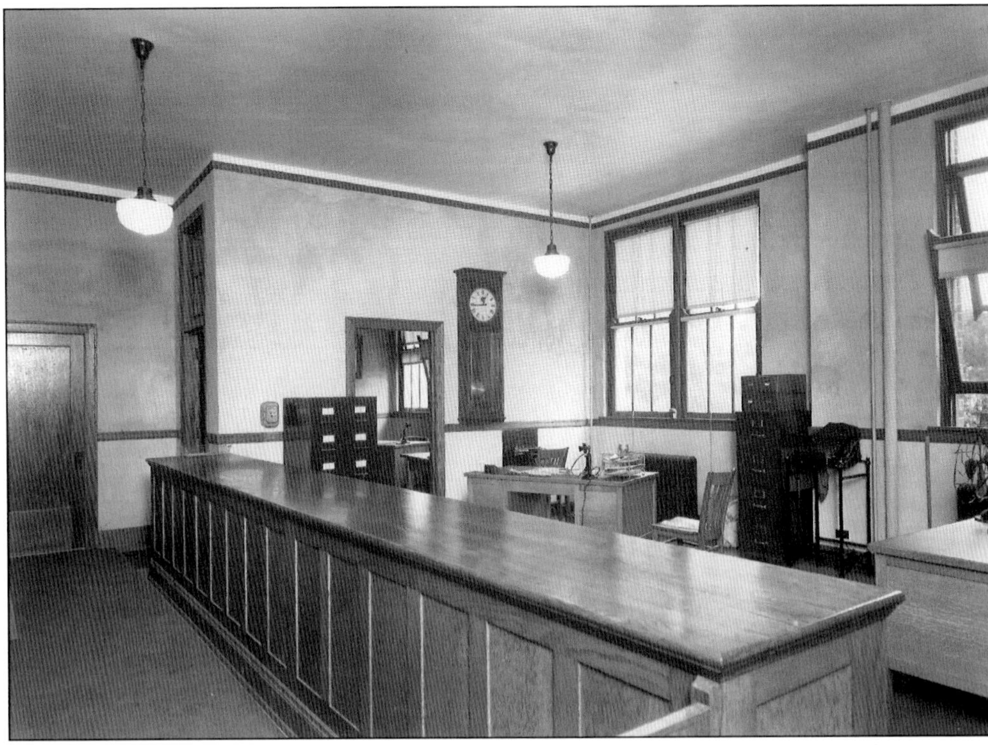

School design was informed by Progressivism. Key to this new way of seeing the work of learning was use of natural light, space, and wood, seen in Chicago architecture's interpretations of modernity. "Modern" didn't mean air conditioning, however. Students and staff alike had to rely on electric fans and open windows to stay cool during the warmer months of the school year, as this 1920s photograph of LTHS's main office shows. (Courtesy of Llewellyn Boardman.)

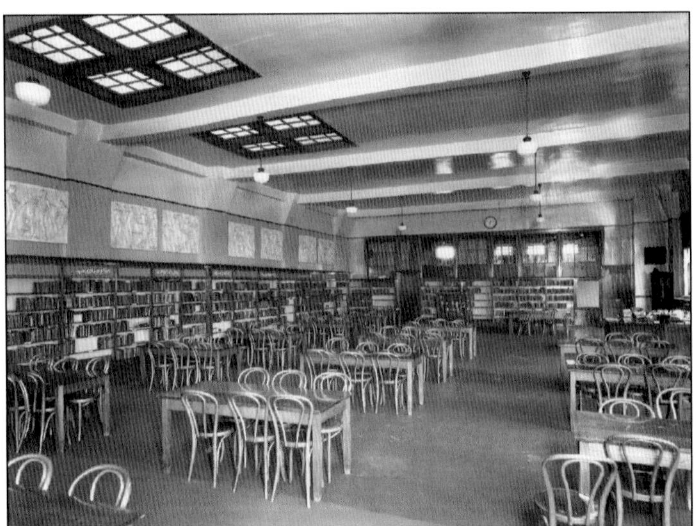

School libraries at the time were a significant investment, exemplifying the shift early Pragmatism had on formal schooling. Science labs, "manual arts" workshops, and school libraries were designed around the skills students needed in a post-agrarian economy. LTHS's library provided ample space for quiet study, as seen in this c. 1924 photograph. (Courtesy of Llewellyn Boardman.)

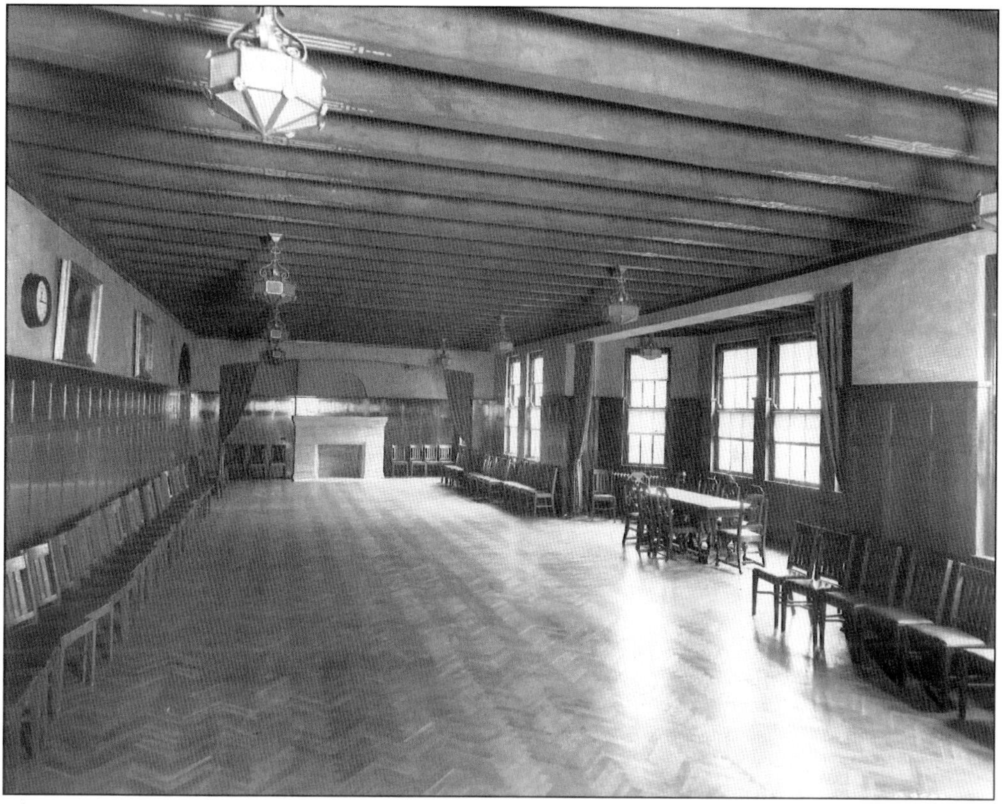

The community room, with its stone fireplace and elegant parquet wood floors, was a linchpin for LTHS in 1928 and remains in use today. A May 1928 student newspaper article quotes Llewellyn: "On the third floor . . . there is a room with bare walls lighted by [a] sky-light that affords ample opportunity for the art society connected with the school for placing of paintings and various objects of art. The auditorium, foyer, and community room gives a unit not surpassed by many other[s] in the state for community purposes. These rooms have been furnished to make them attractive and acceptable to the public. . . . The thought behind the whole plan . . . is that all community organizations interested in educational and cultural activities may here find a place to carry on their work as well and in addition to the regular school activities." (Courtesy of Llewellyn Boardman.)

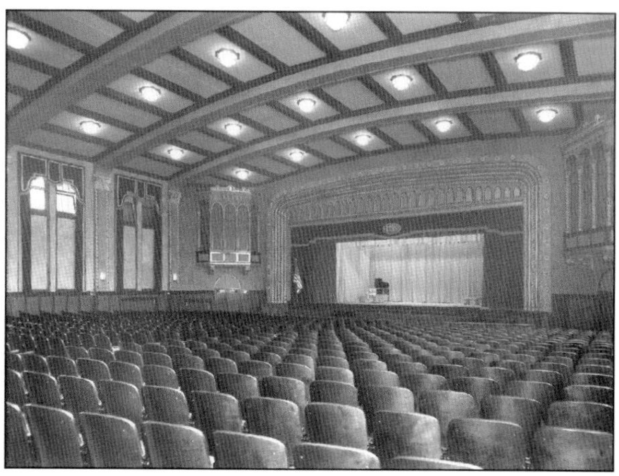

Musical and theatrical performances took place at LTHS's auditorium, photographed in 1928 soon after its opening. The auditorium, library, gymnasium, and offices were all addressed in the 1926–1929 renovations. Llewellyn's firm was at the apex of its popularity and influence and would complete 52 school designs around this time. (Courtesy of Llewellyn Boardman.)

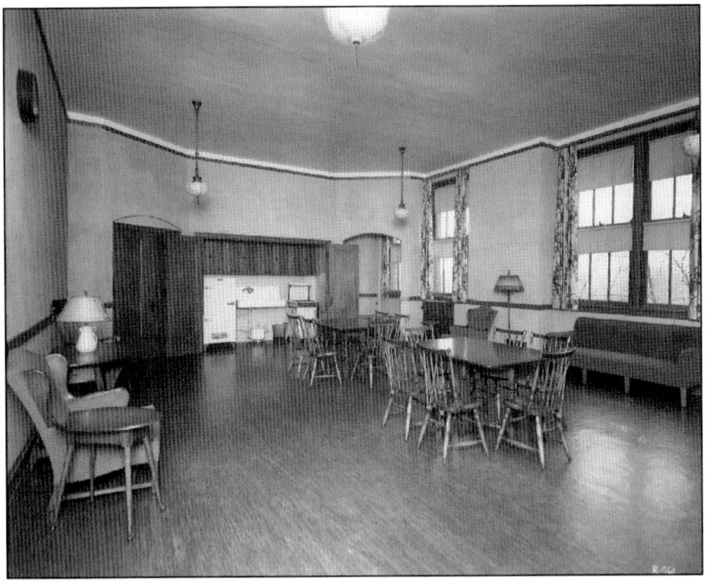

Room 343, the women's lounge, seems quaint today. While female student enrollment was statistically equal to male enrollment in the late 1920s in the areas' schools, having a dedicated—and, perhaps, more collegial—space was a welcome luxury. (Courtesy of Llewellyn Boardman.)

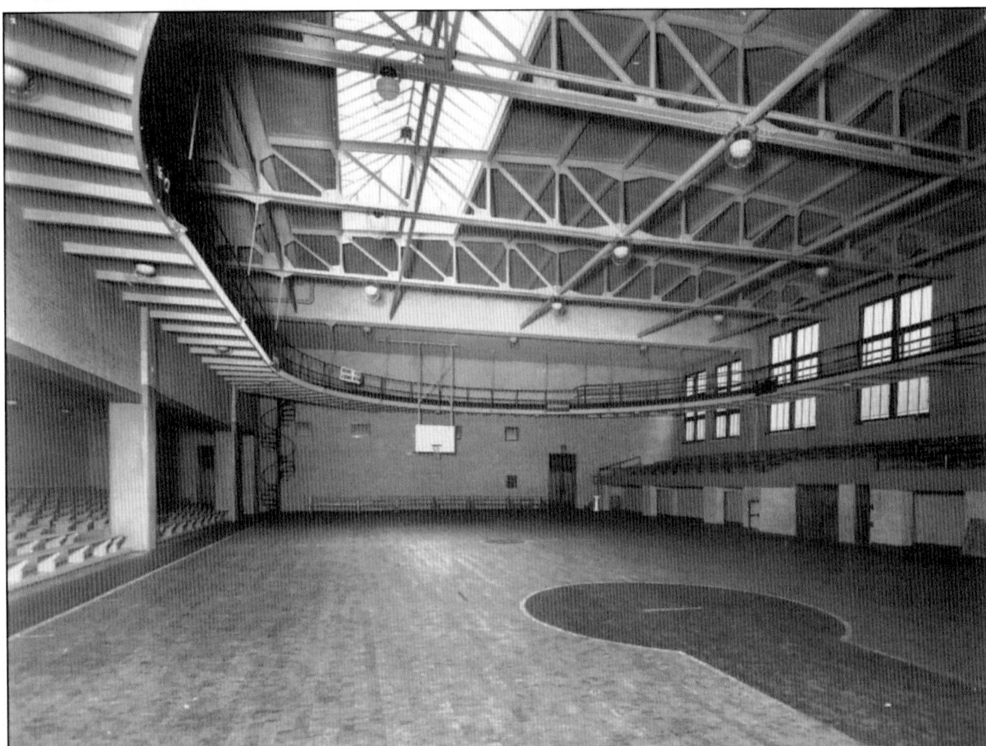

Basketball was made a wildly popular game by leagues in the YMCA and universities before the turn of the 20th century. Interestingly, basketball was initially introduced in Illinois high schools as a young women's sport, with the first local interscholastic teams of Austin High and Oak Park facing off in 1896. However, by 1910, women's teams were no longer allowed to play interscholastic basketball. By the late 1920s, the National Interscholastic Basketball Tournament was hosted each March at the University of Chicago and was a Chicago sports staple. LTHS's 1928 gymnasium was cutting edge to have a basketball court. (Courtesy of Llewellyn Boardman.)

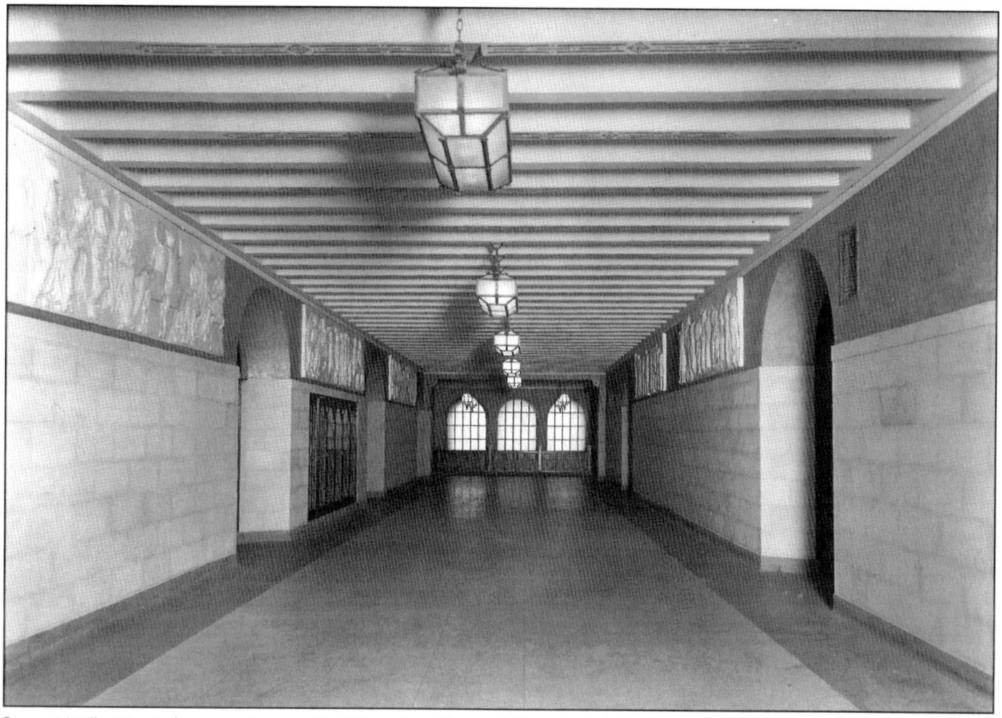

In a 1945–1946 description in LTHS's Gold and Blue Guide, the author writes, "Our foyer is the beauty spot in our building. On the east side are the plaster casts of the sculpted frieze of the Parthenon, a gift from the architect, Mr. Joseph C. Llewellyn, in 1928." The idea of a public space that would be inspiring was the architect's intent. (Courtesy of Llewellyn Boardman.)

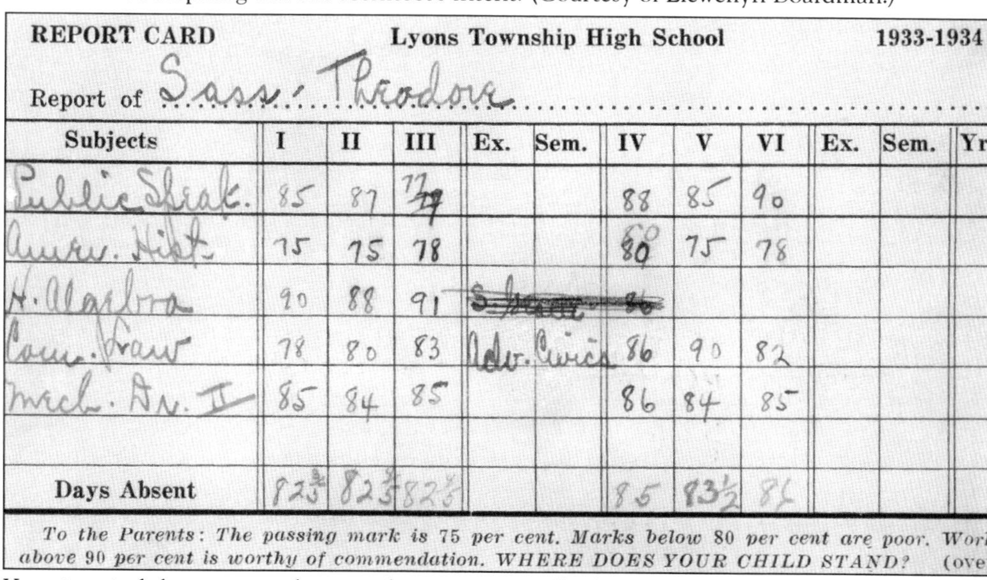

REPORT CARD **Lyons Township High School** **1933-1934**

Report of Sass: Theodore

Subjects	I	II	III	Ex.	Sem.	IV	V	VI	Ex.	Sem.	Yr.
Public Speak.	85	87	77			88	85	90			
Amer. Hist.	75	75	78			80	75	78			
H. Algebra	90	88	91								
Com. Draw	78	80	83	Adv. Civics		86	90	82			
Mech. Dr. II	85	84	85			86	84	85			
Days Absent	[illegible]	[illegible]	[illegible]			85	83½	[illegible]			

To the Parents: The passing mark is 75 per cent. Marks below 80 per cent are poor. Work above 90 per cent is worthy of commendation. WHERE DOES YOUR CHILD STAND? (over

Keep in mind that most students in the area, especially those from "out of town" and along the southern border of what is now Burr Ridge, lived on what was still farm and dairy land. Teens would often help their families with chores before setting foot in school and picked up those same chores right after. So, Theodore Sass can be commended for maintaining passing grades in all of his subjects for the 1933–1934 school year. (Courtesy of Flagg Creek Heritage Society.)

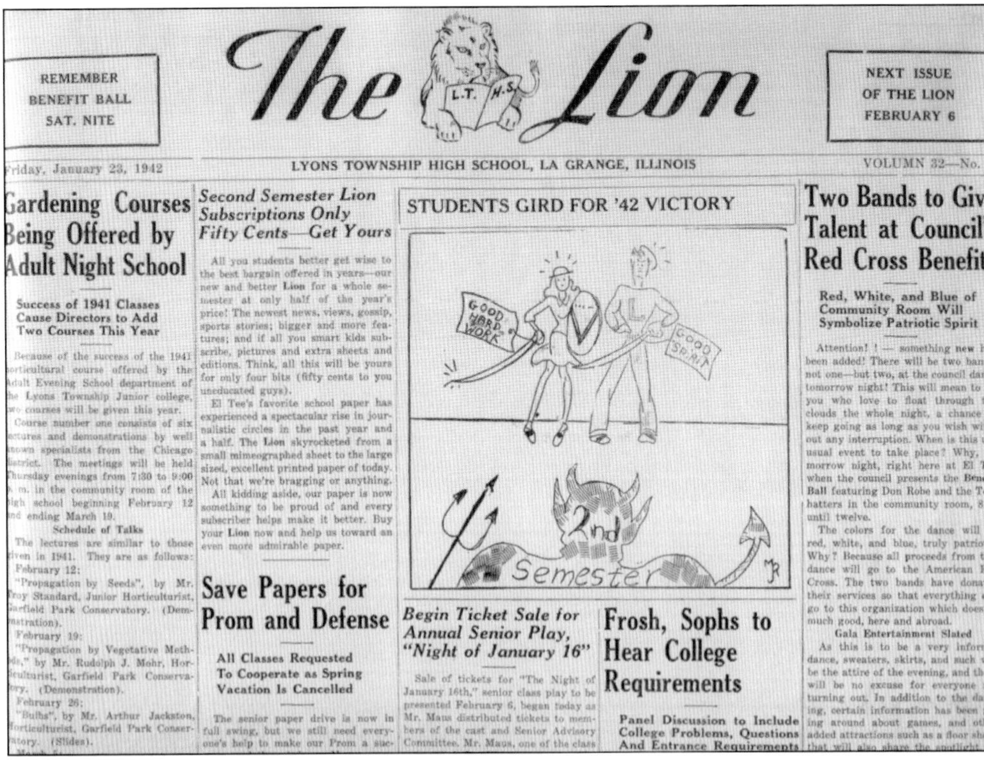

REMEMBER
BENEFIT BALL
SAT. NITE

The Lion

NEXT ISSUE
OF THE LION
FEBRUARY 6

riday, January 23, 1942 | LYONS TOWNSHIP HIGH SCHOOL, LA GRANGE, ILLINOIS | VOLUMN 32—No. 9

ardening Courses Being Offered by Adult Night School

Success of 1941 Classes Cause Directors to Add Two Courses This Year

Because of the success of the 1941 orticultural course offered by the Adult Evening School department of he Lyons Township Junior college, wo courses will be given this year.

Course number one consists of six ectures and demonstrations by well nown specialists from the Chicago istrict. The meetings will be held Thursday evenings from 7:30 to 9:00 . m. in the community room of the igh school beginning February 12 nd ending March 19.

Schedule of Talks

The lectures are similar to those iven in 1941. They are as follows:

February 12:

"Propagation by Seeds", by Mr. Troy Standard, Junior Horticulturist, arfield Park Conservatory. (Demnstration).

February 19:

"Propagation by Vegetative Methds," by Mr. Rudolph J. Mohr, Horiculturist, Garfield Park Conservaory. (Demonstration).

February 26:

"Bulbs", by Mr. Arthur Jackston, Horticulturist, Garfield Park Conseratory. (Slides).

Second Semester Lion Subscriptions Only Fifty Cents—Get Yours

All you students better get wise to the best bargain offered in years—our new and better **Lion** for a whole semester at only half of the year's price! The newest news, views, gossip, sports stories; bigger and more features; and if all you smart kids subscribe, pictures and extra sheets and editions. Think, all this will be yours for only four bits (fifty cents to you uneducated guys).

El Tee's favorite school paper has experienced a spectacular rise in journalistic circles in the past year and a half. The **Lion** skyrocketed from a small mimeographed sheet to the large sized, excellent printed paper of today. Not that we're bragging or anything.

All kidding aside, our paper is now something to be proud of and every subscriber helps make it better. Buy your **Lion** now and help us toward an even more admirable paper.

Save Papers for Prom and Defense

All Classes Requested To Cooperate as Spring Vacation Is Cancelled

The senior paper drive is now in full swing, but we still need everyone's help to make our Prom a suc-

STUDENTS GIRD FOR '42 VICTORY

Begin Ticket Sale for Annual Senior Play, "Night of January 16"

Sale of tickets for "The Night of January 16th," senior class play to be presented February 6, began today as Mr. Maus distributed tickets to members of the cast and Senior Advisory Committee. Mr. Maus, one of the class

Frosh, Sophs to Hear College Requirements

Panel Discussion to Include College Problems, Questions And Entrance Requirements

Two Bands to Give Talent at Council's Red Cross Benefit

Red, White, and Blue of Community Room Will Symbolize Patriotic Spirit

Attention! ! — something new ha been added! There will be two bands not one—but two, at the council danc tomorrow night! This will mean to a you who love to float through th clouds the whole night, a chance t keep going as long as you wish with out any interruption. When is this un usual event to take place? Why, to morrow night, right here at El Te when the council presents the **Benef Ball** featuring Don Robe and the Top hatters in the community room, 8:3 until twelve.

The colors for the dance will b red, white, and blue, truly patriotic Why? Because all proceeds from thi dance will go to the American Re Cross. The two bands have donate their services so that everything ca go to this organization which does s much good, here and abroad.

Gala Entertainment Slated

As this is to be a very informa dance, sweaters, skirts, and such wi be the attire of the evening, and ther will be no excuse for everyone no turning out. In addition to the danc ing, certain information has been go ing around about games, and othe added attractions such as a floor show that will also share the spotlight

This January 1942 issue of LTHS's school newspaper, *The Lion*, demonstrates that teens were well aware of the war. In later issues, many of their fellow students would be shown in uniform, likely heading to the European and the Pacific theaters of war. Later issues would memorialize graduates who had died serving. (Courtesy of Lyons Township High School.)

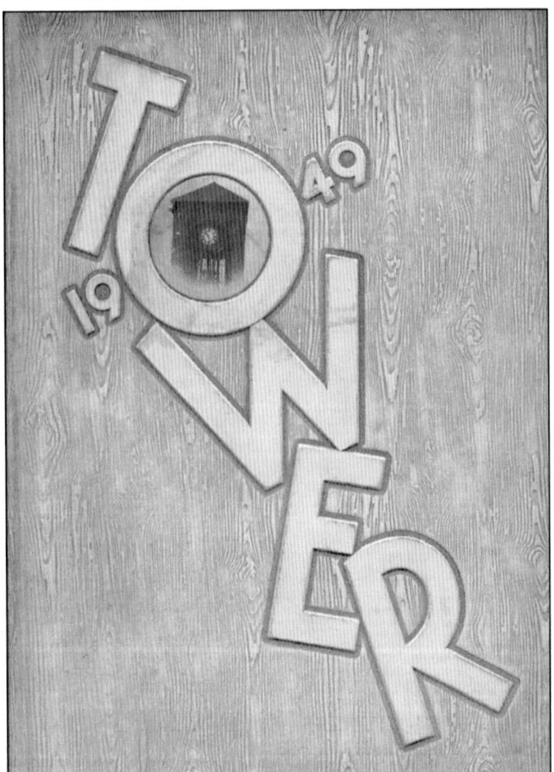

LTHS shared space with the community college, the first in the area. Its yearbook was known as the *Tower*, further cementing the school's clock tower in local lore. (Courtesy of Lyons Township High School.)

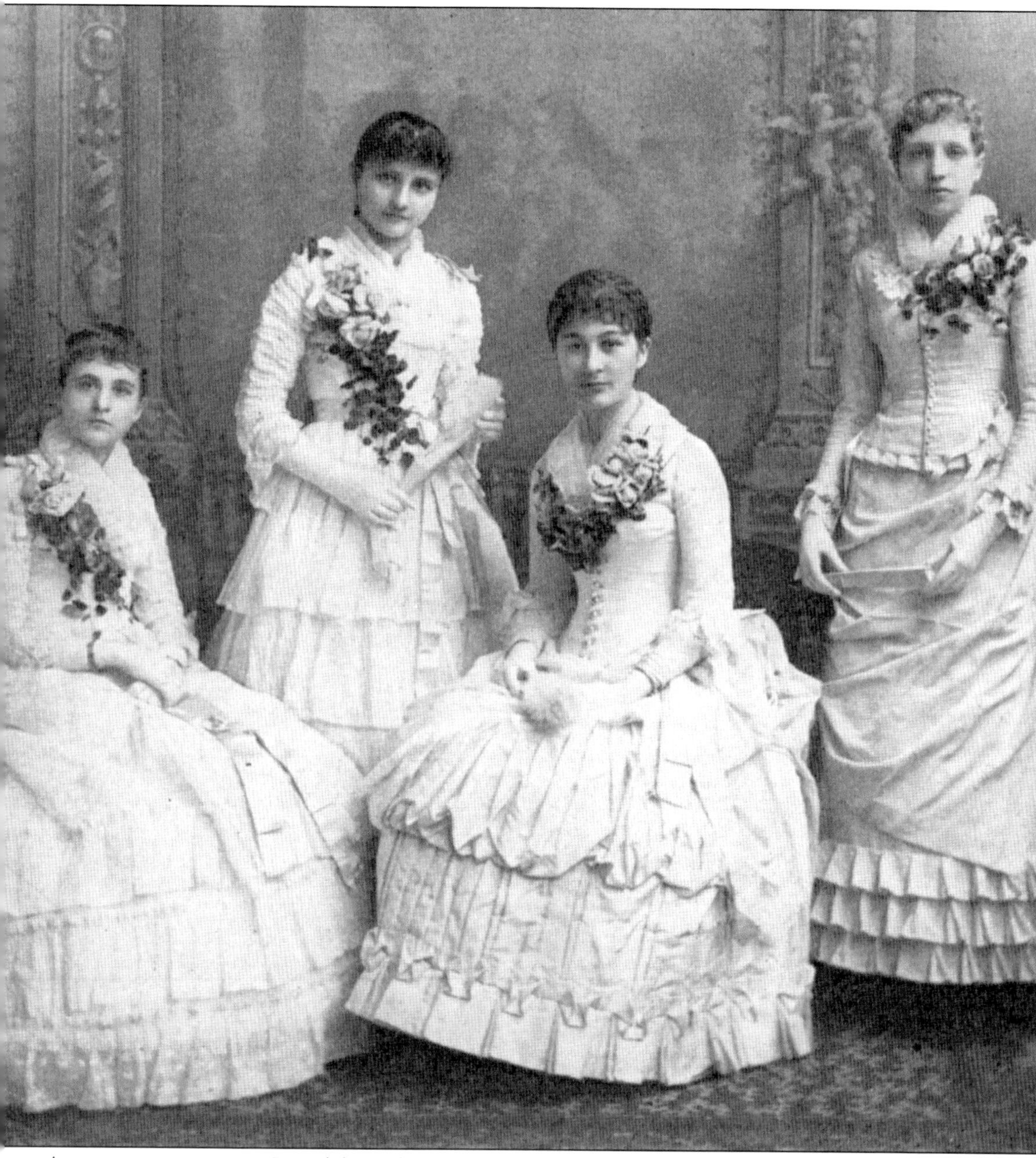

Across town, as it were, Hinsdale High School emerged. Alice Warren, Grace Redfield, Minnie Robinson, and Mrs. John Hall were the first graduates of Hinsdale High School. They graduated in 1893, although the North Central Association would not grant accreditation to the school until 1908. (Courtesy of Indian Prairie Public Library.)

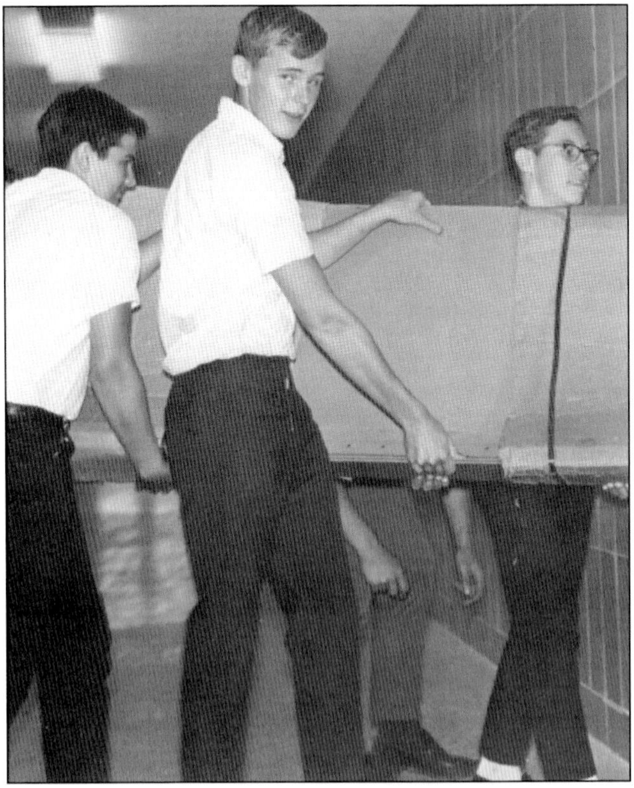

During Hinsdale South's inaugural 1965–1966 school year, 418 students attended the high school. Moving in continued on the first day of opening in the fall of 1965. (Courtesy of Hinsdale South High School.)

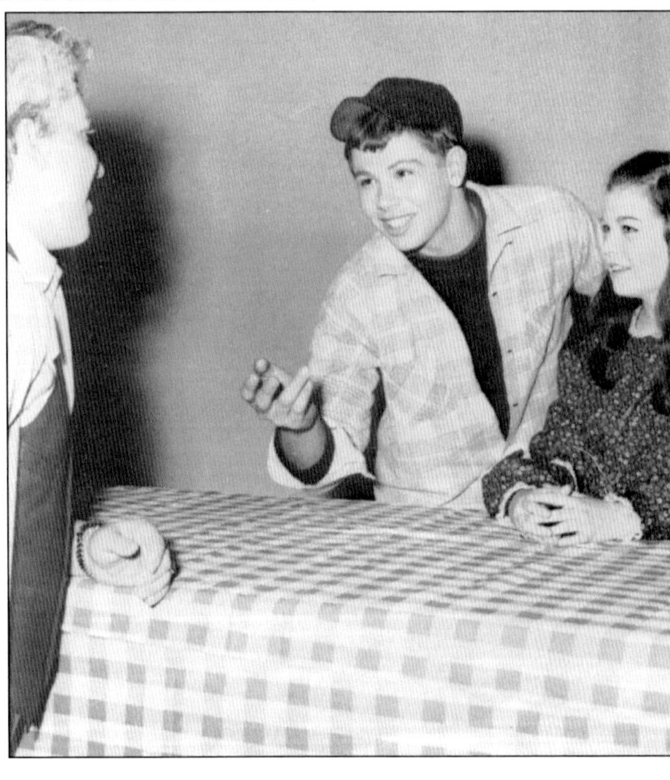

Hinsdale South's first yearbook recorded scenes from the school's daily life. From its beginnings, it set itself apart from Hinsdale Central despite sharing the same district. The Hornets had arrived on the scene. (Courtesy of Hinsdale South High School.)

Nine

Farms to Farmalls

International Harvester. The name is known worldwide, not just in Burr Ridge. In some ways, it put what became Burr Ridge on the map. In 1902, International Harvester Company (now Case New Holland, or CNH) was formed by Cyrus McCormick Jr. and included farm equipment manufacturer Deering. It quickly came to dominate the farming equipment market. International Harvester purchased 414 acres of land in 1917 for its research facility that included a working experimental farm to test new tractors and other farming equipment on Plainfield Road between County Line and Madison Roads.

It was there that, according to CNH, "the world's first all-purpose, row-crop tractor" was perfected: the one and only Farmall. The Farmall was such an engineering advancement that the site was dedicated in 1980 as an Agricultural Engineering Historic Landmark. With its invention, global production of food increased, and efficiency soared.

The Farmall, or "Big Red," was painted red for safety reasons early in its history, but it came to define the image of the iconic American farmer. Harvester Red No. 50 (designed in 1936 and revised over the years) was the famous model. A 1943 version of it is even in the Smithsonian. Kile Martin, who worked the Burr Ridge farm from 1940 to 1967, was featured in most IH photographs, advertising, and imagery.

But the 1940s meant more than IH. The decade brought another shift. Returning veterans from World War II were the next new generation of arrivals to buy land, build homes, raise families, work hard, and make better lives.

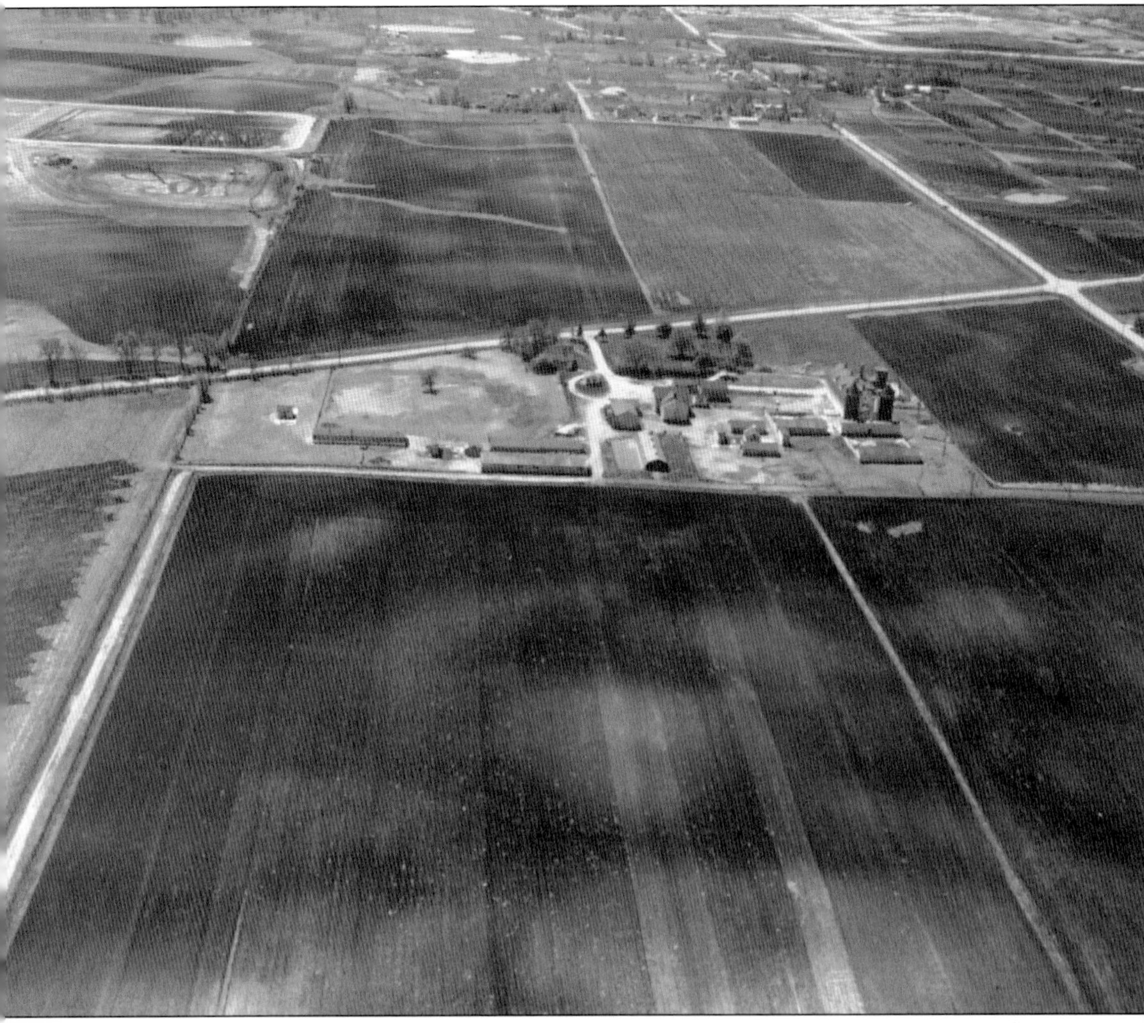

International Harvester is pictured here as it appeared in the late 1940s, showing what was called the Hinsdale Farm. The home on this site once belonged to Peter Craigmile. (Courtesy of International Harvester.)

The families whose husbands, fathers, and grandfathers once worked the family farms that became International Harvester had retired or moved into non-farming professions. Ruth C. Hoyt, Sarah Craigmile Snyder, Esther Craigmile, and Nellie Craigmile Vial pose at a late afternoon picnic as the men pitch horseshoes. (Courtesy of Flagg Creek Heritage Society.)

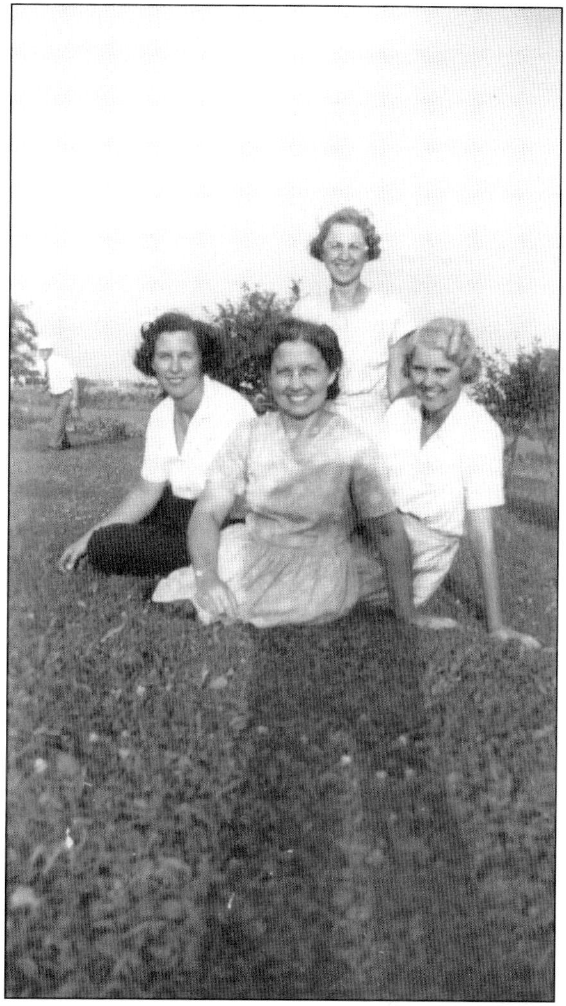

Most families still maintained family plots with gardens, and children had the run of the land, like these boys in 1941. (Courtesy of Sandra Browning.)

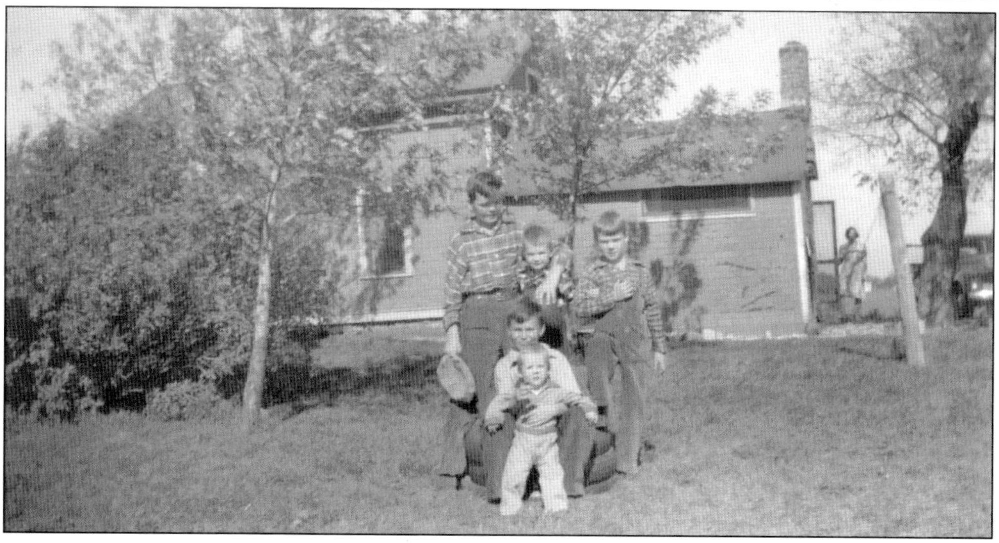

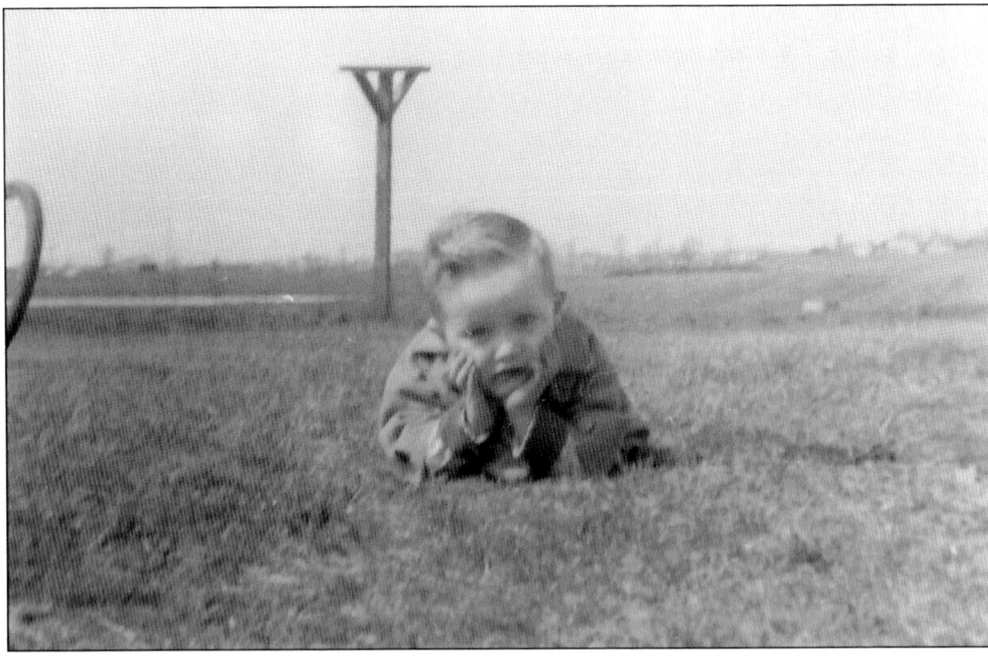

Surrounding acres circling International Harvester (what is now Burr Ridge Park District Harvester Park) were platted and sold. This yard on Giddings Street once backed against the wetlands and pond where this young boy—like many of the time—fished. (Courtesy of Katie and John McHugh.)

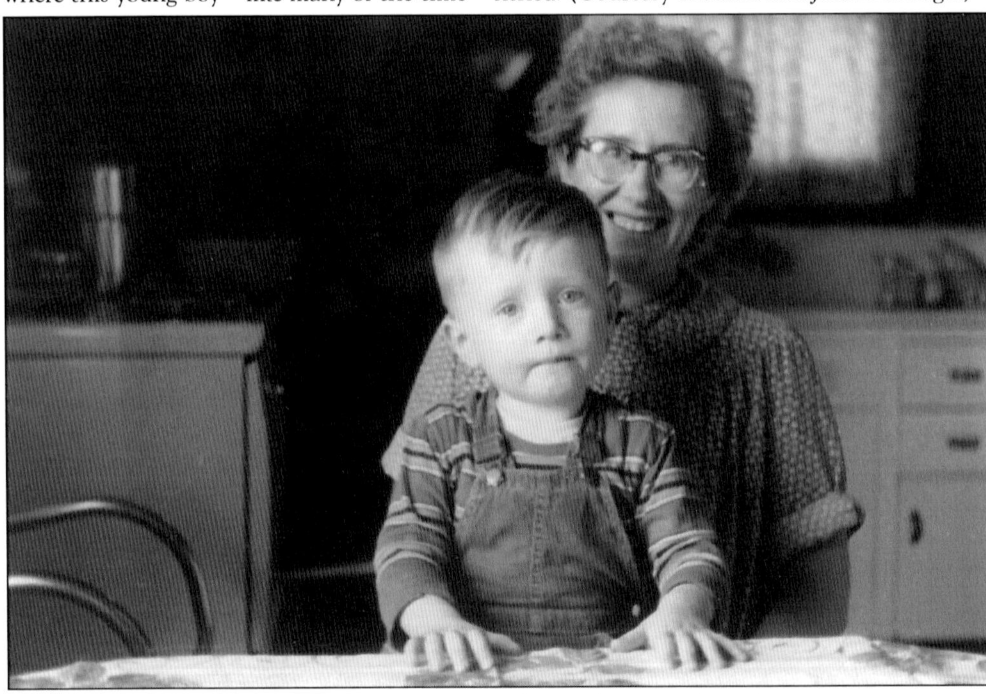

The joy of owning one's own home on acreage with woods, wetlands, and room to raise a family is evident in this mother's face. Nina (Bonham) McHugh and her husband, Sam, built their home by themselves on Giddings Street, living in the basement until they completed it. (Courtesy of Katie and John McHugh.)

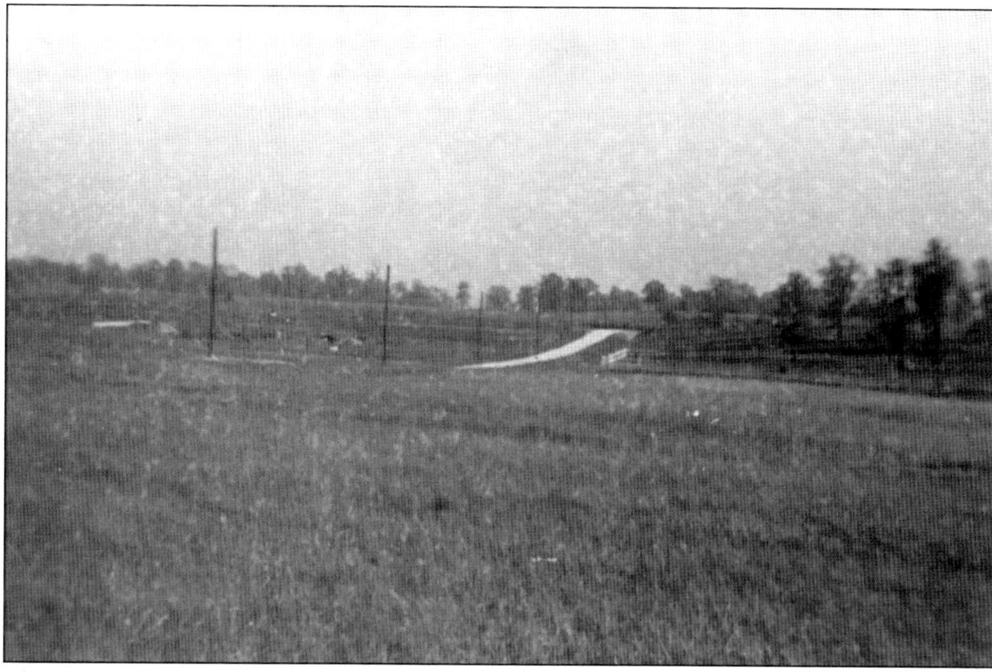

This view accentuates the seeming emptiness in 1946, when family farms had been divided but not yet sold. That would soon change, with new families eager to build new homes. (Courtesy of Reynolds Chadwick family.)

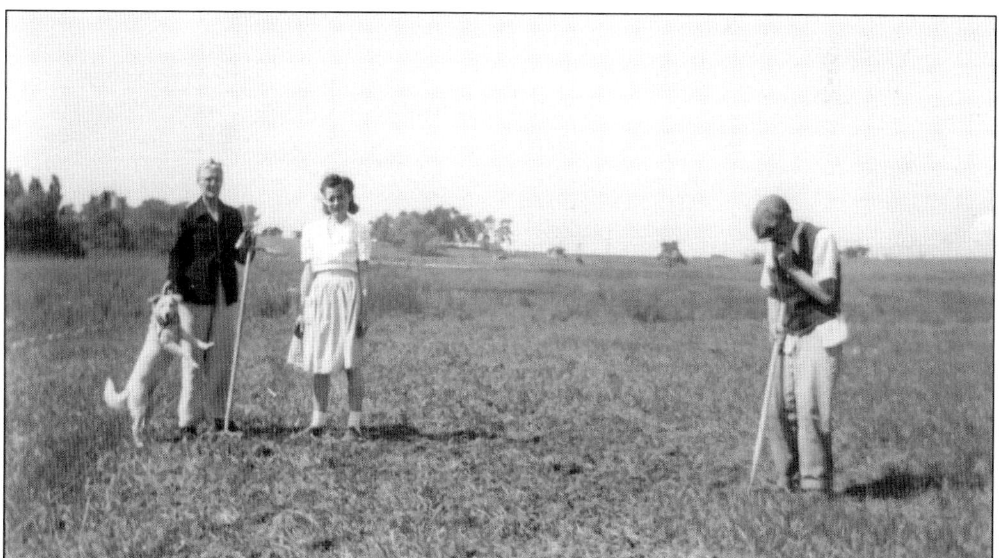

The Chadwick family lived near 77th and Hamilton Streets in the early 1940s. Their son served in World War II. (Courtesy of Reynolds Chadwick family.)

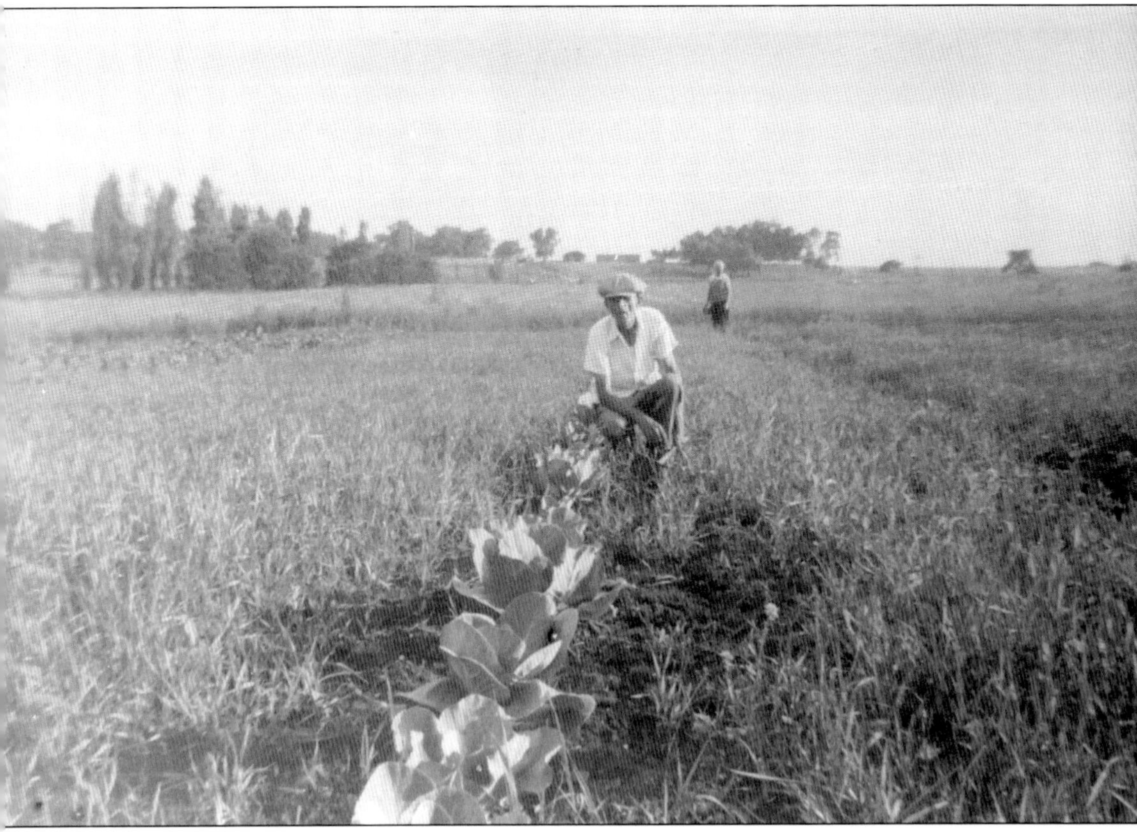

Victory gardens were one way to support the troops throughout the war. Growing more than was needed and sharing was an ordinary ethic for most people at the time. (Courtesy of Reynolds Chadwick family.)

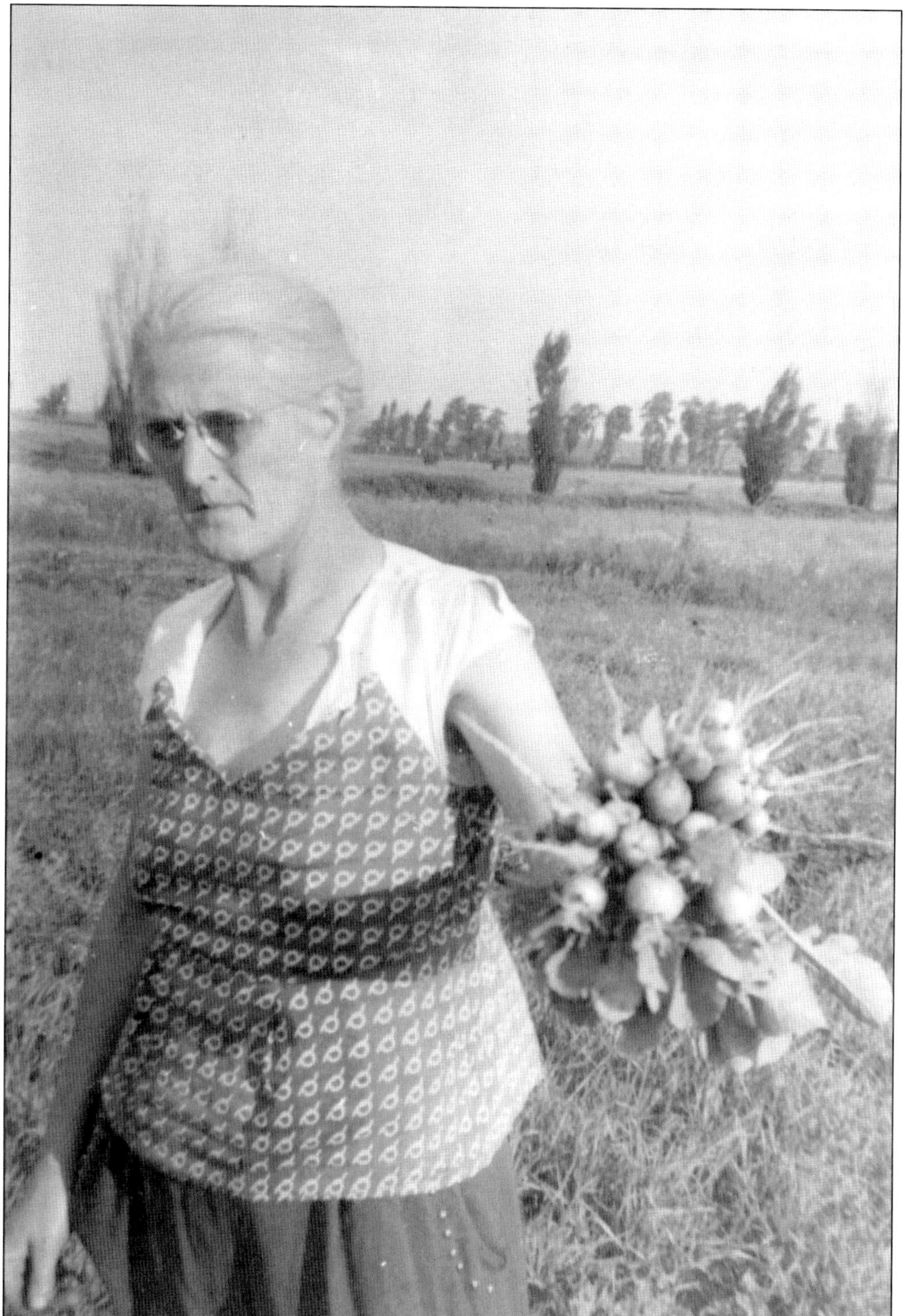

Pictured in 1947, Mrs. Chadwick represents in some ways life on the land at the end of an era. (Courtesy of Reynolds Chadwick family.)

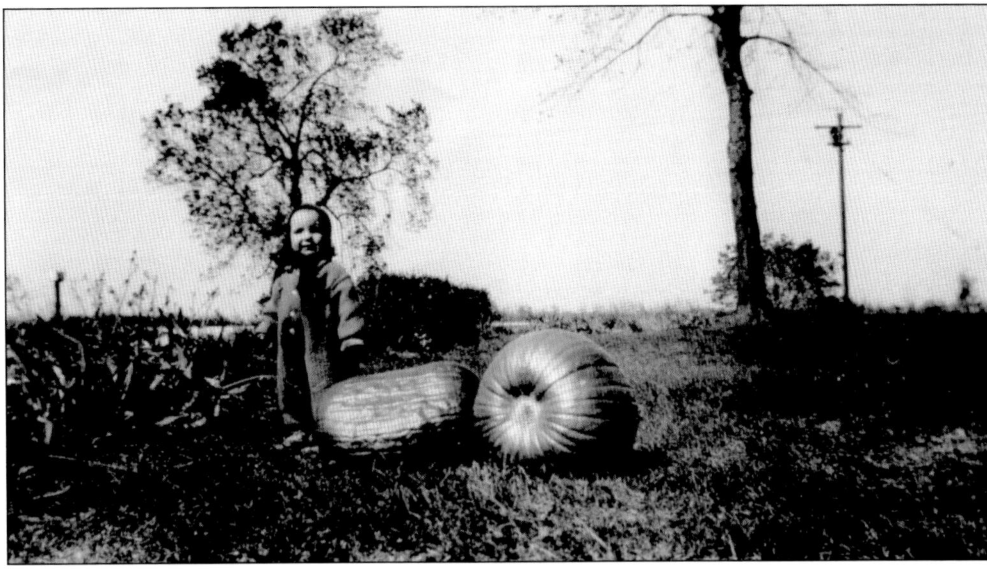

New generations were now being raised without the future prospect of living on a farm. About the closest they would have is a garden like this pumpkin patch in 1946. (Courtesy of Sandra Browning.)

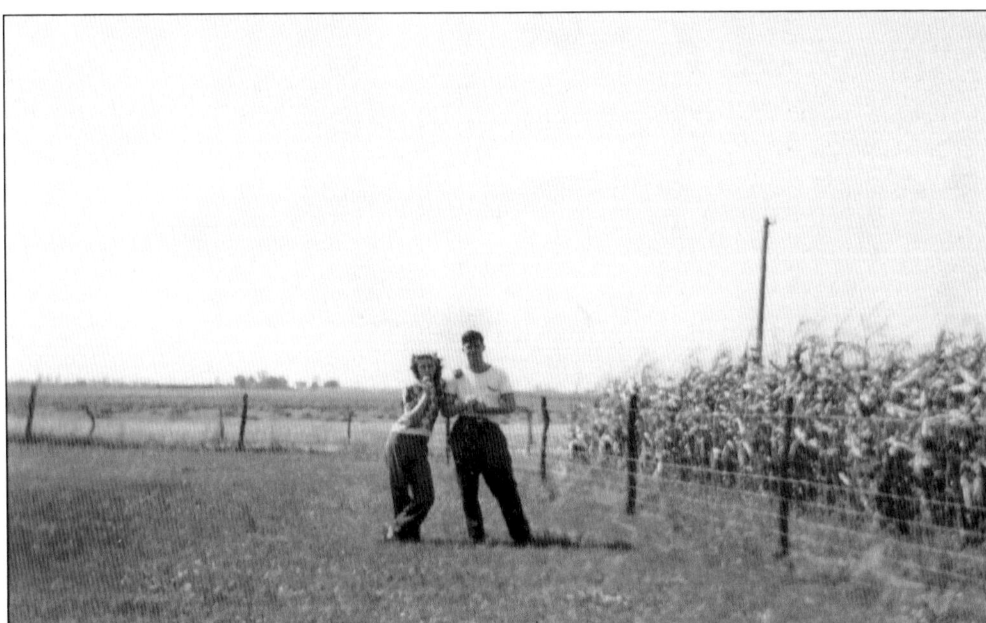

Teens of the era were also shifting away from traditional farming. The corn at right represents the edge of International Harvester crops for testing equipment. (Courtesy of Reynolds Chadwick family.)

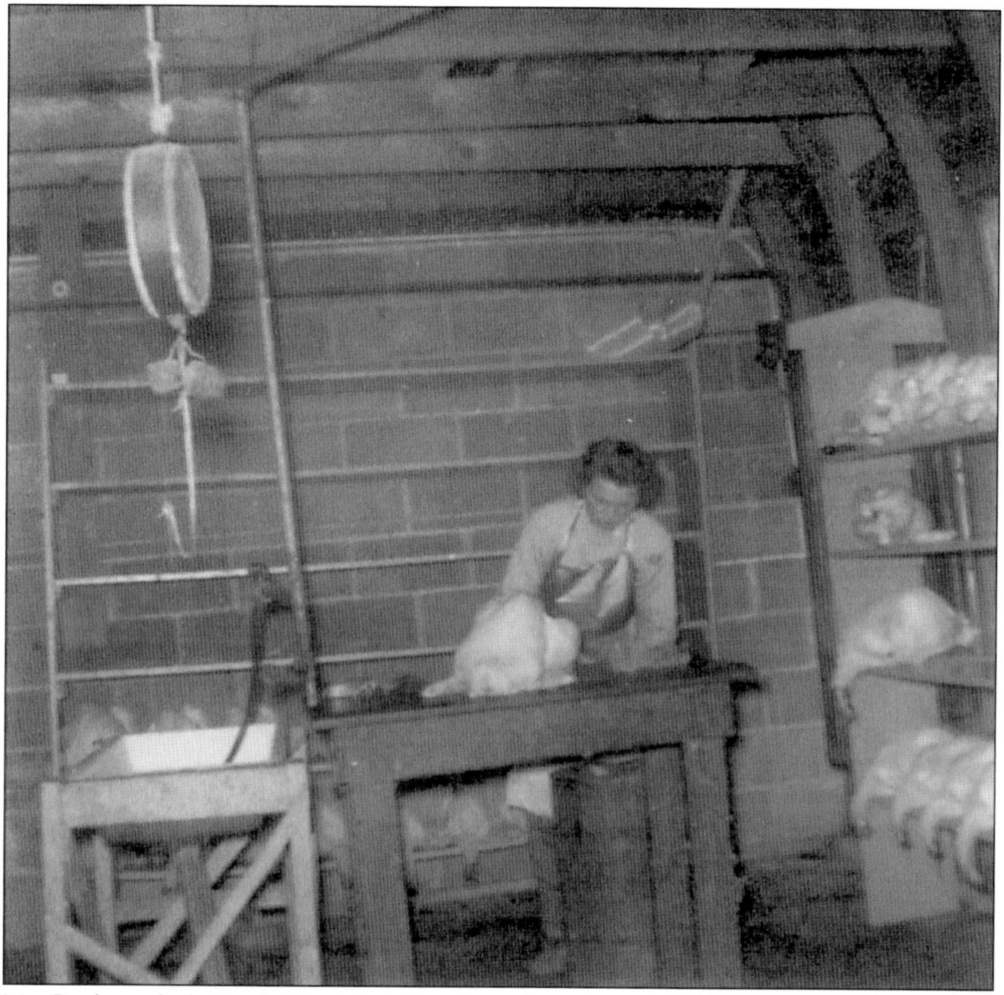

Mrs. Banks worked a South Hinsdale chicken farm, shown here in 1945. Women worked throughout the war. (Courtesy of Flagg Creek Heritage Society.)

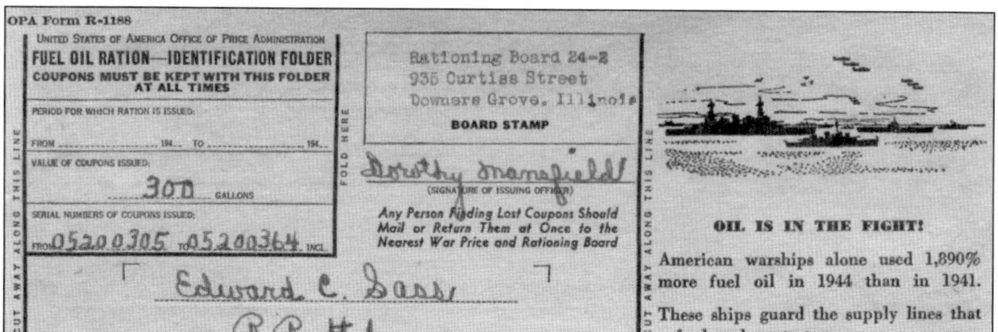

OPA Form R-1188

UNITED STATES OF AMERICA OFFICE OF PRICE ADMINISTRATION

FUEL OIL RATION—IDENTIFICATION FOLDER

COUPONS MUST BE KEPT WITH THIS FOLDER AT ALL TIMES

PERIOD FOR WHICH RATION IS ISSUED:

FROM .... 194.. TO .... 194..

VALUE OF COUPONS ISSUED:

300 GALLONS

SERIAL NUMBERS OF COUPONS ISSUED:

FROM 05200305 TO 05200364 INCL.

FOLD HERE

Rationing Board 24-2
935 Curtiss Street
Downers Grove, Illinois

BOARD STAMP

Dorothy Mansfield

(SIGNATURE OF ISSUING OFFICER)

Any Person Finding Lost Coupons Should Mail or Return Them at Once to the Nearest War Price and Rationing Board

Edward C. Sass
R.R. #1
Hinsdale, Ill.

Size of folder optional—use entire card, or cut away along lines indicated 16—43168-1

CUT AWAY ALONG THIS LINE

OIL IS IN THE FIGHT!

American warships alone used 1,890% more fuel oil in 1944 than in 1941.

These ships guard the supply lines that feed and protect our men overseas.

USE NO MORE FUEL OIL THAN YOU MUST

Fuel rationing was expected and followed during the war, as evidenced by Edward Sass's card from 1944. (Courtesy of Flagg Creek Heritage Society.)

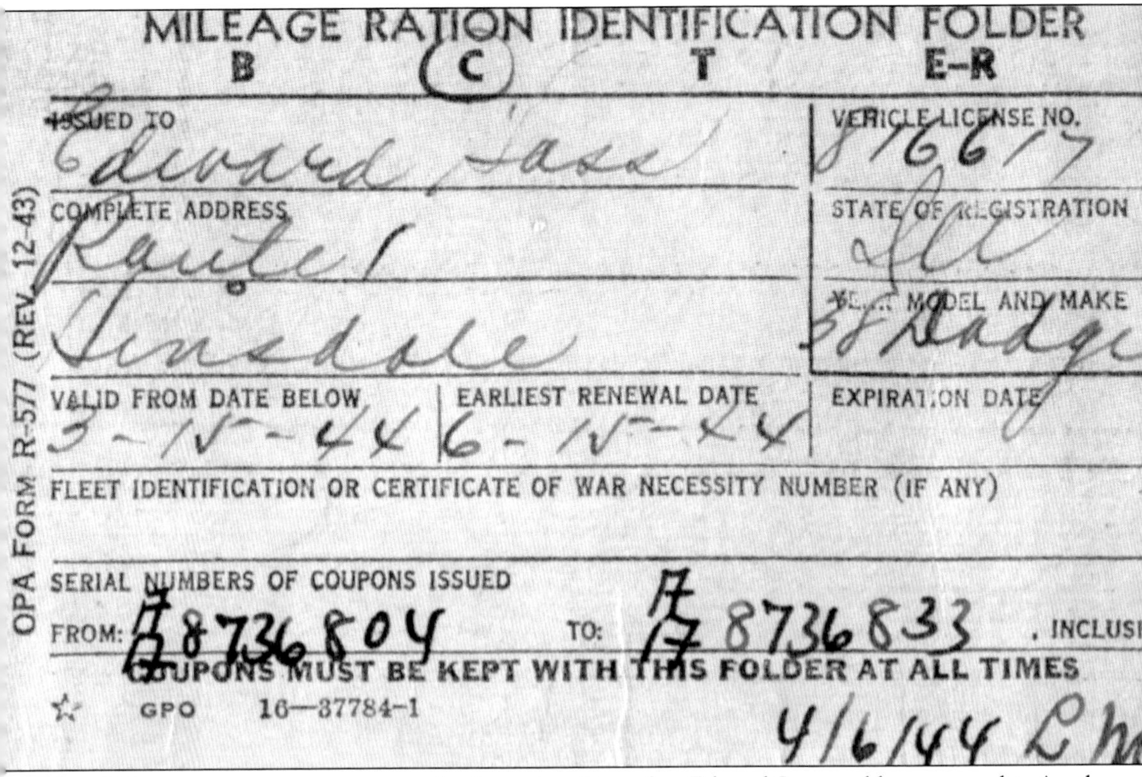
MILEAGE RATION IDENTIFICATION FOLDER

B (C) T E-R

ISSUED TO Edward Sass | VEHICLE LICENSE NO. 876617

COMPLETE ADDRESS Route 1 Hinsdale | STATE OF REGISTRATION Ill

YEAR, MODEL AND MAKE 38 Dodge

VALID FROM DATE BELOW 3-15-44 | EARLIEST RENEWAL DATE 6-15-44 | EXPIRATION DATE

FLEET IDENTIFICATION OR CERTIFICATE OF WAR NECESSITY NUMBER (IF ANY)

SERIAL NUMBERS OF COUPONS ISSUED

FROM: A 8736804 TO: A 8736833 , INCLUSI

COUPONS MUST BE KEPT WITH THIS FOLDER AT ALL TIMES

OPA FORM R-577 (REV. 12-43)

☆ GPO 16—37784-1

4/6/44

Mileage rationing, too, was standard practice. Note that Edward Sass could not renew his April 1944 card until June. (Courtesy of Flagg Creek Heritage Society.)

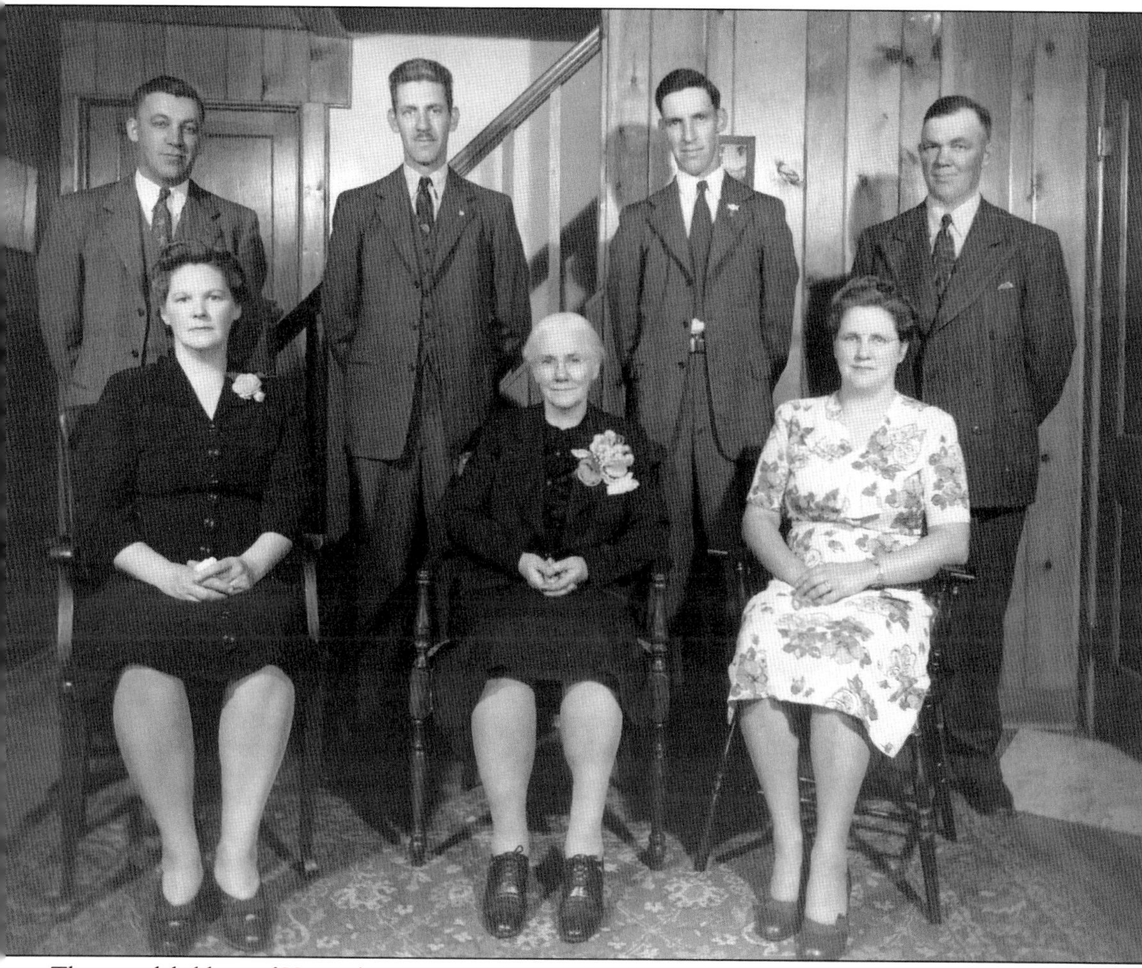

The grandchildren of Howard Hoyt, who had worked the Four Pines Farm and had a dairy herd on land at the corner of County Line and Plainfield Roads, now were grown up. Mike Hoyt, pictured second from left in 1947, served in World War II, landing in Normandy only days after D-Day. (Courtesy of Sandra Browning.)

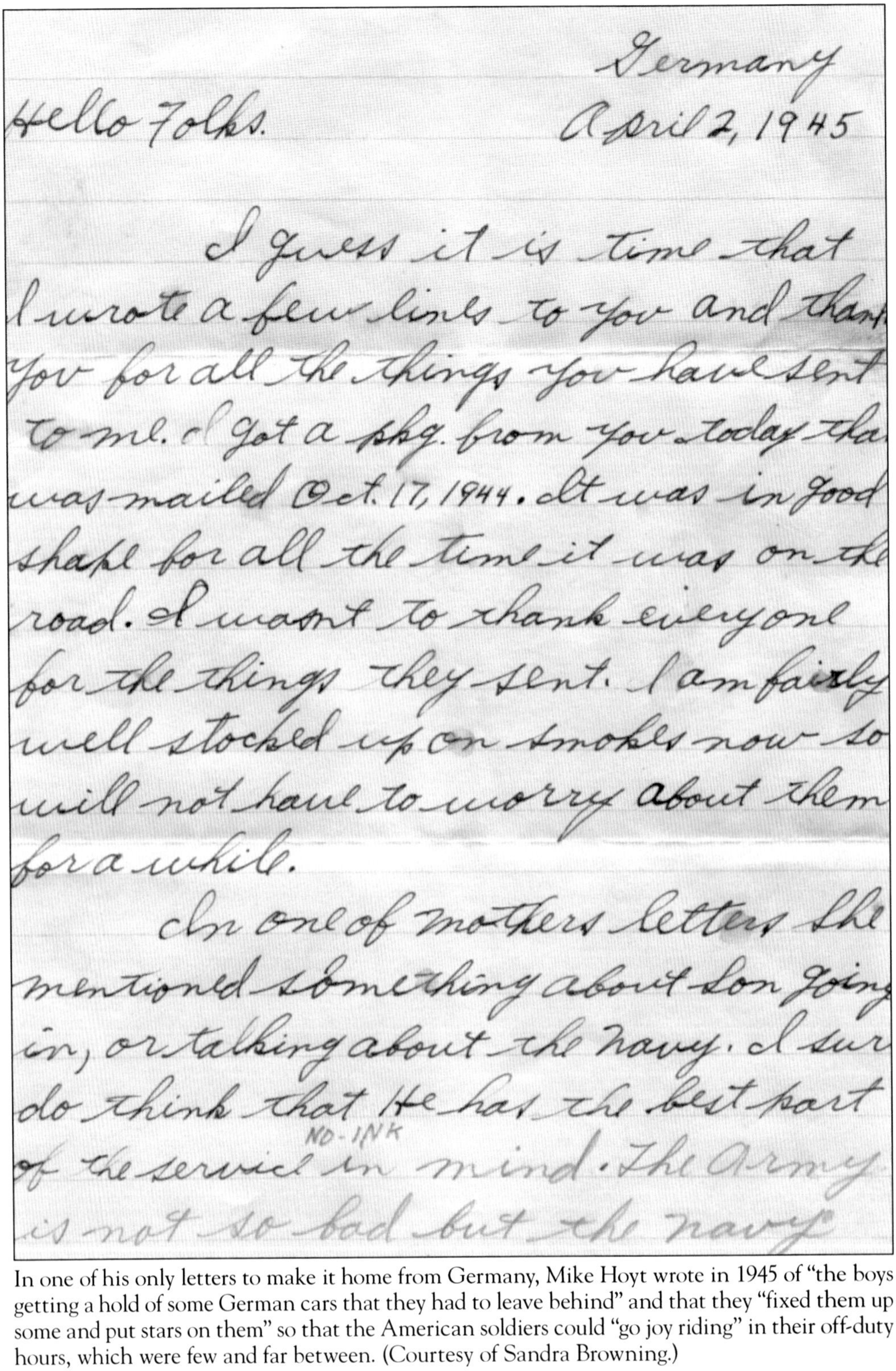

Germany

Hello Folks. April 2, 1945

I guess it is time that I wrote a few lines to you and thank you for all the things you have sent to me. I got a pkg. from you today that was mailed Oct. 17, 1944. It was in good shape for all the time it was on the road. I want to thank everyone for the things they sent. I am fairly well stocked up on smokes now so will not have to worry about them for a while.

In one of mothers letters she mentioned something about Son going in, or talking about the navy. I sure do think that He has the best part of the service in mind. The Army is not so bad but the navy

NO-INK

In one of his only letters to make it home from Germany, Mike Hoyt wrote in 1945 of "the boys getting a hold of some German cars that they had to leave behind" and that they "fixed them up some and put stars on them" so that the American soldiers could "go joy riding" in their off-duty hours, which were few and far between. (Courtesy of Sandra Browning.)

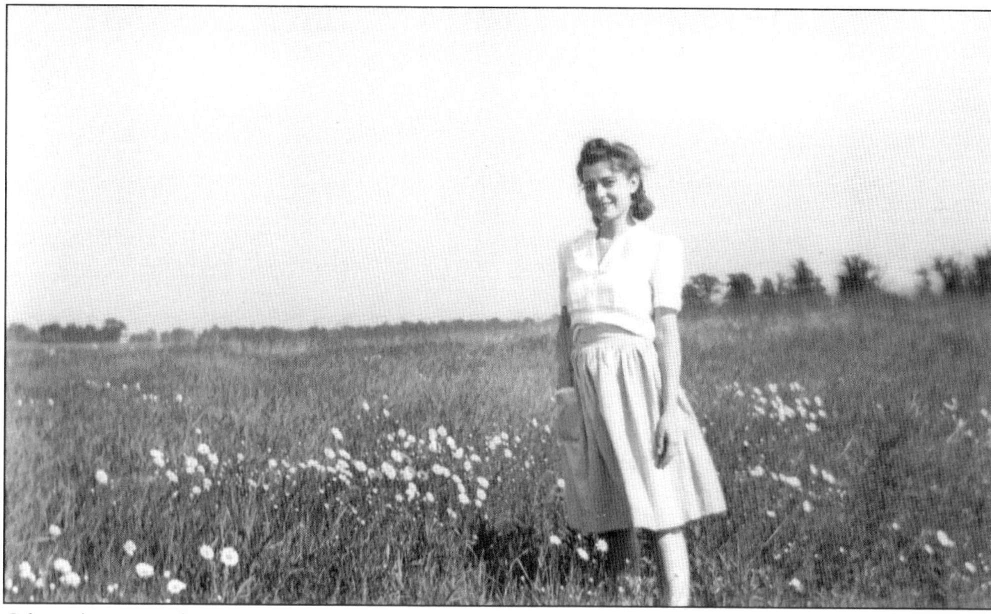

Often the men who went to war would imagine the young women they left behind. It is believed this photograph was taken in the vicinity of 77th Street looking south. Soldiers home on leave, if they were fortunate to come home, would take pictures of their girl for powerful keepsakes. (Courtesy of Reynolds Chadwick family.)

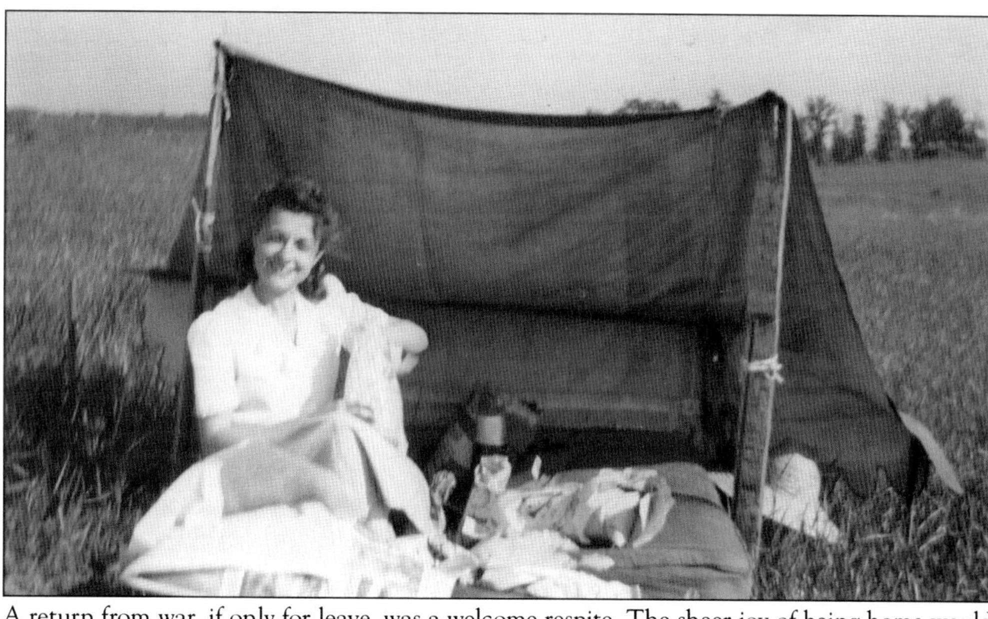

A return from war, if only for leave, was a welcome respite. The sheer joy of being home would be captured and revisited when duty called again. The Chadwick family saw their son serve and return home, and they remained in the area for decades after the war was over. (Courtesy of Reynolds Chadwick family.)

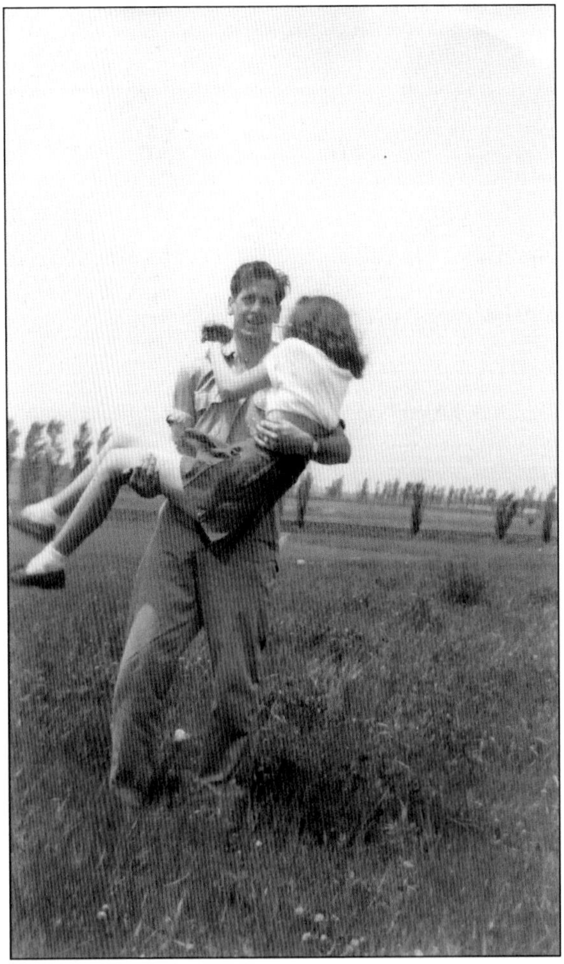

After World War II, a new postwar boom began, with GIs returning and being supported via the Serviceman's Readjustment Act. Land—and housing that followed—became an attainable dream. Surveying was a common sight, as pictured below near 77th Street. (Courtesy of Reynolds Chadwick family.)

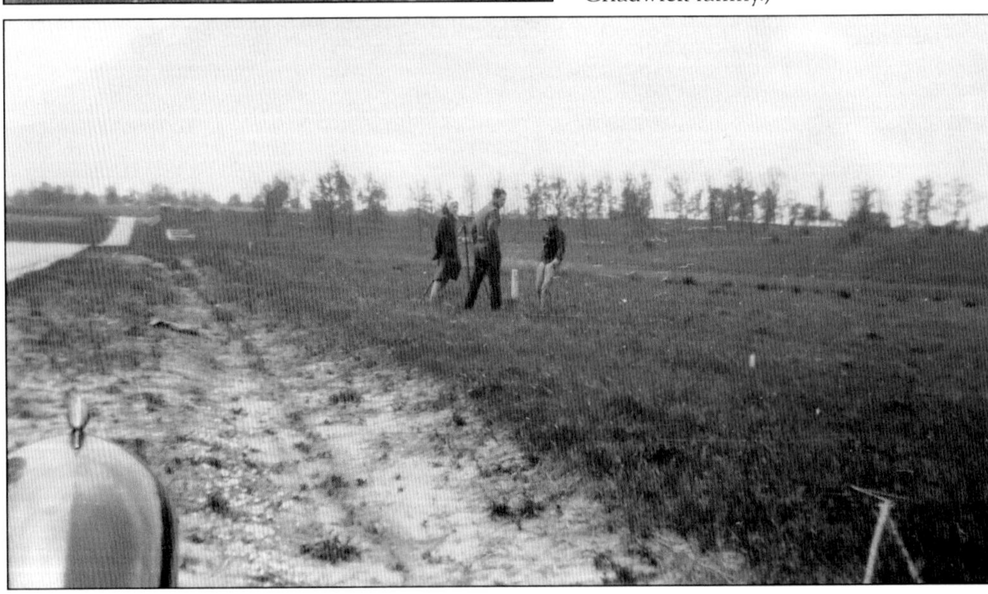

By 1947, what would become known as the Baby Boom had begun. New houses were dotting the area, and developers such as Robert Bartlett entered the landscape. Bartlett's Hinsdale Countryside Estates would soon follow. (Courtesy of Reynolds Chadwick family.)

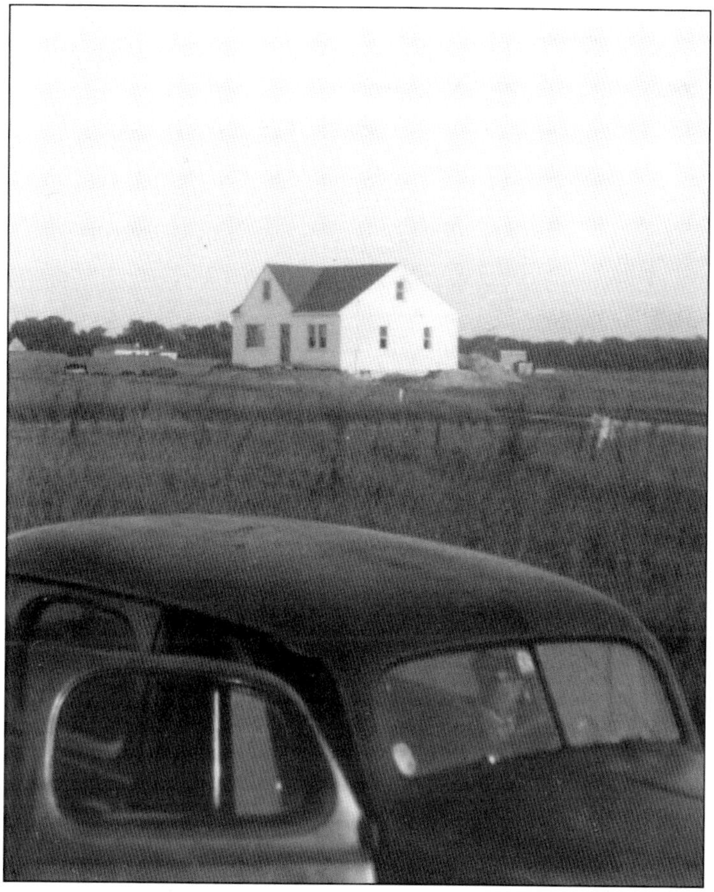

"Lawns" hadn't quite grown so small as to only require a mower, but in the distance, homes are beginning to fill in as lots are sold at a faster pace around 1950. At this time, developer Denver Busby made his mark with estate-sized lots of five acres each. (Courtesy of Reynolds Chadwick family.)

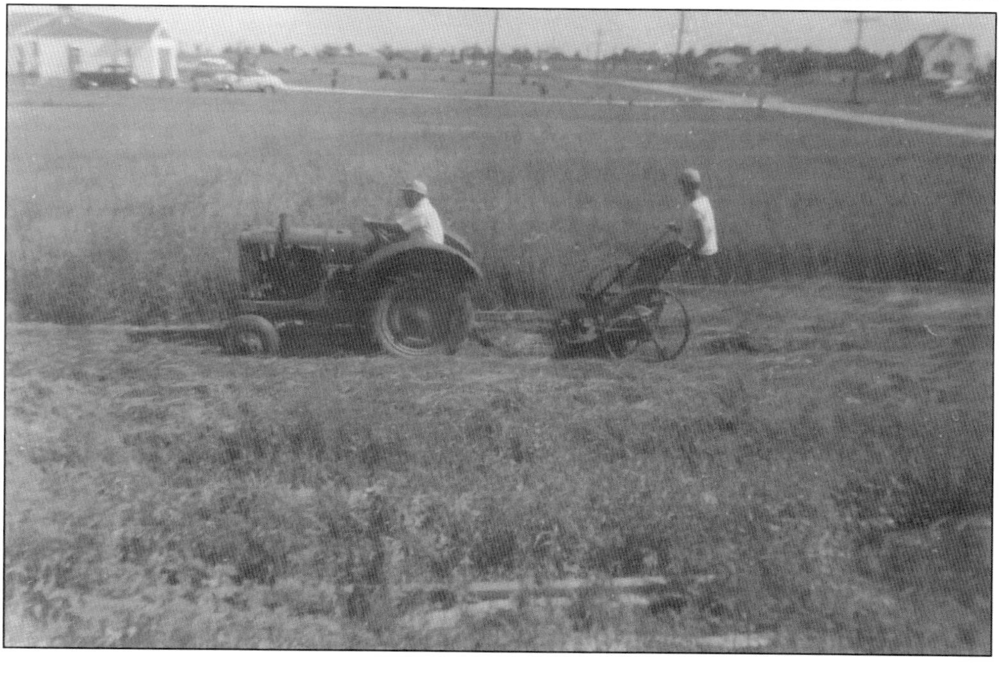

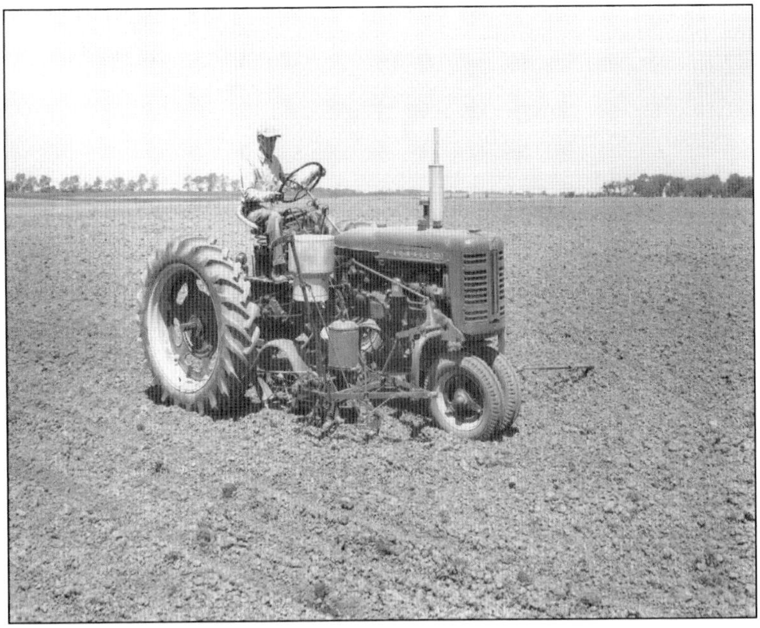

What many don't realize is that International Harvester wasn't only a globally significant research farm developing equipment that changed world food production. It was also a home. From 1940 to 1967, Kile Martin worked the Hinsdale Farm, as it was called, raising his sons, Jim and John, on the land. (Courtesy of Jim Martin.)

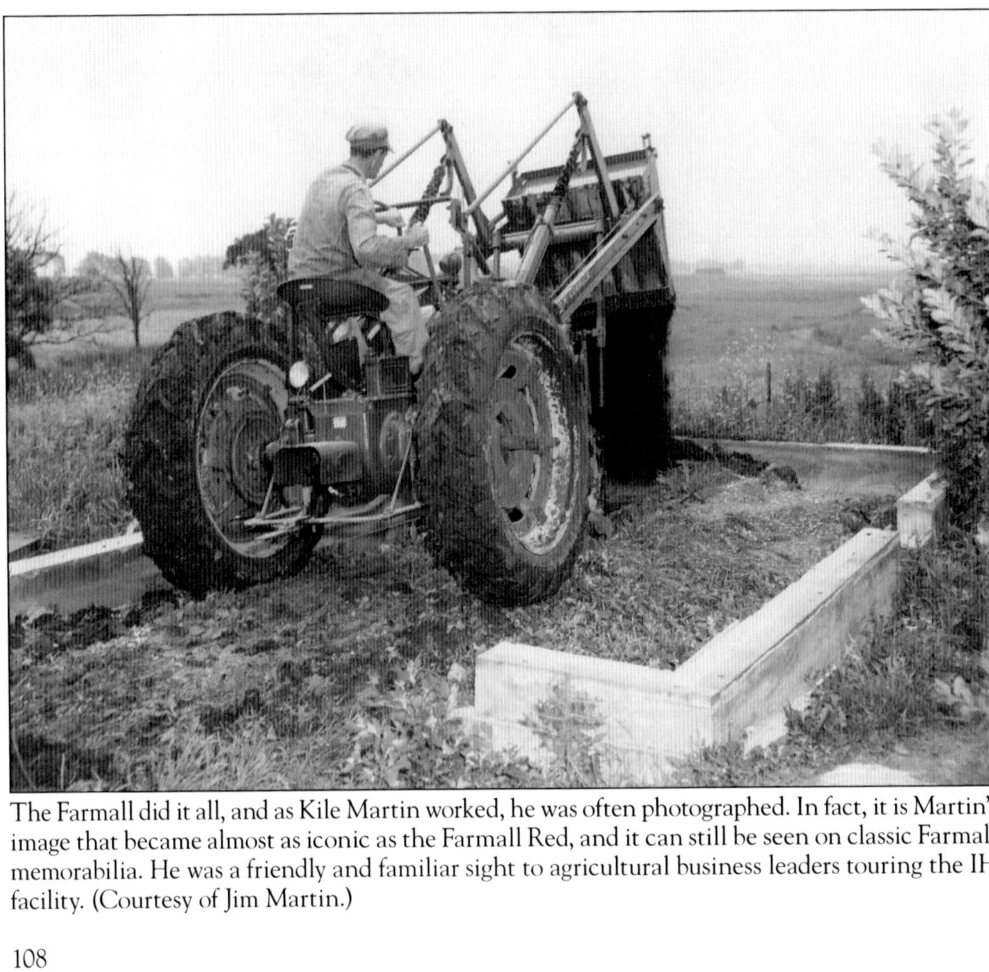

The Farmall did it all, and as Kile Martin worked, he was often photographed. In fact, it is Martin's image that became almost as iconic as the Farmall Red, and it can still be seen on classic Farmall memorabilia. He was a friendly and familiar sight to agricultural business leaders touring the IH facility. (Courtesy of Jim Martin.)

Jim and John Martin grew up in the 1940s in almost idyllic Midwest conditions: tractors and open land. For the children, it was (mostly) all fun, with their dad being, in many ways, at the center of what was a close-knit family of International Harvester workers. Jim (left) and John, all smiles, are pictured on—what else—a Farmall. (Courtesy of Jim Martin.)

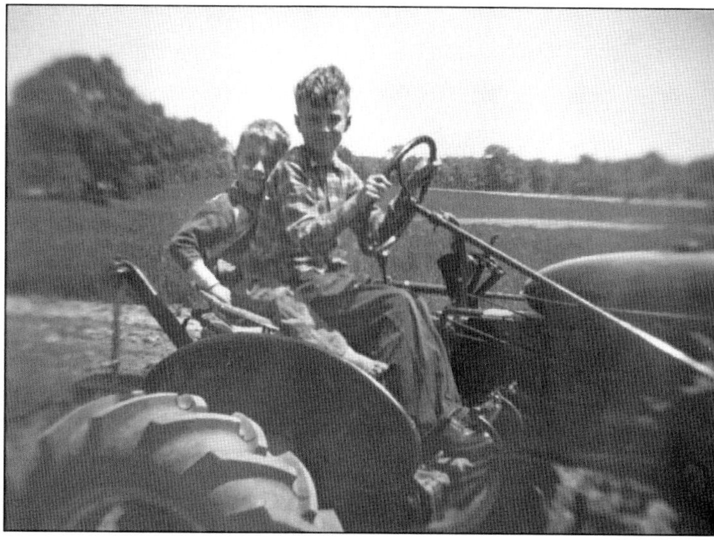

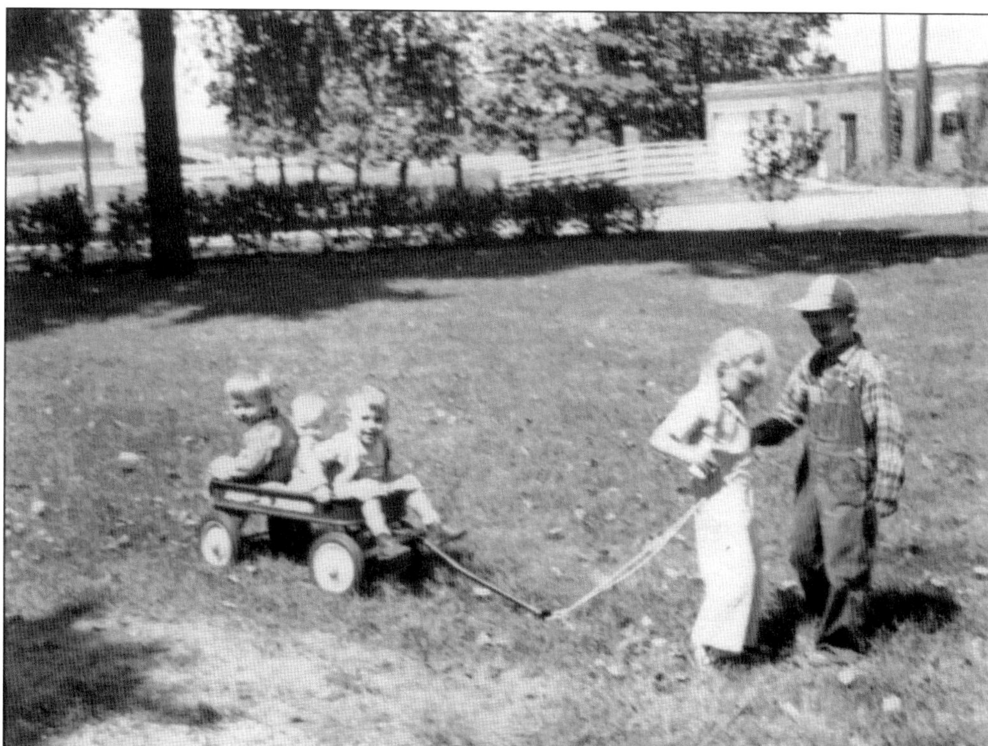

Children of other International Harvester workers often played together on the Hinsdale Farm. Like the Martins, most attended Gower School, so school friendships were naturally extended. Jim Martin is pictured on the right in 1941. (Courtesy of Jim Martin.)

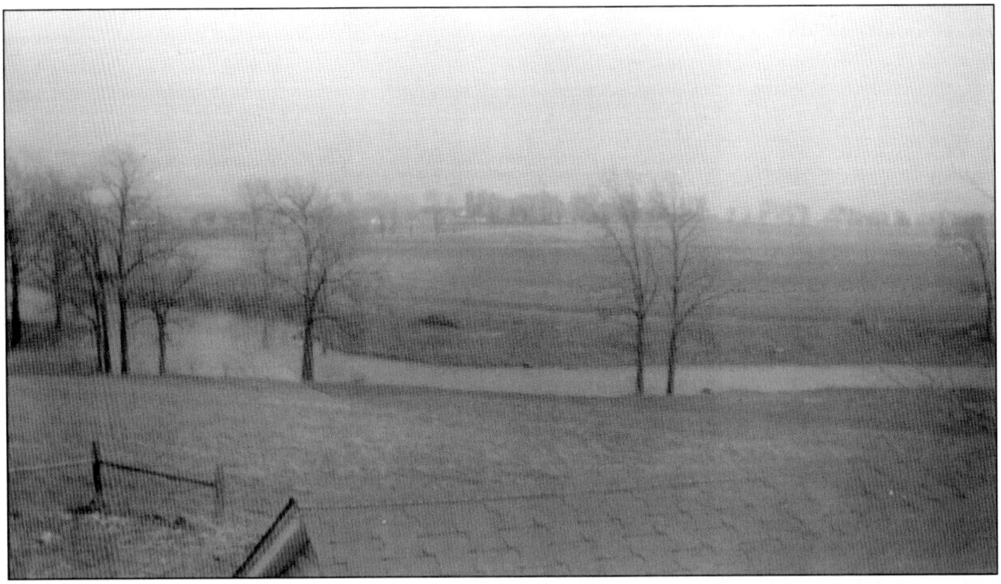

This view from the Peter Craigmile home, in which the Martins lived on the Hinsdale Farm, has an almost haunting, nostalgic look. The Hinsdale Farm and home would be torn down in the coming decades. (Courtesy of Jim Martin.)

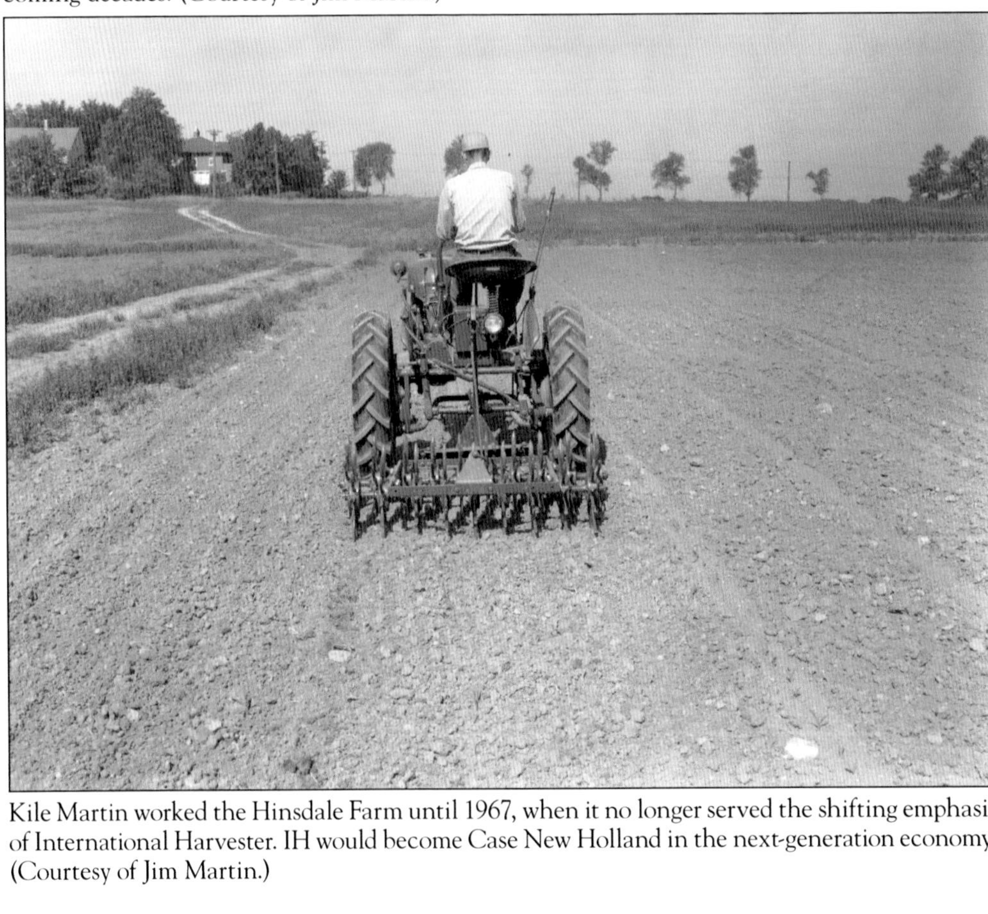

Kile Martin worked the Hinsdale Farm until 1967, when it no longer served the shifting emphasis of International Harvester. IH would become Case New Holland in the next-generation economy. (Courtesy of Jim Martin.)

Ten

Harvester and Burr Ridge

A new period of growth had arrived by the 1950s. New families, attracted by real estate and a booming economy, became some of the first to purchase fresh starts. This ushered in an era of civic building not seen since the turn of the last century: schools grew and facilities were fresh and modern. Young families arrived from the city, eager to escape the crowding. Employees of emerging industrial corridors on the south and west sides of Chicago were drawn farther west into the suburbs. This is the time one can begin to recognize Burr Ridge as it is today, largely because this is recent enough to be in living memory. Village founders and leaders still live and serve. Strategic growth, hard decisions, sustained effort, and no little amount of challenges along the way all created the backdrop of the narrative we hear and see around us. While the story might not have begun with the founding of the village of Harvester and the christening of Burr Ridge proper, it makes a perfect end.

When Robert Bartlett purchased land and developed Hinsdale Countryside Estates in 1947, he could not have known what would come. Nor could Denver Busby have anticipated it when he purchased those 190 acres for Burr Ridge Estates with five-acre lots. Or perhaps they did, and that was the foresight and planning that inspired Burr Ridge.

In a garage on Drew Avenue on October 20, 1956, votes were cast, and the incorporation of the new village of Harvester passed. The 300 residents at the time were but a beginning. In 1962, after much discussion with International Harvester and village leaders, the name "Burr Ridge" was chosen.

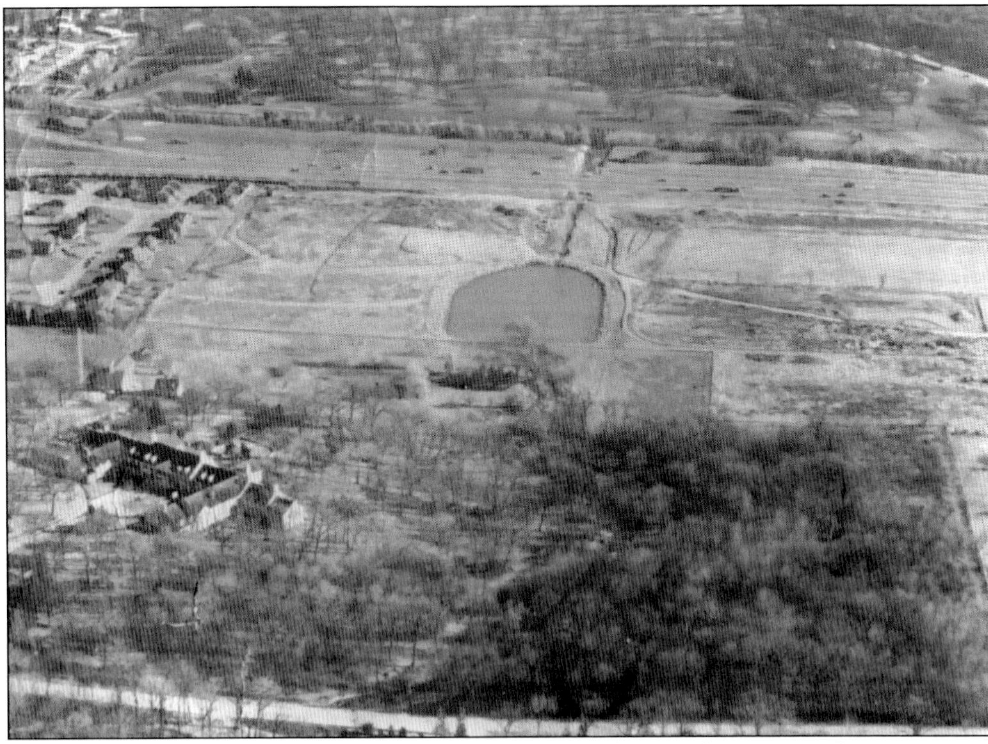

In this aerial view, King-Bruwaert is easily seen at left, with the new I-294 under construction at top. (Courtesy of King-Bruwaert.)

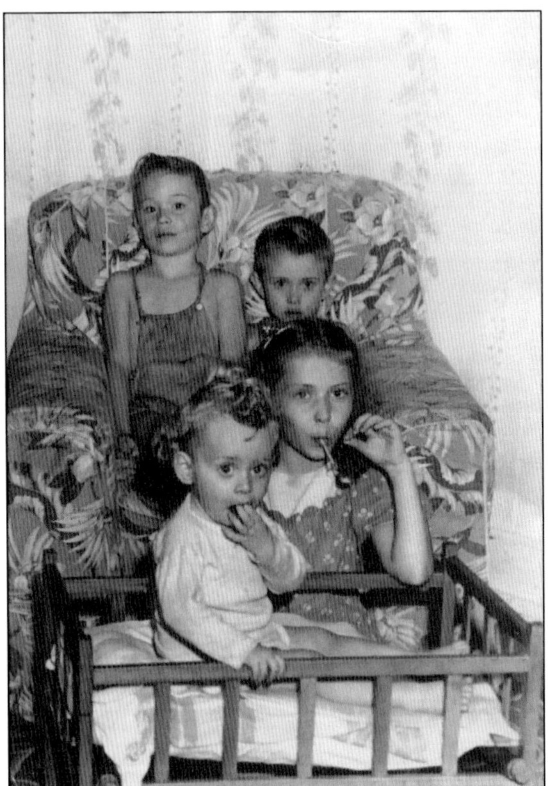

Working-class families like the McHughs flocked to the area, appreciating its wide-open spaces and safe streets. Here Pat McHugh watches over her younger brothers around 1949. (Courtesy of Pat McHugh.)

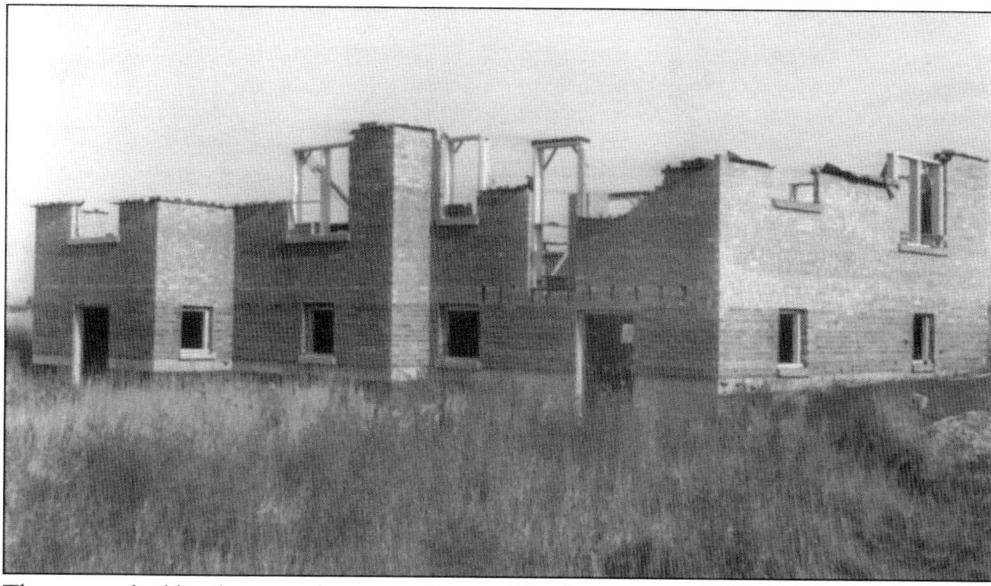

The postwar building boom made construction sites like this one, a single-family home near Hamilton and 77th Streets, a common sight around 1950. (Courtesy of Reynolds Chadwick family.)

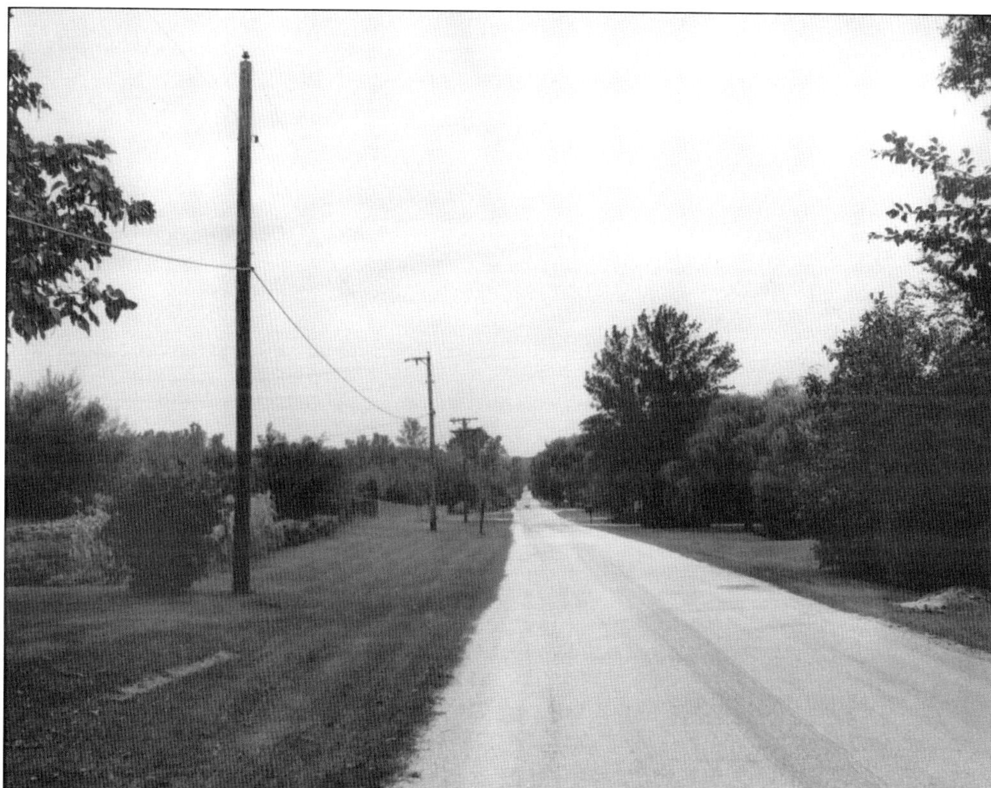

This peaceful view looking south down Madison Street shows evidence of a growing community: by 1960, what was once farmland had become home to fences, street signs, and mailboxes. (Courtesy of Reynolds Chadwick family.)

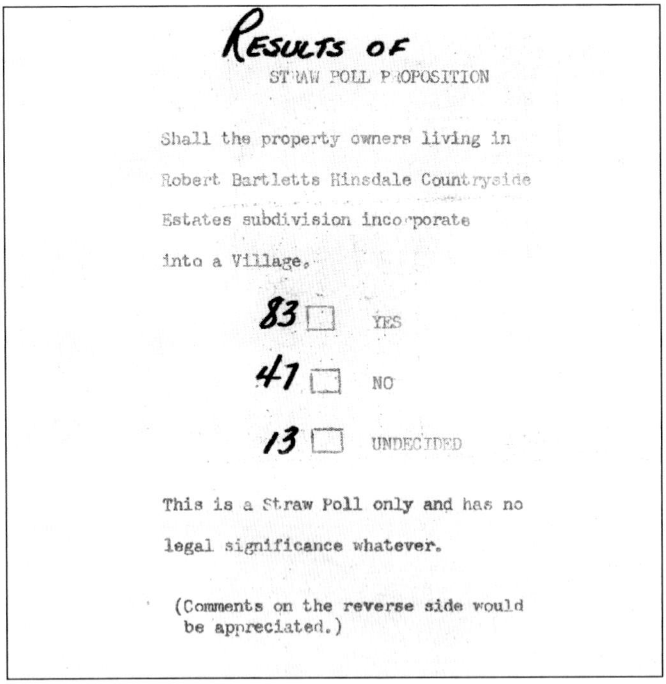

RESULTS OF

STRAW POLL PROPOSITION

Shall the property owners living in Robert Bartletts Hinsdale Countryside Estates subdivision incorporate into a Village.

83 ☐ YES

47 ☐ NO

13 ☐ UNDECIDED

This is a Straw Poll only and has no legal significance whatever.

(Comments on the reverse side would be appreciated.)

A non-binding 1953 straw poll revealed that a strong majority of the Hinsdale Countryside Estates subdivision was in favor of incorporating into a village. But it was not without some level of door-to-door politicking and canvassing, according to village records. When all was said and done, however, official incorporation was achieved (Courtesy of Village of Burr Ridge.)

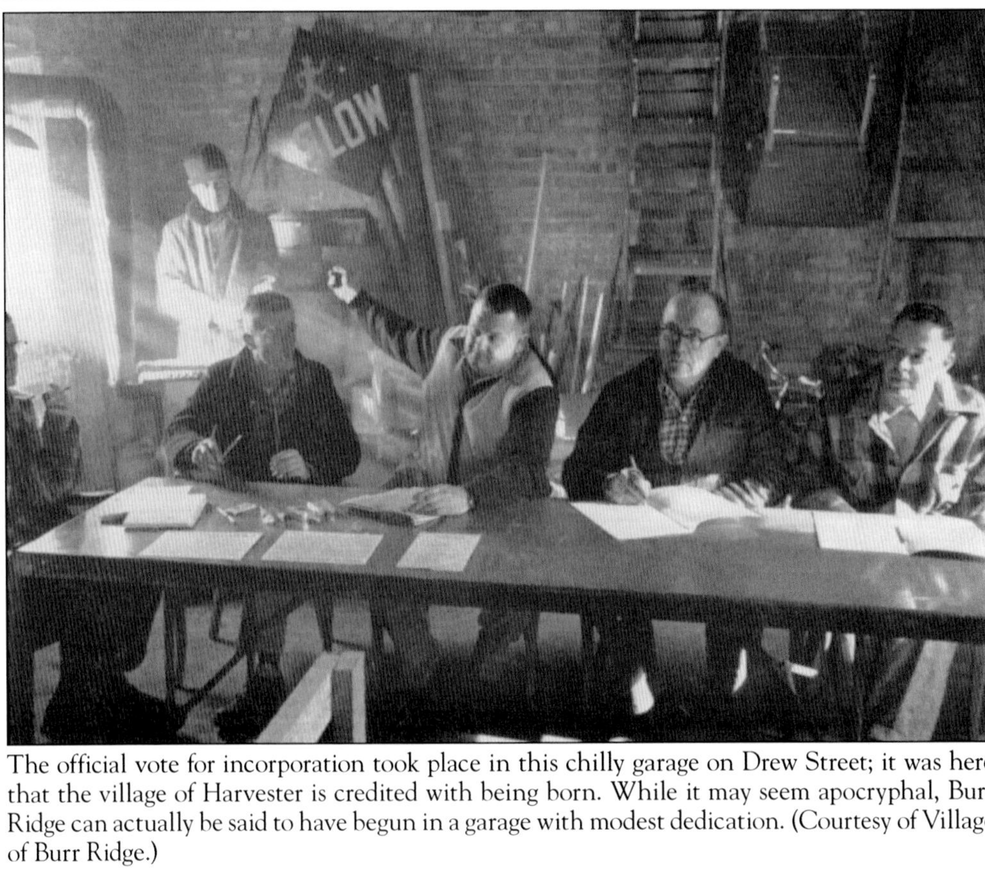

The official vote for incorporation took place in this chilly garage on Drew Street; it was here that the village of Harvester is credited with being born. While it may seem apocryphal, Burr Ridge can actually be said to have begun in a garage with modest dedication. (Courtesy of Village of Burr Ridge.)

A new village meant new village officers. This 1956 sample ballot, Harvester's first, familiarized voters with the candidates for village president, clerk, and trustees. In a newsletter for International Harvester employees, the candidates were noted. One copy of that newsletter has attached to it a handwritten note on IH letterhead. The note is addressed to one of the candidates from a manager, who gently teased him about all the attention the election was giving him. It was all in good fun. (Courtesy of Village of Burr Ridge.)

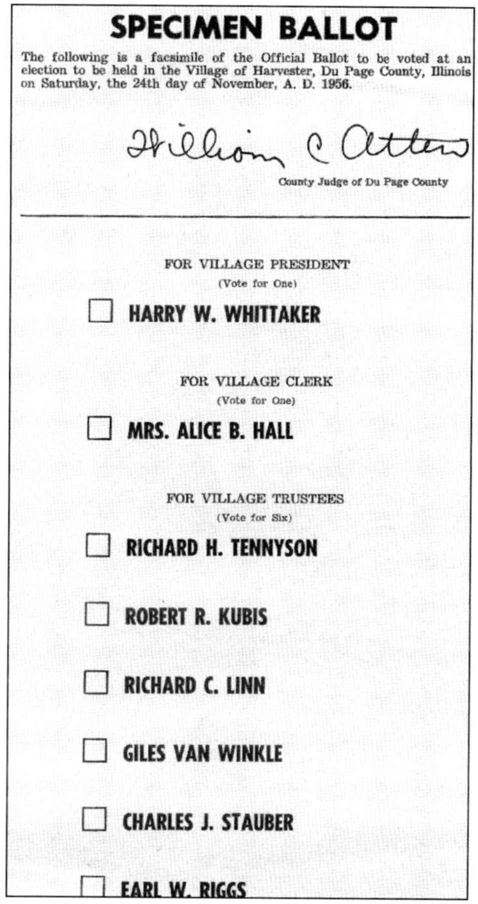

SPECIMEN BALLOT

The following is a facsimile of the Official Ballot to be voted at an election to be held in the Village of Harvester, Du Page County, Illinois on Saturday, the 24th day of November, A. D. 1956.

William C Atten

County Judge of Du Page County

FOR VILLAGE PRESIDENT
(Vote for One)

☐ HARRY W. WHITTAKER

FOR VILLAGE CLERK
(Vote for One)

☐ MRS. ALICE B. HALL

FOR VILLAGE TRUSTEES
(Vote for Six)

☐ RICHARD H. TENNYSON

☐ ROBERT R. KUBIS

☐ RICHARD C. LINN

☐ GILES VAN WINKLE

☐ CHARLES J. STAUBER

☐ EARL W. RIGGS

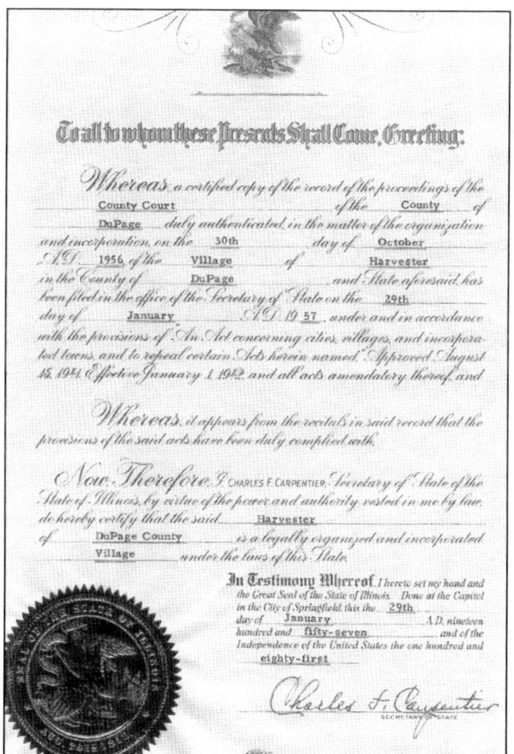

To all to whom these Presents Shall Come, Greeting:

Whereas, a certified copy of the record of the proceedings of the County Court of the County of DuPage duly authenticated, in the matter of the organization and incorporation, on the 30th day of October A.D. 1956, of the Village of Harvester in the County of DuPage and State aforesaid, has been filed in the office of the Secretary of State on the 29th day of January A.D. 1957, under and in accordance with the provisions of "An Act concerning cities, villages, and incorporated towns, and to repeal certain Acts herein named." Approved August 15, 1941, Effective January 1, 1942, and all acts amendatory thereof, and

Whereas, it appears from the recitals in said record that the provisions of the said acts have been duly complied with,

Now, Therefore, I, CHARLES F. CARPENTIER, Secretary of State of the State of Illinois, by virtue of the power and authority vested in me by law, do hereby certify that the said Harvester of DuPage County is a legally organized and incorporated Village under the laws of this State.

In Testimony Whereof, I hereto set my hand and the Great Seal of the State of Illinois. Done at the Capitol in the City of Springfield this the 29th day of January A.D. nineteen hundred and fifty-seven and of the Independence of the United States the one hundred and eighty-first.

Charles F. Carpentier
SECRETARY OF STATE

Following the successful vote, Harvester was officially incorporated in 1957. In many ways that was just the beginning of committed civic effort. Now the work of managing budgets, village services, and—soon—zoning and growth were next on the agenda. (Courtesy of Village of Burr Ridge.)

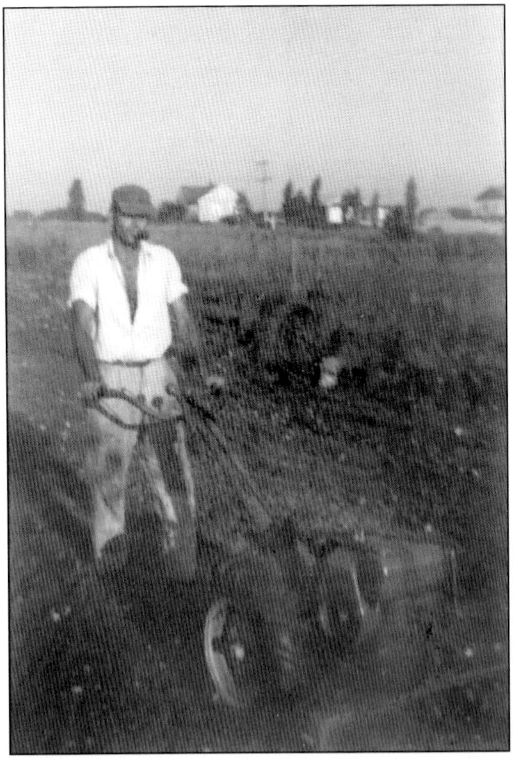

International Harvester equipment, large and small, helped farmers increase yields in the 1950s. Even small backyard farms like this one, seen in 1955, could afford something from the IH catalog. But by now, these acreages were lots that required tending, not harvesting, and were less necessary as food and consumer goods weren't grown and made as they were in the lean decades before. (Courtesy of Reynolds Chadwick family.)

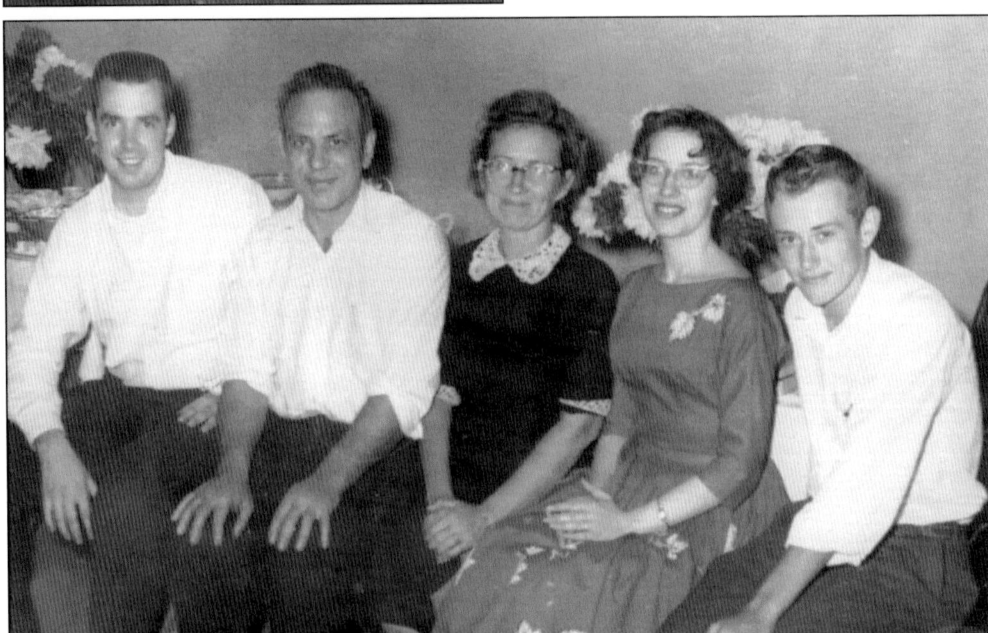

Sam and Nina McHugh (second and third from left) and family attend a wedding party on Giddings Street in 1960. Nina sold real estate in the budding neighborhood, persuading her sister to purchase nearby property. Often, that is how the area grew: one resident was asked to invite, persuade, and sell land for a larger landholder/developer. No real estate license was required. (Courtesy of Pat McHugh.)

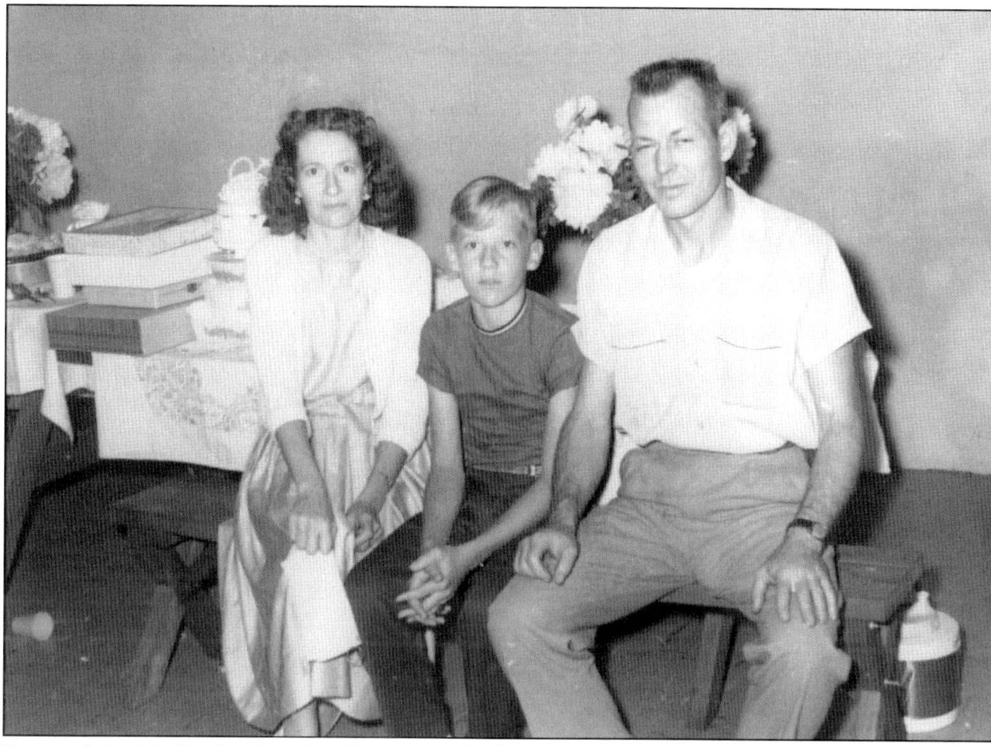

Etta and Art McHugh take a break at the end of a party in 1960. Art was a World War II Marine veteran and purchased land and built a house on Hamilton Street in the growing neighborhood within the Gower School district. By this time, the school's enrollment had soared with children born after the war—the Baby Boom was swelling local schools. (Courtesy of Pat McHugh.)

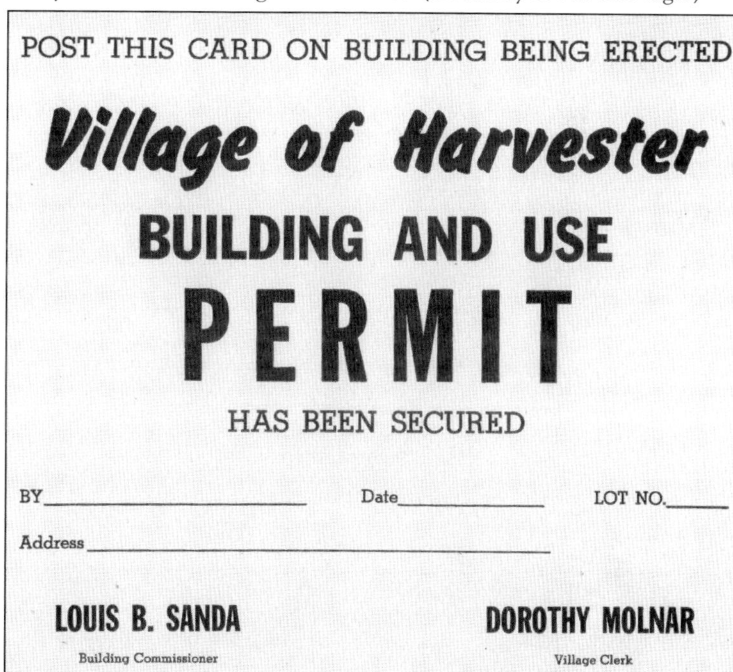

POST THIS CARD ON BUILDING BEING ERECTED

Village of Harvester

BUILDING AND USE

PERMIT

HAS BEEN SECURED

BY______________________ Date______________ LOT NO.______

Address____

LOUIS B. SANDA
Building Commissioner

DOROTHY MOLNAR
Village Clerk

From its inception, one of Harvester's key challenges was managing the village's rapid growth. Building permits like this one were a prerequisite for any new construction. Zoning, like now, was one of the key commitments to residents. (Courtesy of Village of Burr Ridge.)

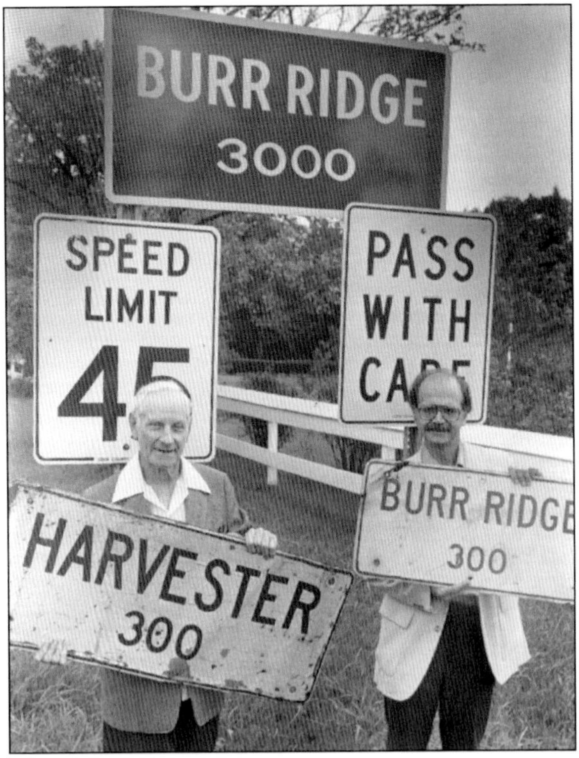

A watershed moment for the village was the decision to change its name. While the history of that decision remains unclear, according to board minutes and reports of the time, there is no question about the result. Harvester changed its name to Burr Ridge, becoming official in 1962. Village founders and leaders were asked to pose with the signs as they were changed. These signs remain in the village archive to this day. (Courtesy of Village of Burr Ridge.)

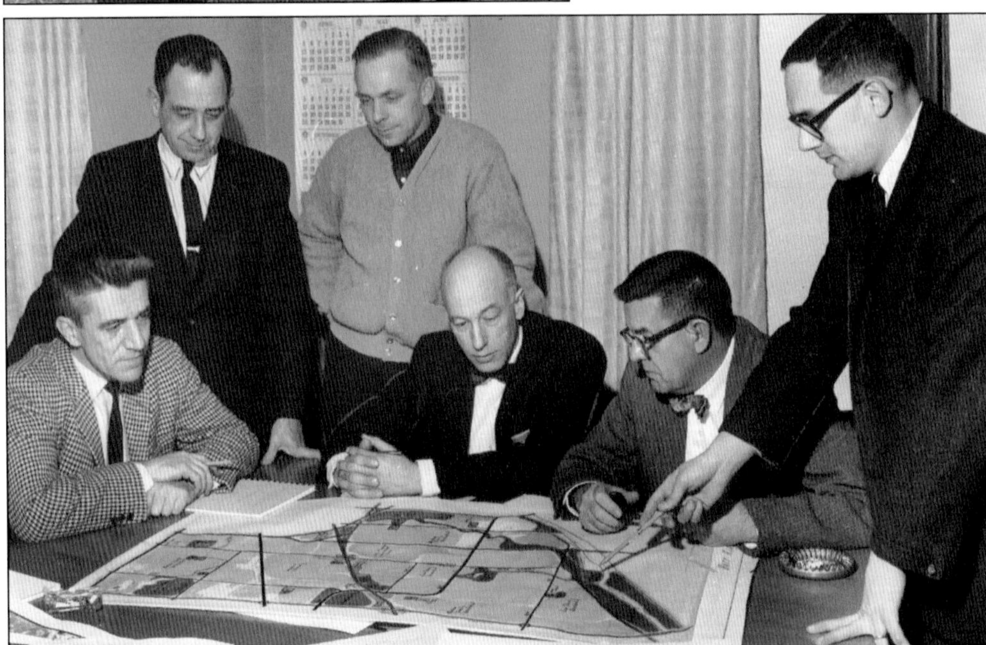

The Burr Ridge Planning Commission regulated the village's growth throughout the 1960s. Its zoning decisions still shape the landscape of Burr Ridge today. What developed, where it developed, why, and when were choices all made with deliberation and much discussion. (Courtesy of Village of Burr Ridge.)

Burr Ridge's first administration building was a point of civic pride. This humble building may not seem grand by today's standards, but to have a dedicated space where the village could conduct the very busy business of civic management was another turning point on the path to a prosperous future. (Courtesy of Village of Burr Ridge.)

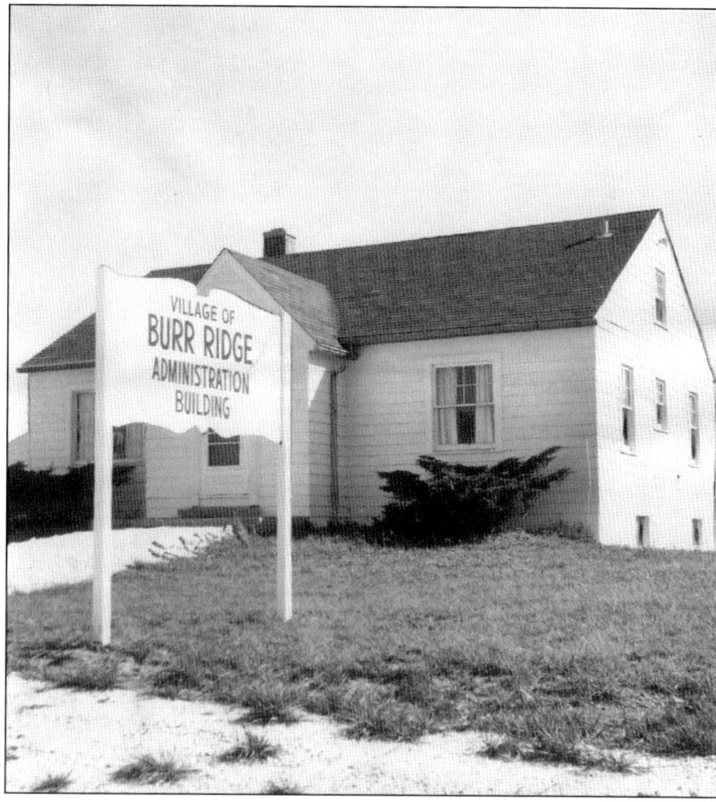

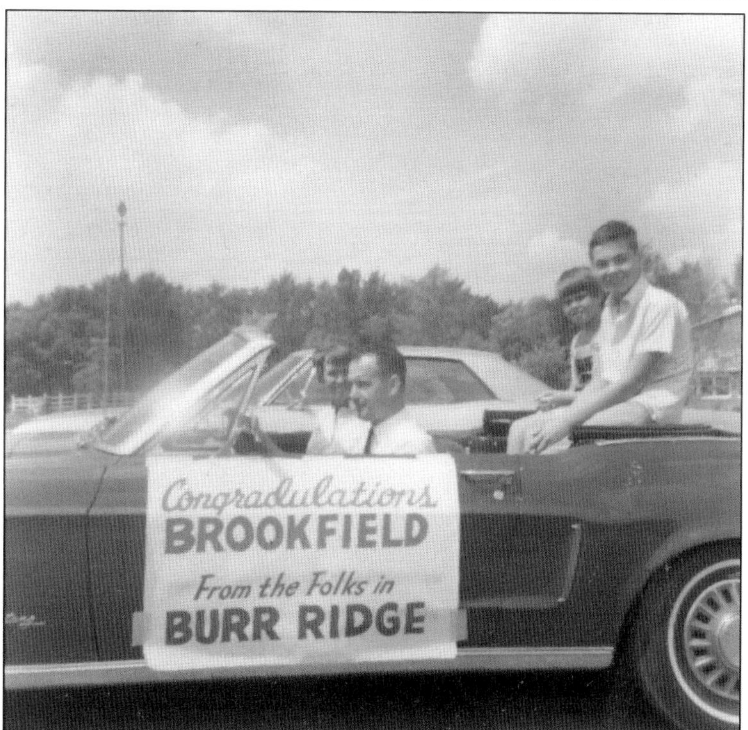

Leonard Ruzak, Burr Ridge's village president, prepares to drive a Ford Mustang in a parade in 1968. Civic pride shows in this one glimpse of photographic ephemera in the archives, revealing a genuine sense of growing village identity. (Courtesy of Village of Burr Ridge.)

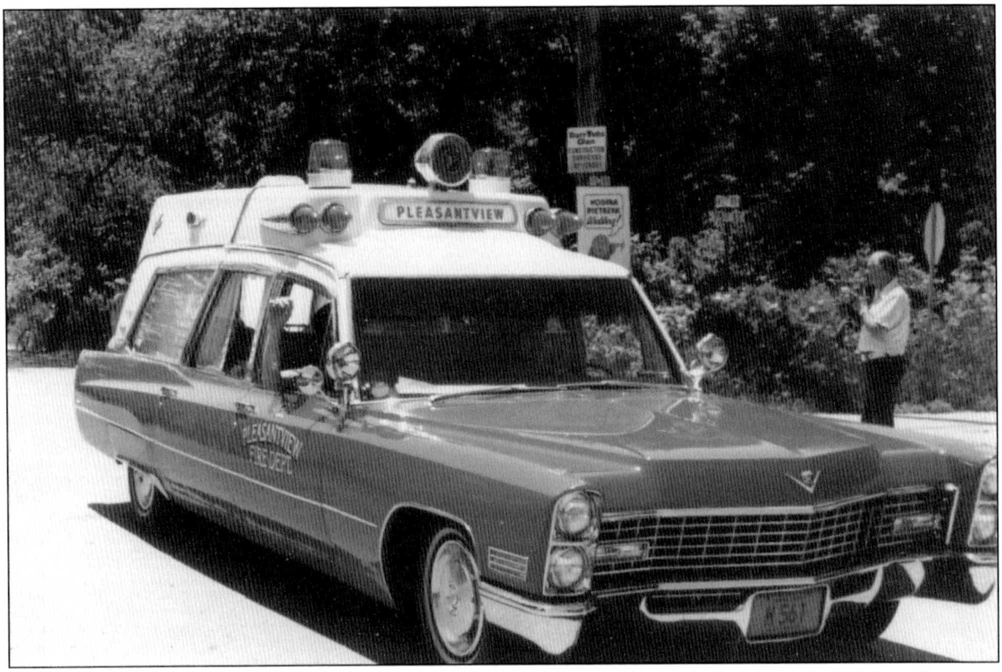

Fire, emergency, and police protection was and is very real and serious work. The early years required volunteer firefighters, with many area families seeing their husbands and sons answering the call. On this occasion, however, duty was of a lighter nature, as an ambulance lines up for a parade from the Pleasantview Fire Department near Burr Oaks Glen during the late 1960s. (Courtesy of Village of Burr Ridge.)

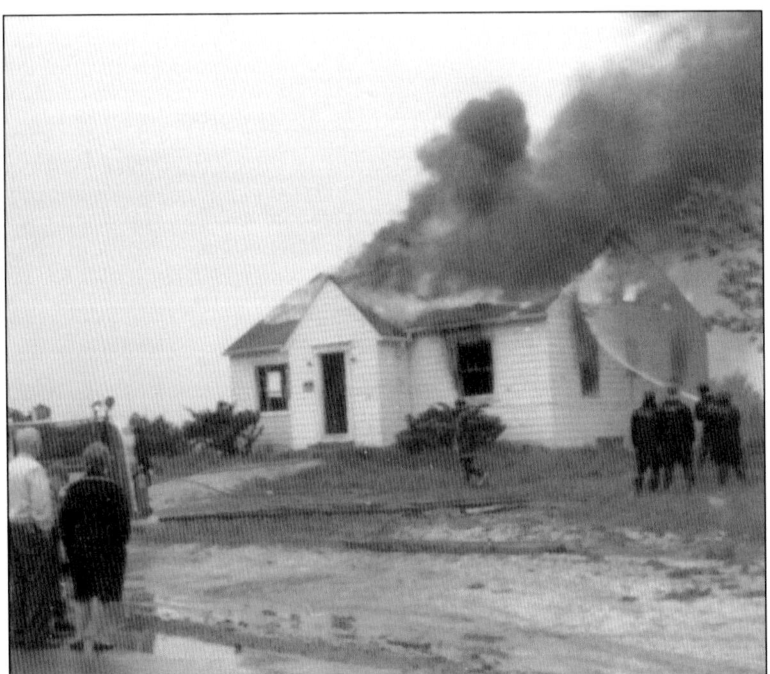

Those firefighters were needed, however, on May 25, 1969, when Burr Ridge's first village hall burned down. It was good fortune no one was hurt and records were rescued. (Courtesy of Village of Burr Ridge.)

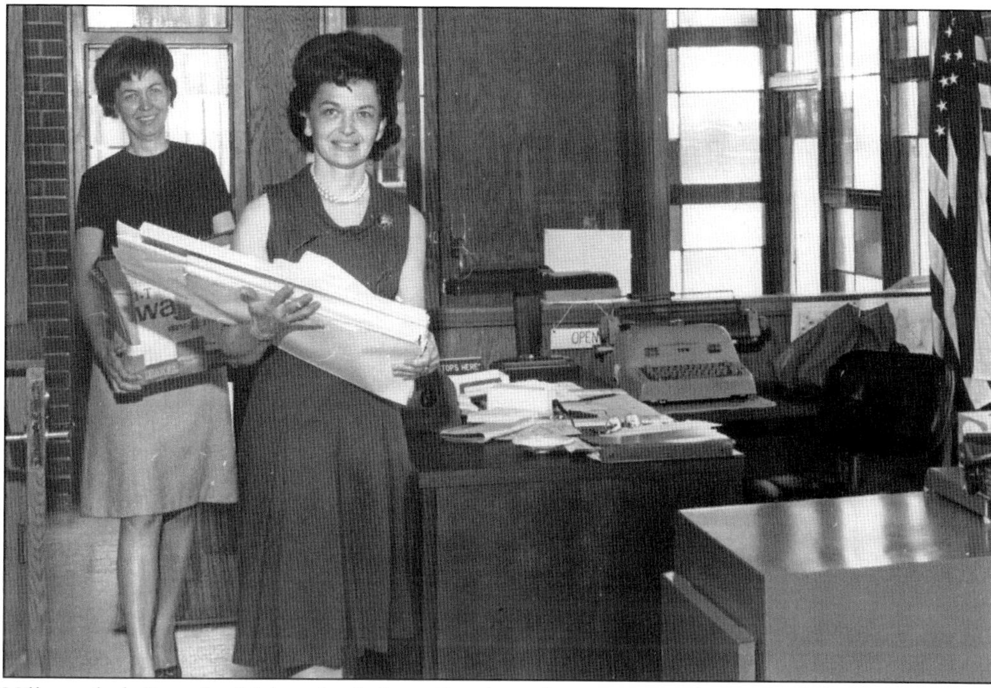

Village clerk Dorothy Molnar leads Joan Ruzak as they carry on the work of the village in the temporary offices offered by the then-new Burr Ridge United Church of Christ. The administration was kept running smoothly throughout the construction of a new building. (Courtesy of Village of Burr Ridge.)

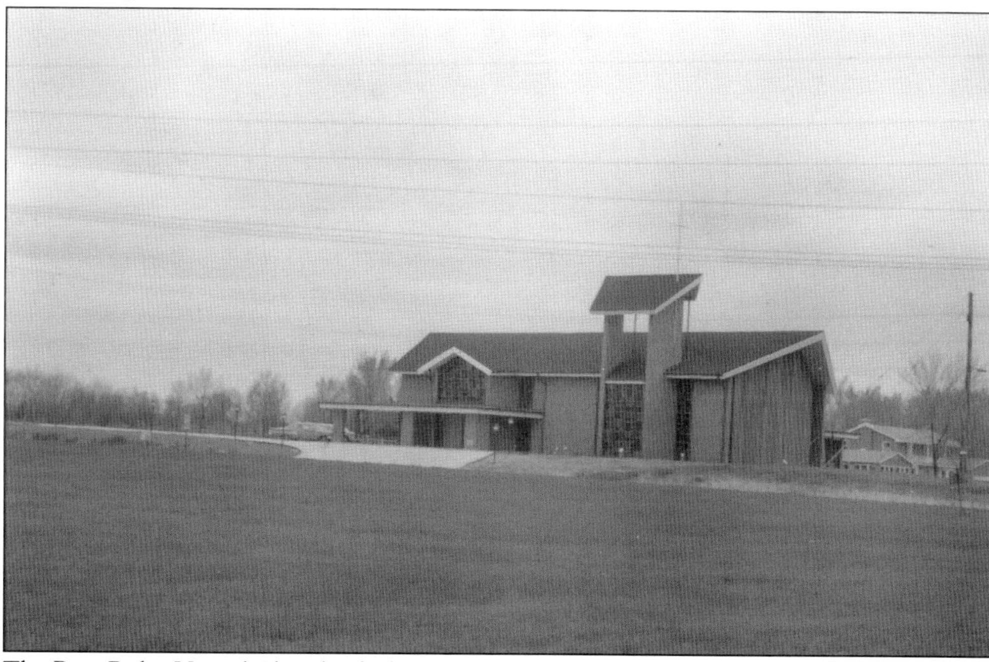

The Burr Ridge United Church of Christ, located at the intersection of Plainfield and County Line Roads, barely had time to serve its congregation before the village itself needed tending. (Courtesy of Village of Burr Ridge.)

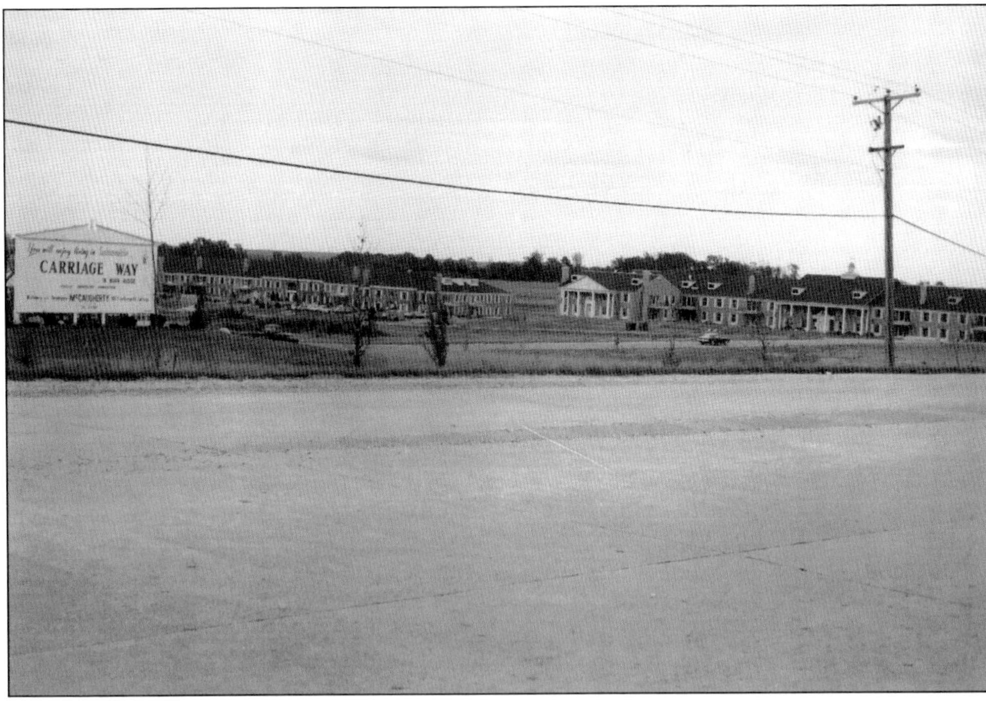

Signs advertising new housing were springing up all over Burr Ridge in the 1960s. Carriage Way was one of the earliest developments during the decade. The Cleary House, an original home, remains on the site, however. (Courtesy of Village of Burr Ridge.)

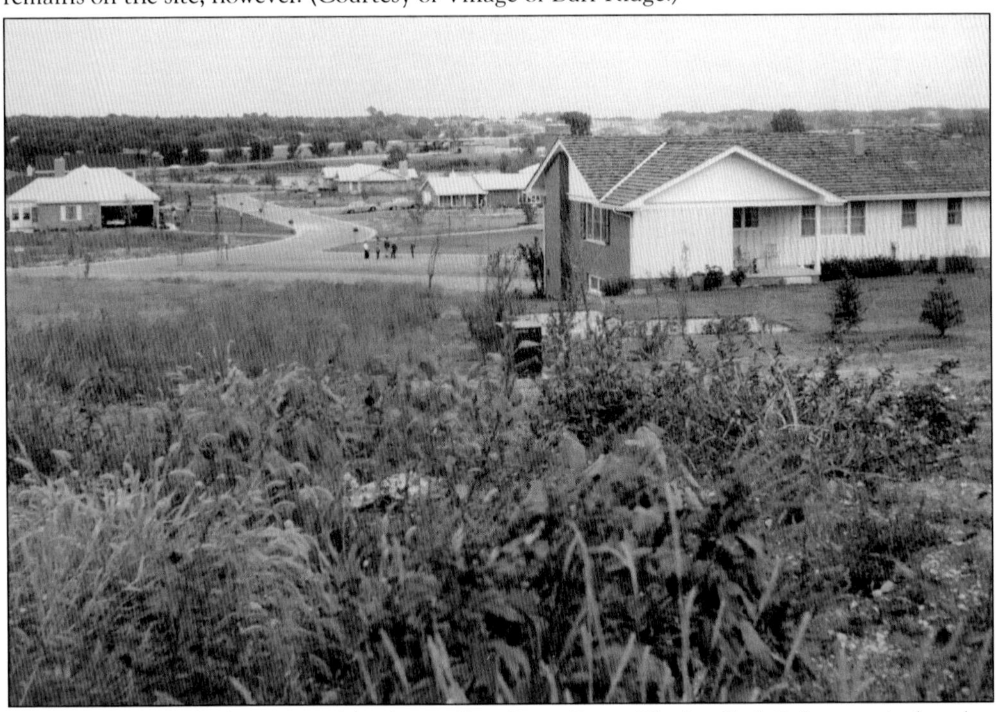

Carriage Way was built on part of the former Four Pines Dairy. The land's shift from agricultural to residential usage exemplified this latest shift in the economy. (Courtesy of Village of Burr Ridge.)

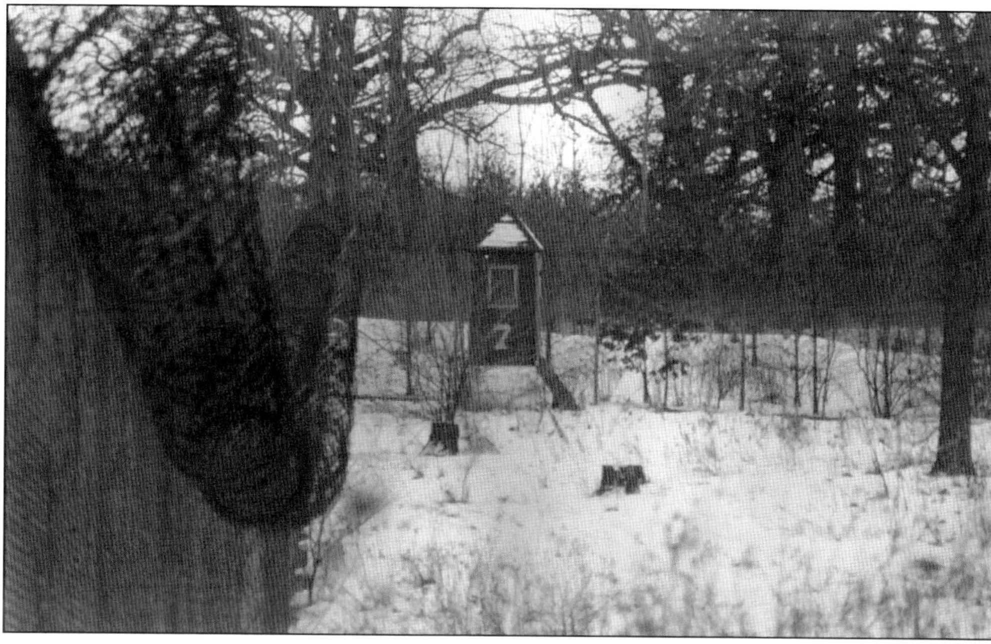

Much has been made of the fact that Burr Ridge once had a prison. The Bridewell Prison Farm was created from 371 acres in 1918. It used to stand east of County Line Road. Yes, it did have pigs, hence the oft-noted "pig farm" references. But it was a fully functional honor prison farm, with chickens and a working dairy. It operated through 1950 but was not used after. These photographs from 1973 are the last remaining images known. (Both, courtesy of Guy Franzese.)

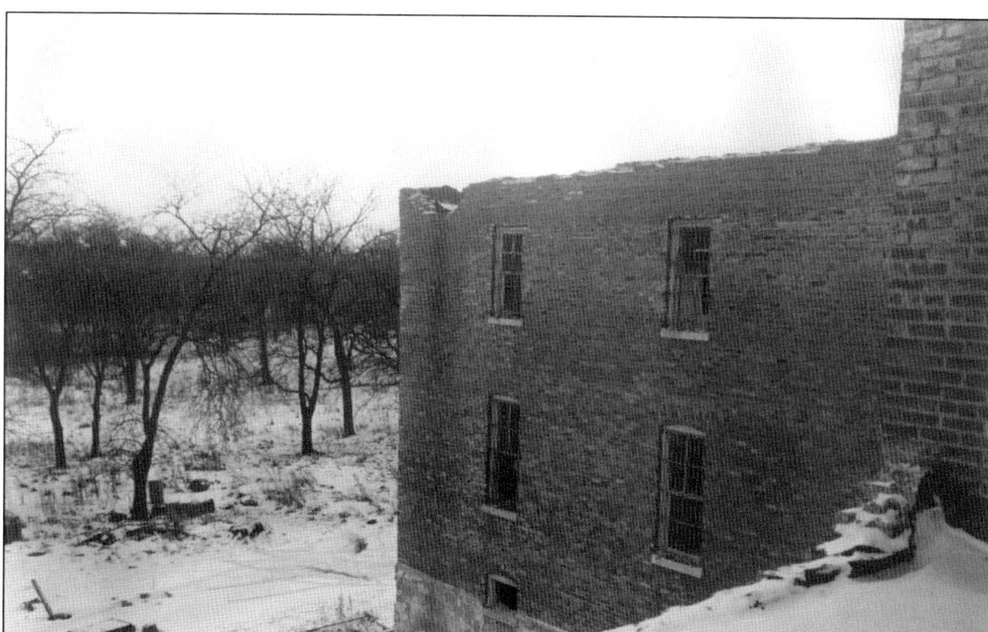

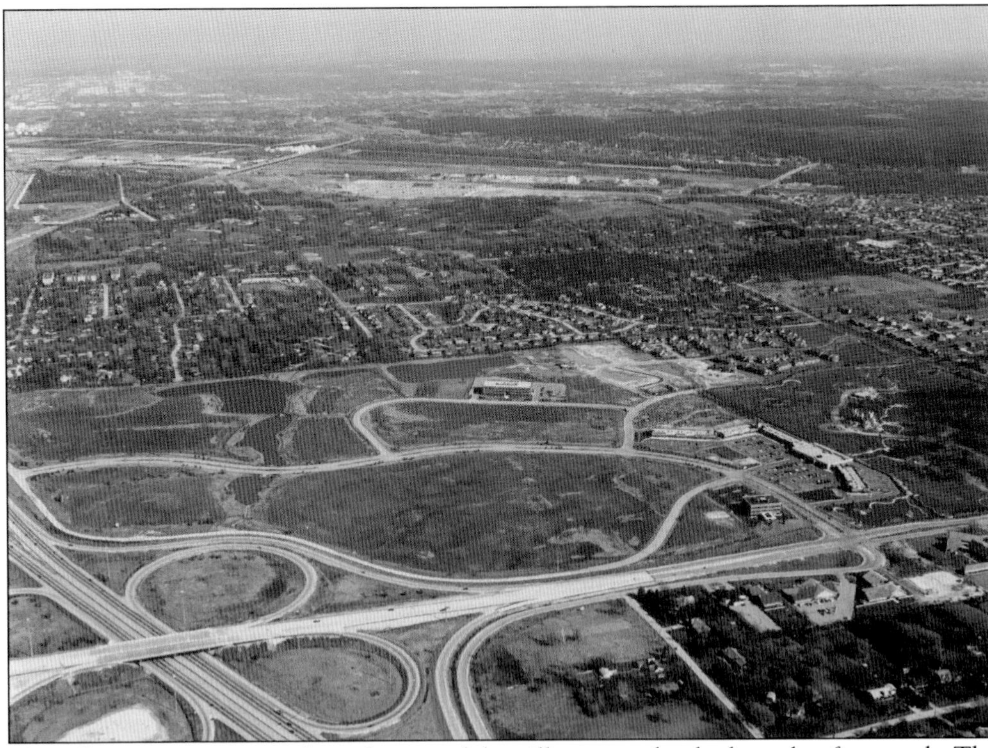

The village commission used aerial views of the village to make the best plan for growth. The area is shown just before major development began. Where Village Center stands today appears cleared and open. (Courtesy of Village of Burr Ridge.)

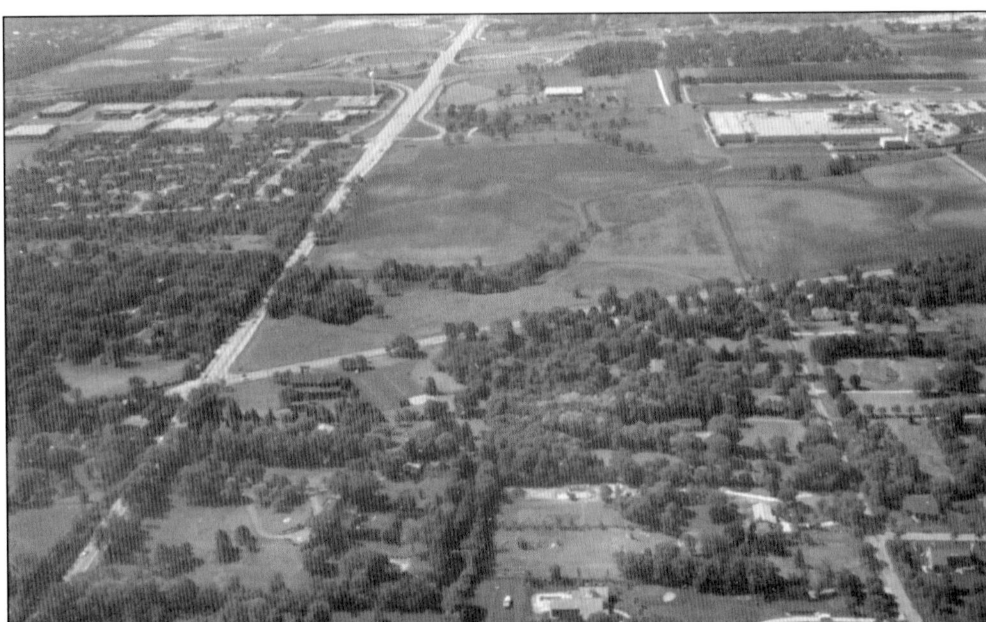

This aerial shot from 1987 shows International Harvester still in the center of its fields. At lower left, Burr Ridge United Church of Christ is visible. (Courtesy of Jim Martin.)

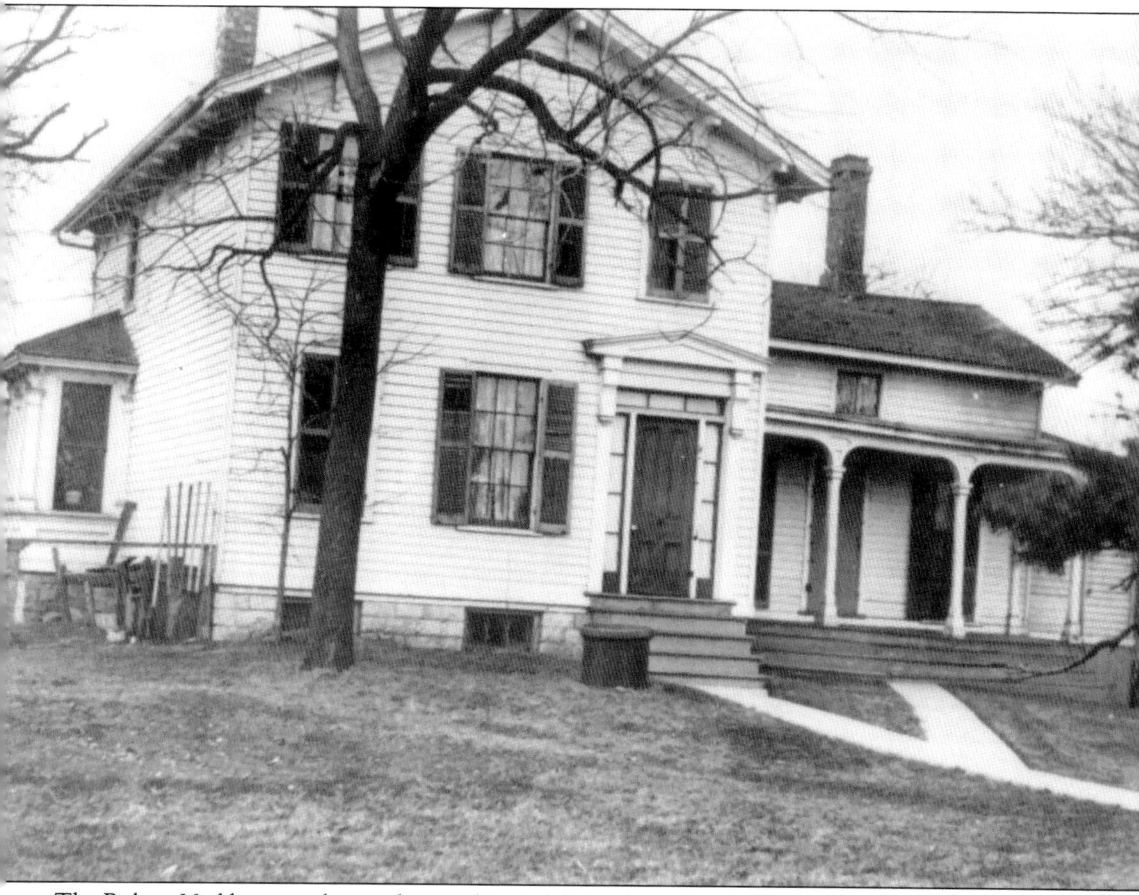

The Robert Vial home is the residence of one of the earliest settlers in the area. In the 1880s, the home stood on Plainfield Road near Wolf Road. (Courtesy of Flagg Creek Heritage Society.)

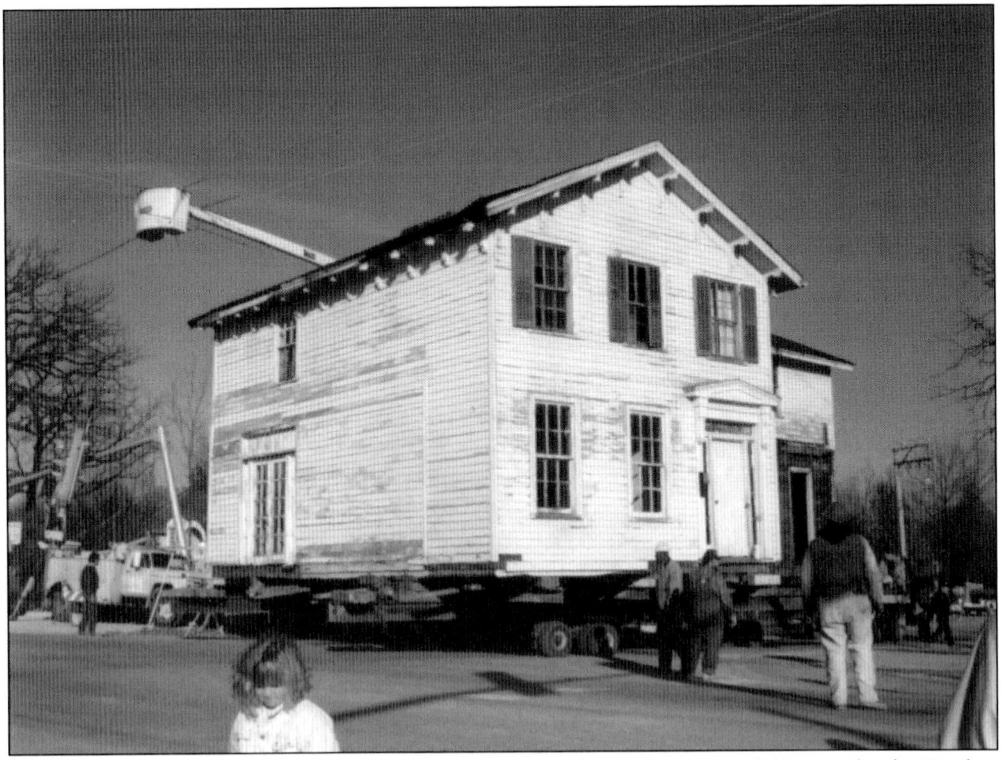

The Robert Vial home was lived in last by Alice Vial, and then became a clubhouse for the Timber Trails Golf Course. Ruth Vial Martin fought to have it rescued and restored as a fitting piece of founding history. Flagg Creek Heritage Society obtained new land and the home for $1 but spent $20,000 to move it. One July 1989 day, neighbors watched the home crawl down Wolf Road toward its current location at 7425 South Wolf Road. (Courtesy of Flagg Creek Heritage Society.)

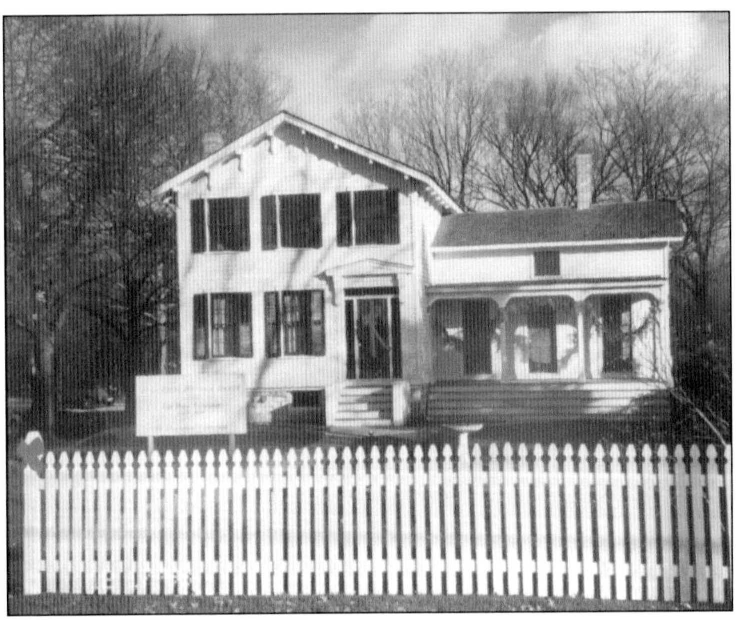

The Robert Vial house is shown in Christmas décor after its full restoration by the Flagg Creek Heritage Society. It is now listed in the National Register of Historic Places. (Courtesy of Flagg Creek Heritage Society.)

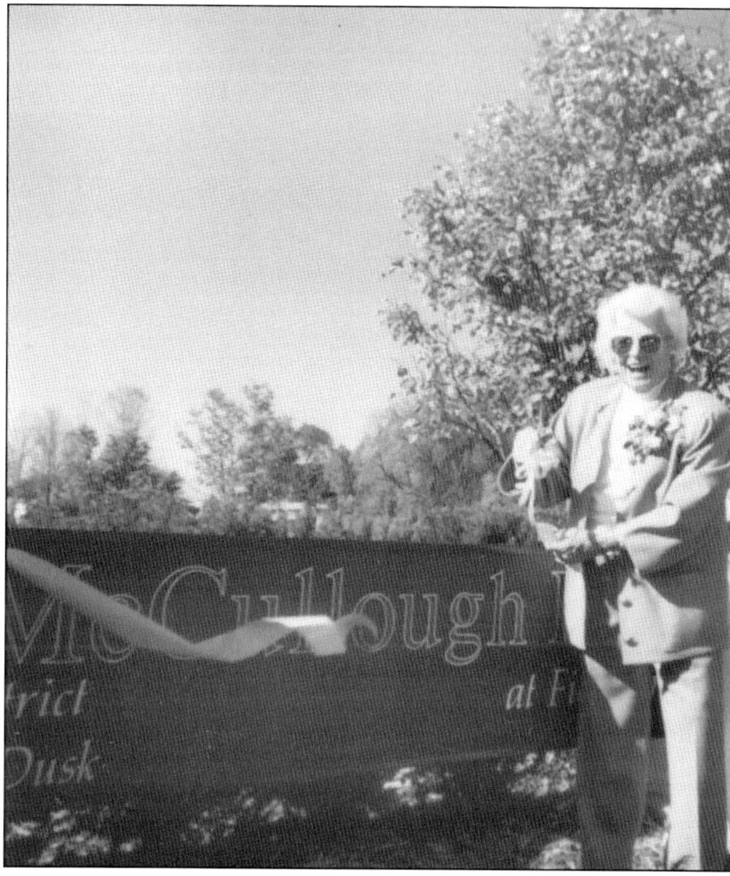

Purdie McCullough, former village clerk and author of Burr Ridge's 1976 anniversary booklet "A Very Special Place," celebrates with a yellow ribbon cutting at the park named after her at the corner of Plainfield and County Line Roads. (Courtesy of Village of Burr Ridge.)

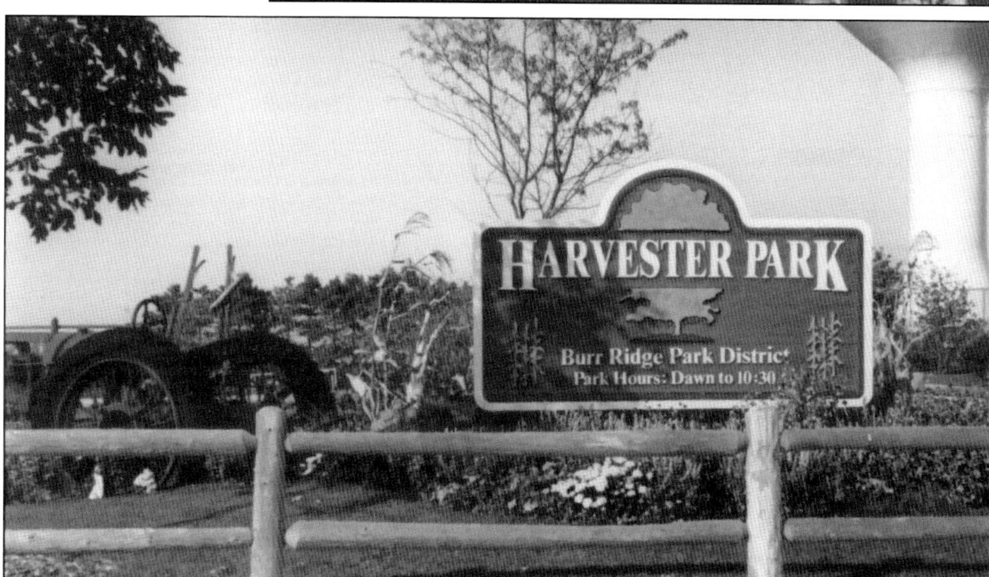

Case New Holland pays homage to Burr Ridge's roots, and much of Harvester Park in the Burr Ridge Park District is former IH land. A Farmall is a fitting welcome to Burr Ridge's past and future. (Courtesy of the Village of Burr Ridge.)

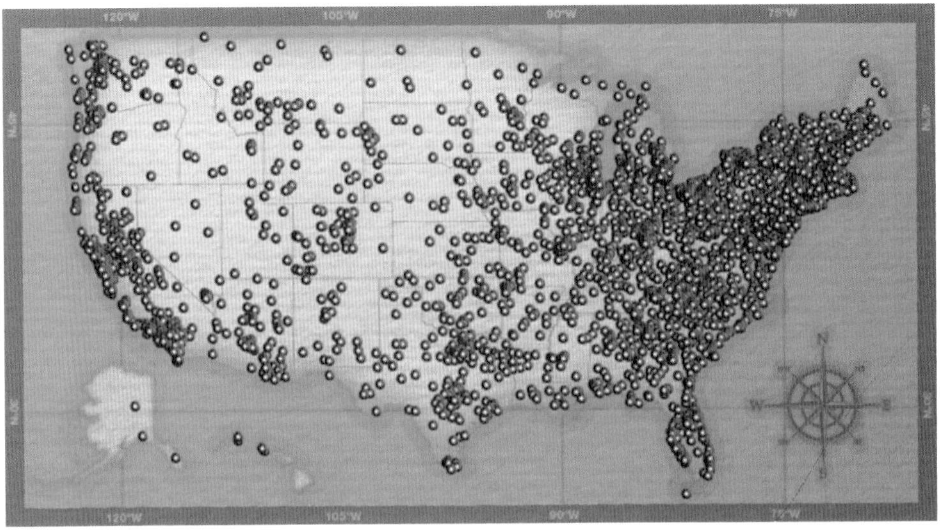

Consistent with our mission to preserve history on a local level, this book was printed in South Carolina on American-made paper and manufactured entirely in the United States. Products carrying the accredited Forest Stewardship Council (FSC) label are printed on 100 percent FSC-certified paper.

MADE IN THE USA